Terwilliger BUNTS ONE

Wayne Terwilliger

with Nancy Peterson and Peter Boehm

Please return to:

JAMES A PALMER OR
DORAIN H PALMER
2360 SCENIC HILL DR
SPRING HILL, FL 34606

(352) 666-0862
or
~~(___) ___-____~~

INSIDERS' GUIDE®

GUILFORD, CONNECTICUT
AN IMPRINT OF THE GLOBE PEQUOT PRESS

INSIDERS' GUIDE®

Copyright © 2006 by Wayne Terwilliger, Nancy Peterson, and Peter Boehm

Text design: Peter Boehm

This book is neither affiliated with nor endorsed by Major League Baseball.

Excerpt on pages 272–73 is from page 110 of *An American Childhood* by Annie
Dillard ("One Sunday afternoon . . . 'Death to privilege.'"). Copyright © 1987 by
Annie Dillard. Reprinted by permission of HarperCollins Publishers.

Excerpt on page 274 from *Lake Wobegon Summer 1956* by Garrison Keillor,
copyright © 2001 Garrison Keillor. Used by permission of Viking Penguin, a
division of Penguin Group (USA).

Library of Congress Cataloging-in-Publication Data
Terwilliger, Wayne.
  Terwilliger bunts one / Wayne Terwilliger with Nancy Peterson and
Peter Boehm.—1st ed.
    p. cm.
  Includes index.
  ISBN-13: 978-0-7627-4310-0
  ISBN-10: 0-7627-4310-7
  1. Terwilliger, Wayne. 2. Baseball players—United States—Biography.
3. Baseball team owners—United States—Biography. 4. Baseball
coaches—United States—Biography. I. Peterson, Nancy. II. Boehm,
Peter. III. Title.
  GV865.T43A3 2006
  796.357092—dc22

                                    2006004483

Manufactured in the United States of America
First Edition/First Printing

To Marcie
hippie, Harley rider, environmentalist,
and starving artist

and Steve
emergency paramedic with hands like a surgeon,
and avid hunter and fisherman

with lots of help from
Lin,
Nancy,
and Peter

and special thanks to all
the U.S. armed forces,
especially
the Marines

Contents

Acknowledgments

Many people have helped with this book, knowingly and unknowingly. Jim Caple's wonderful 1998 *Saint Paul Pioneer Press* story celebrating Twig's first fifty years in baseball inspired this project. Lin Terwilliger helped us persuade Twig that it was worth doing and then helped in the process. Brian Motiaytis hunted up valuable sources and clippings. We were able to check facts and context through great Internet sources including www.baseball-almanac.com, www.baseball-reference.com, www.baseballlibrary.com, and Stew Thornley's on-line history of the Minneapolis Millers. Neal Karlen, Mike Veeck, Nanette Peterson, Tom Whaley, and Paul Higbee provided advice about getting published, and Erin Turner at Globe Pequot has been a true champion in rushing this book into production in time for the baseball season. The Saint Paul Saints and Fort Worth Cats were generous with access to photos and other assistance —thanks Dave Wright, Emil Moffatt, and David Hatchett. David Nordrum was always willing to help with computers and photos. Submissions to our Web site, www.wayneterwilliger.com, provided information and assured us there is a receptive audience. We thank Eric for reading early chapters and Abby for bringing muffins. Many others have helped and encouraged us, and we thank you all. Most of all: Thank you, Wayne Terwilliger, for allowing us to help you tell your stories. It is an honor.

—Nancy Peterson and Peter Boehm

Editors' Note

Twig is a natural storyteller, and in this book, we've made every effort to preserve his voice and personality throughout the text. A sampling of interesting newspaper quotes and other references to Terwilliger's career are sprinkled throughout. Where no source is named, that's us, as co-authors/editors, adding historical background to aid in understanding the events surrounding Terwilliger's remarkable life. Historical background found in Chapter 4, "San Diego to Suribachi—a Gung-Ho Marine," was compiled from *2nd Armored Amphibian Battalion USMC WWII Saipan Tinian Iwo Jima,* produced by 2nd Armored Amphibian Association, 1991.

—Nancy Peterson and Peter Boehm

1

Ancient History and Current Events

Shoes got holes, no sandwich sacked
Ball all scuffed . . . bat's cracked
Glove needs a web, no jock or cup
Where's the field . . . Batter Up!

Ted Williams used to say to me, "Wayne, you gotta have enthusiasm to play this game."

He was talking *to* me, but not *about* me. Enthusiasm is something I've had as long as I can remember. I was small for my age and my talents were modest, but even as a kid I loved working on my skills, I loved to compete, and I loved to hustle. My approach to every-thing—"Don't just walk when you can run"—got me into the game and into a twelve-season playing career in the majors and Triple A. It opened the door to coaching and managing, and it brought me expe-riences and opportunities I could never have imagined, including both a job and a friendship with Ted Williams. It has kept me feeling young, and it has kept me in the game for fifty-seven seasons.

I was helping out at spring training with the Washington Senators in 1969 when their new manager, Ted Williams, asked me to be his third-base coach. During our four years together, we had many a conversation about players who don't hustle, don't run out every ball, don't work as hard as they can to develop their talent. Neither of us could understand why somebody with the opportunity to play wouldn't give it everything he's got. Despite the obvious differences in our skills and accomplishments, Ted and I both knew we had gotten where we were through hard work. *Really* hard work. Our successful first season with the Senators was the highlight of my career, and in our four years working together, he gave the word "enthusiasm" a whole new meaning for me.

Growing up in Michigan in the 1920s and '30s, I used to toss a ball against the steps of our house hour after hour. As it bounced back, I pretended it was coming off some major-leaguer's bat. I tried to anticipate the bounce and to be ready for whatever direction it took. Learning to get a good jump on the ball was part of what made me a good defensive infielder. Meanwhile in California Ted was taking batting practice off anyone who would pitch to him or squeezing a rubber ball to strengthen his hands and forearms or swinging a bat in front of a mirror and analyzing his swing. He wanted to be *the greatest hitter ever,* and he pictured himself hitting game-winning home runs off major-league hurlers. I saw myself at second base, surrounded by the beautiful green grass of the Detroit Tigers' Navin Field, making great defensive plays like my hero, Charlie Gehringer.

Charlie's autograph was one of many that I collected as a kid, and when I first took the field against boyhood heroes and giants of the game like BoBo Newsom, Stan Musial, Red Schoendienst, and Whitey Ford, it took me a while to stop thinking like a starstruck kid. I never *really* got over it. To this day the thing I love about my playing career is that I played with, and against, so many of the all-time greats.

A few years back, a Minneapolis radio sports guy named Mike Max was interviewing me about my career, and he said, "Well, you could say you had a cuppa coffee in the major leagues." Whoa. I let that comment go by, and I'm still mad at myself. To me "a cup of coffee" means a few days or weeks with a big-league club—maybe getting called up when the roster expands in the fall and playing out the season. I don't like to brag, and I don't exaggerate, but I like the record to be accurate. I should have said, "Wait a minute, Mike. Let's get the facts straight. I spent five full seasons in the majors and parts of four others. With only four months of Triple A experience in 1949, I became the starting second baseman for the Chicago Cubs. The Brooklyn Dodgers acquired me to back up a guy named Jackie

Not much has changed! Enthusiasm and enjoyment are apparent in 1935, as young Wayne Terwilliger tosses a baseball against the steps—this time at his grandparents' home in Lansing, Michigan—to develop his skills. Seventy years later he demonstrates his knack for ball-handling at LaGrave Field in Fort Worth, where he managed the Cats to a 2005 league championship.

Photo on left, Wayne Terwilliger personal collection; photo on right by Vishal Malhotra

Robinson. I spent two seasons as a starter for the Washington Senators, where President Eisenhower commented on how well I was playing—and the *Washington Post* quoted him. I was on the New York Giants with a teammate named Willie Mays and on the Kansas City Athletics with a guy named Roger Maris. I was there to see 'The Shot Heard 'Round the World' at the Polo Grounds and Mickey Mantle's mile-long homer at Griffith Stadium. I got a game-winning single off Satchel Paige and a home run off Whitey Ford, and I turned double plays *against* Pee Wee Reese and Jackie Robinson one season and *with* them the next. Some people compared me defensively with three or four of the all-time great second basemen, including my hero, Charlie Gehringer. I had a lot more than a cup of coffee!"

As much as I loved playing, I discovered that I liked managing even more. I love being The Man in Charge, I love helping young players develop, I love game strategy, and I love winning. What worked in Greensboro in 1961 worked with the Fort Worth Cats in 2005, and with ten other clubs in between. I spent eighteen years coaching in the majors, including two World Championship seasons with the Minnesota Twins. The money was better in the majors, and the accommodations were nicer, but winning is sweeter when you're the manager, even if it's in the minor leagues.

My career almost ended in 1994 when the Twins fired me at age sixty-nine. Everyone assumed I was retiring. The players gave me a fishing boat, which took away some of the sting of being let go, but I wasn't done. I went across the river and coached with the independent Saint Paul Saints for eight seasons. When my wife and I moved to Texas in 2002, everybody thought I was finally bowing out gracefully. Instead, twenty-two years after my last managing job, the Fort Worth Cats of the independent Central Baseball League gave me another chance.

When the Cats announced my hiring, one Fort Worth reporter wrote that the Cats were changing the seventh-inning stretch to the seventh-inning nap. Now, that's funny. Not true, but funny. Steve Rushin said about me in *Sports Illustrated,* "His *career* is eligible for an AARP card." They told me I was the oldest active manager in baseball, the oldest ever in the minors and the second oldest in all of baseball behind Connie Mack, who managed his Philadelphia Athletics until he was eighty-seven. I didn't take the job to become "the oldest." I didn't even feel old. I took the job because I felt good, I still loved working with young players, and I was pretty sure I could still manage and win.

As I write this in 2005, I've just finished my third year with the Cats. It was quite a season. In June I got a huge amount of press just for turning eighty. In July the league chose me to manage our All-Star team in an inter-league competition in Massachusetts, and in September they named me Manager of the Year. Best of all, we

Like many other boys his age, Twig admired Ted Williams, wrote for his autograph, listened to his games on the radio, and even saw his game-winning home run in the 1941 All-Star Game. Unlike other boys, Twig got to be an on-field opponent, batting student, fellow Marine, co-worker, and friend of The Greatest Hitter Who Ever Lived—and the beneficiary of advice about beer, salad making, aftershave, and so much more.

Wayne Terwilliger personal collection

compiled the best record in franchise history and won the league championship for the first time since 1948.

It couldn't get better than that, and in October, with a lot of mixed emotions, I decided to retire as manager. In December I "unretired," rejoining the team as first-base coach. I may not be on the bus for twelve-hour trips to Pensacola, but I'll still be at the ballpark, coaching and hitting fungoes for infield drills, because—in spite of eighty candles on my birthday cake, in spite of cancer surgery in 2004, and in spite of hundred-degree Texas afternoons—I *still* have enthusiasm for the game.

Looking back, I have only two regrets. I should have been a better hitter. A little more patience might have made me one. Managers would have kept me around longer, and my playing career might have been even more satisfying.

The more important regret is that I didn't appreciate my family in my early years. I often acted like a jerk. I thought I was just being competitive and intense. It took me a long time to learn that even when you lose and you're mad as hell, you don't have to take it out on your family, your friends, or the fans. If I had grown up sooner, I'd have enjoyed everything more and so would the people around me.

The game has seen a lot of changes since I started—batting helmets, artificial turf, the designated hitter, huge player salaries, even the way fans dress for the ballpark. But the important things don't change—the crack of the bat, the slap of the ball hitting the glove, the adrenaline rush of stealing a base, the strategizing, the losing, the winning—the game itself.

As a kid, I knew I wanted to be part of it. Unlike Ted Williams, I wasn't absolutely sure I'd make it. But I did everything I could to be ready if I ever got the opportunity, and every time somebody gave me another chance I showed that I wasn't going to let *anybody* work harder than me. I'm still amazed at the people I've met, the places I've been, the fun I've had. While I was coaching with the Saint Paul Saints, I would tell my stories to some of the tailgaters at Midway Stadium, and they'd say, "You oughtta write a book." After hearing that enough times, I did.

So here it is, the story of a kid who went from bouncing a ball off the steps on North Main Street in Charlotte, Michigan, to playing at

Ebbets Field, the Polo Grounds, and Yankee Stadium. A kid who went from choosing up sides on the playground to playing with and against some of the all-time major-league greats. A kid who saw the U.S. flag hoisted on Iwo Jima and remembers that moment every time the "Star-Spangled Banner" is sung before a game. A kid who was thrilled to see Ted Williams hit a game-winning home run in the 1941 All-Star Game at Detroit and found himself coaching for him three decades later. A kid who cheered his Detroit Tigers to a World Series championship when he was ten and steered his Fort Worth Cats to the Central League championship when he was eighty, with a couple of other World Series and league championships along the way.

Is this a great game, or what?

2

Ivan the Terrible, Tigers, and Mom

How many balls hit the steps each day?
How many one-man games did I play?
How many times did Detroit beat the Yanks?
For the fan in the window—Mom—a big thanks.

My father must have been the most surprised guy in the world when I got seriously interested in baseball. I started life as a mama's boy. My mother, Doris, let my blond hair grow into curls and dressed me in fancy clothes, and people would comment about how pretty I was. She taught me to memorize nursery rhymes, and I would recite them for relatives and friends with very little urging. Mom had been valedictorian of her high school class. She played the violin and piano, and before long she had me taking violin, piano, and tap-dancing lessons. She also wrote poetry, and as soon as I learned to write, I started making up my own "rhymers." I sometimes wrote them for school, and I still write them for special occasions. (Some of the rhymers in this book were written when I was a kid, others more recently.)

Mom and my father, Ivan, were a very unlikely twosome, and I never understood how they got together. He was a tough guy who spent nearly all of his time working. He never said anything about it to me, but I'm sure that for the first few years of my life he wondered what kind of boy he had fathered.

Dad was a husky guy—not more than 5-foot-10 but 240 pounds and strong as a bull. When my folks were married in Clare, Michigan, he was a mail carrier, a part-time drummer in a local band, and a semi-pro pitcher in a county league. (He never discussed it, but eventually somebody told me he had been pretty good.) When I was about a year old we moved a couple of hours away to Charlotte—accent on the second syllable. He rented a store and turned it into a bar, selling iced-down beer out of a tub and tobacco from a big box. Eventually he bought a place called the Dearborn Bar and gradually built up a business that featured beer, wine, tobacco, the best hamburgers in town, and a small sign in the front window reading MEN ONLY. Card playing was allowed in the back, euchre being the game of choice. He enjoyed his regular customers, but he didn't take crap from anybody. If somebody tried to make trouble, he'd challenge them to finger wrestle. His fingers were strong from pulling a beer tap all day; he'd bend their fingers over and push them right off their stool. The bar was his kingdom and maybe his refuge.

At home my dad stayed to himself a lot and kept his bottle of muscatel in the kitchen. He never raised a hand against us, but he made sure he got his way. On Sundays, when the bar was closed, he would listen to the Detroit Tigers on the big radio in the living room. When I was five or six, I began to listen with him. Before long I was listening to every Tigers' game, living and dying with every play by Hank Greenberg, Mickey Cochran, Goose Goslin, Tommy Bridges, Schoolboy Rowe, and the rest of the Tigers of the 1930s and early '40s. Second baseman Charlie Gehringer became my hero, and I found myself wanting to play the game. Despite the best efforts of my teachers and my mother, I only managed to make the damnedest squeaking noises with the violin, and although I wish I had stuck with the piano, I didn't. I'd look out the window and see somebody go by with a ball and a glove, and that's where I wanted to be.

When I was still very young, I began to spend most of my free time throwing a ball against the steps of the house. Some of the other kids did the same, but I did it day after day from early morning until dark. I never got tired of it. I used a rubber ball, a tennis ball—I even tried a golf ball, but it came close to the bay window a couple times and my mother "suggested" I not use that one any more. I began to

Young Wayne with dad, Ivan, and mom, Doris. "Dad was so tough he ate Limburger cheese without crackers and washed it down with muscatel," Twig says. "Mom was a saint; there's no other way to describe her. The older I got, the more I noticed the distance between them." Twig's sister, Mary Lou, was born when he was five; an athletic youngster, she won national honors showing quarter horses. *Wayne Terwilliger personal collection*

imagine that I was playing in a major-league game; the ball bouncing off the step was coming off Gehrig's bat, and I was Charlie Gehringer trying to field it. If I caught the ball it was an out; if it bounced over my head it might be a double. I played like that hour after hour, year after year, developing skills an infielder needs: anticipating and getting the jump on the ball. Sometimes I'd catch a glance at Mom looking out the front window and I'd take time for a quick wave; she would just smile, shake her head, and disappear for another hour or two.

Sometimes my friend Bob Baker and I would grab a stick, find a brick wall for a backstop, and take turns pitching to each other from about 15 feet. We used a ball that really moved, and it was a challenge to connect with it. We started meeting at the park for pickup games. Usually eight or ten kids would show up, and the two best players—I was one of them—would choose up sides. We used the time-honored hand-over-hand method of gripping the bat to determine who got first pick, and if I won I always took the fastest kid—if he could catch the ball—over the big hitter. Our games would last all day, although sometimes if one team got way ahead, we'd start a new game. Usually a few kids had to go home before the game was over, but we'd adjust and keep playing.

I also made up a baseball game that I played on the living room floor using marbles and baseball cards. I'd lay the cards in position like a team on the field, with a marble beside each card. Then I'd "pitch" a marble with my left hand and I'd "hit" it with a marble from my right hand, and if it rolled through without hitting any of the cards or any of the marbles out in the field, it was a hit. When it got too easy, I added a short-right fielder and a short-left fielder. I'd get very absorbed in the game until my younger sister, Mary Lou, would come by and kick the marbles around.

I usually played the marble game while I was listening to the Tigers on the radio. I wouldn't leave that radio for anything while a Tigers game was on. Sometimes I listened to Ty Tyson, but I preferred Harry Heilmann, a great Hall of Fame outfielder and slugger for the Tigers in the 1920s. I liked Heilmann's descriptions of the action, and he offered great insights into the game. When I was ten, the Tigers played the Cubs in the 1935 World Series, and I hung on every pitch. Goose Goslin singled in Mickey Cochrane to win the final game, and the next day there was a big picture of him in the paper with pitcher Tommy Bridges kissing one cheek and Cochrane kissing the other. I pictured myself there some day. But not as Goose Goslin. I was always Charlie Gehringer, making the plays at second base and getting a timely hit.

Once a year, my Cub Scout troop would pile into the back of some Army trucks to go see the Tigers play, usually against the White Sox. I loved being at the ballpark, and I paid attention to everything. I remember being amazed by the arm of Bob Kennedy, the White Sox third baseman, when he threw across the infield. But mostly I watched the Tigers. I loved those guys. I kept my eyes on Gehringer every minute that he was on the field. He was one of the all-time great second basemen, and I knew it even then. Everything he did was so smooth. He anticipated the ball. He had a fast pivot and a quick release on the double play. I appreciated that, and I patterned myself after him, then and later. I even noticed that he wrote his name very carefully for every autograph, and I still do that. Watching him, I dreamed that some day I'd play right where he was, and eventually I did. All those boyhood memories came back to me in 1953 when I was on the Washington Senators and we played the Tigers in Detroit. The stadium was called Navin Field when Gehringer played and Briggs Stadium after that, and it was Tiger Stadium when I got there as a Senator. The name didn't matter. I thought, "Geez, here I am, in the very same spot on the same infield where Charlie Gehringer used to play." If there was ever a single moment when I realized that my dream had come true, that was it. I had a chance to talk with Gehringer once, when I was with Brooklyn and he had retired from baseball. I was glad I had the chance to tell him what a role model he had been to me.

My dad took me to a couple of games when I was young. One was against the Yankees. Lou Gehrig hit a home run right toward us in the upper deck of the right-field bleachers. My dad kept saying, "Here it comes, here it comes," and he reached for it, but it landed two rows in front of us. While he was going for it, I ducked. He didn't say anything, but I could tell from his expression that he was disappointed in me, and I was disappointed with myself. I made up my mind that I would never duck again.

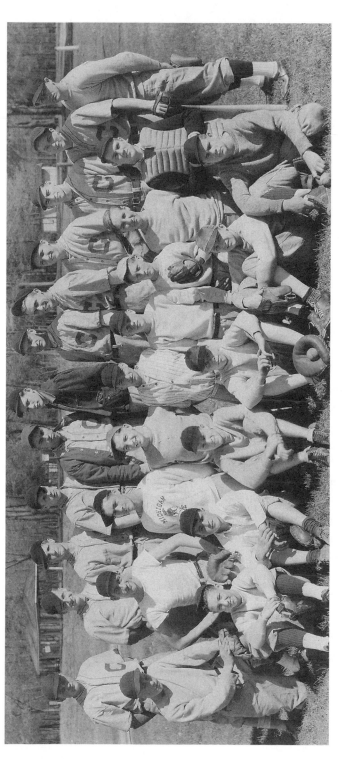

A high school freshman at age thirteen, Twig was backup third baseman for the 1939 Charlotte Orioles. Front row, from left: Twig, Bob Hague, George Howe, Ed Hughes, Willard Mikesell, Laurence Hall. Second row: Carrol Wilmore, Charles Harshman, Jim Durner, Lynn Fowler, Clarence Betts, Russell Steinman, B. Marshall, Max Dowker, Jack Morris. Third row: John Wellman, Jack Mate, Bob Ladd, Fred Wieting, Frank Loucks, Lyle Kane, Wendell Dickenson, Dale Shumaker, Lowell Shumaker, Eldred Toutant, Bob Baker, and Coach Wilford Rohlfs. *Photo courtesy of Charlotte High School*

Hi, Mom, just juice, game starts at eight
Big one today so can't be late
Got beat last week, 19 to none
Guarantee we'll win this one!

Kindergarten and the earliest grades were a snap, so they moved me up a year. I had to work a lot harder after that. I was small for my age, so being younger than my classmates didn't exactly help me in school sports. An older kid at school—Eldred Toutant, who later became the town's recreation director—talked me into coming out for intramural basketball when I was in fifth or sixth grade. That got me into organized competition and into showering with "the guys"—overcoming my shyness about that was a big accomplishment. Soon I found myself on the junior varsity; we played just before varsity games. I remember coming off the floor at the end of our game just as the varsity came out in their fancy uniforms and thinking, "In a couple years I'll be doing that." I was right, and basketball became my best sport. As a sophomore I was already playing a lot; I still wasn't very big, but I was quick and had good hands. In my junior year we won the district and regional tournaments for the first time ever, and in my senior year we ran off sixteen straight wins before losing in the regional.

I played football, although I was really too small. (My coach once suggested that I sit out a year so I could grow, but I said no thanks.) In my senior year I "ballooned" to 147 pounds and became the quarterback in a single-wing offense. We finished that year 6-1-1 and I made the All-Conference team despite completing only about a dozen passes all season. The football was a lot fatter than it is now and my hands were too small to grip it. But I could run and I called my own number pretty often, especially when we got near the goal line. I wrote up all of our games, too, because I was the sports editor for the high school paper. I gave myself whatever credit I deserved, but I'd also make sure to say there was excellent blocking by so-and-so, to give credit to the guys I would be counting on in the next game.

Baseball was my favorite sport, although I didn't stand out the way I did in the other two. In my freshman year I was in the team picture and that was about it. But by senior year we won the conference

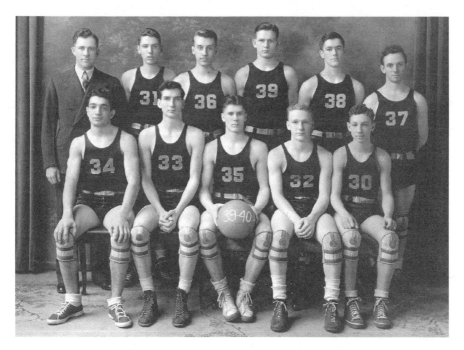

High school basketball coach Malcolm Gobel became a role model for Twig because of the way he commanded players' respect. This is the team during Twig's sophomore year. Front row, from left: Jimmy Spaniolo, Clarence Squibb, Fred Wieting, Jack Mate, Twig. Back row: Coach Gobel, Leland Wendell, Kenneth Bruce, Lyle Kane, James Durner, Raymond Snyder.
Photo courtesy of Charlotte High School

championship and I was playing well enough that I decided to focus on baseball in college.

If my mother was disappointed when I quit violin and piano and dance lessons, she never showed it. Instead, she became my most enthusiastic and reliable fan. She liked basketball because it was indoors, so she was at nearly all of those games, and quite a few football and baseball games, too. My dad only made it to a couple of football games during my whole high school career, but I'd stop in at the bar after every game, home or away. He'd fix me a couple of hamburgers and I'd give him the play-by-play. He didn't compliment me or brag about me, but occasionally my mother would tell me, "You know, he's thrilled about that hit you had." When he put up a picture on the back bar of me in a Cubs uniform, I knew he was proud.

High school wasn't only about sports. I was president of my class in my sophomore, junior, and senior years. I've always thought it was a combination of being a three-sport star and being a little shy. I didn't have a girlfriend, although I did notice girls, including one who sat behind me in history class. She had nice legs and she often crossed them. I'd find some reason to turn around—dropping a pencil was always good—and there they were. I guess I've always been a "leg man." More than once, I had to tell the teacher that I wasn't prepared to give a report, because I didn't want to embarrass myself getting up in front of the class. At the bell, I'd have to carry my books low and in front. It made me mad to have to lie to the teacher, though, because I *was* prepared. I did my work, and my mom helped me if I needed her to, but I was as average a student as you can be—I graduated 52nd in a class of 103!

Sometime during high school my fantasies about being a professional player began to turn into some real hopes for a career. I knew it would not be easy to get there, so I also thought about alternatives. I liked writing for the school paper, and when I got to be sports editor I enjoyed planning the coverage and laying out the pages, so I thought being a sports reporter would be fun. I also admired Malcolm Gobel, our football and basketball coach, and I started to picture myself doing what he did. He was tough, he demanded a lot from his players, and he didn't tolerate any nonsense. I saw him kick a basketball player in the backside for shooting one-handed—we used two hands back then and he wasn't going to have anybody doing it differently. He also expected us to behave away from school. A bunch of us were at the pool hall one day, and somebody whispered, "Coach is coming." We managed to scatter before he got there; we knew we were in for it if he caught us. He commanded his players' respect, and I thought maybe I could do that, too. Twenty years later, I would get the chance. The players I managed and coached would be a little older, but not necessarily any more mature.

First, though, there were lots of other adventures in store for me, including college, a war, and a professional playing career.

3

The Fall of
Western Civilization

Was Alexander so great
when he stepped to the plate?
Would Hannibal's nerve
show up for the curve?

My first try at college didn't go exactly as planned. I encountered a
history professor who didn't know a ground ball from a popup and
didn't care. In other words, he wasn't a guy who would change a
grade for an athlete. I learned a lot from him, but not about history.

I had graduated from Charlotte High School in the spring of
1942, and by that fall, my folks had scraped up enough money to
send me to Western Michigan College of Education, now Western
Michigan University, in Kalamazoo. Western had a good baseball
program, so I was really looking forward to the second term when
the season would start. Because I had skipped an early grade, I had
just turned seventeen during the summer before college. I really wasn't
prepared for college, and my first-term grades showed it: I got an A
in physical education; a B, C, and D in some other courses; and an F
in history. When I flunked that history course, I became ineligible to
play baseball in the spring.

The course I failed was Foundations of Western Civilization,
taught by Dr. Russell Seibert. I took it because I needed a history
course and it fit my schedule. The title alone should have scared me
off. I liked recent history and current events, but I just couldn't relate

to the ancient stuff we were studying. I got a D on the final paper, which left me with an F for the course. When I found out, I went to talk to Professor Seibert. I said I thought a D on the paper should be enough to get a D for the class. He said no, that wasn't the way it worked. I explained, in case he didn't know, that failing the course would mean I couldn't play baseball, and baseball was the main reason I had come to college. He explained to me that athletes didn't get special treatment. I told him I would quit school and join the Marines. He wished me well.

So in December 1942, I went directly from the office of Dr. Russell Seibert to the Marine Corps recruiting office in Kalamazoo and signed up. Then I went home and waited eight months for them to call.

4

San Diego to Suribachi—
a Gung-Ho Marine

What to do and where to go . . .
How about a little gung-ho?
Might as well be with the best—
U.S. Marines—won't flunk this test!

I've had some long road trips in my life, but the one to Saipan, Tinian, and Iwo Jima was definitely the longest—and the one of which I'm most proud.

In August 1943, two months after my eighteenth birthday, the Marines called me to active duty and I reported to San Diego for boot camp. I had never used a gun, but thanks to a great instructor I became an expert shot with the M-1 rifle. I went to radio school and turned out to be good at Morse Code, although I never did use it in combat. With this preparation I became a radioman-machine gunner in a tank for the duration of the war.

I'd had two choices when I signed up: sea duty or infantry. I thought sea duty sounded great—I'd ride around on a battleship and wear dress blues. Instead, I found myself in a tank. In March 1944 I went to Oceanside, California, assigned to the Second Armored Amphibian Battalion (attached to the Second Marine Division), a new unit created specifically to be the assault wave on several operations in the Pacific. Our job was to lead the way for the infantry as we landed on each of several islands. The United States needed the islands to provide airstrips for our planes to use on their way to Japan.

Twig enlisted in the Marines at age seventeen and was called to active duty in August 1943, just after his eighteenth birthday. He trained at San Diego to be a radio operator and machine gunner in an amphibious tank unit; the unit served as the advance landing force at Saipan, Tinian, and Iwo Jima in the South Pacific. *Wayne Terwilliger personal collection*

Our unit was to operate amphibious tanks, a brand-new assault vehicle designed to travel in water and on land. We had only a few to train on at Oceanside. The guys assigned to be drivers practiced taking them out into the breakers and then trying to bring them back in without stalling or getting swamped. Among other problems, the huge waves pushed the tank sideways, which could cause it to tip over. Our practice tanks had no guns, so we couldn't train with those until we got to Maui.

It didn't take long to start forming the tight friendships that would carry us into combat. A lot of our time was spent just hanging around reading our mail and talking, but we also did some sightseeing and some partying. The big deal was going to Tijuana, which I did only once with some buddies. We had heard all the wild stories, but I don't know what we thought we were going to do there. When we went through the border checkpoint, they gave each serviceman a package of condoms and a little flier talking about things to watch out for—warnings about venereal diseases, mostly. Even today, when I see a sign, I believe it. When it says STOP, I stop, and when it says BE CAREFUL, I'm careful. So when they gave us these warnings, I believed them. Getting a venereal disease sounded like about the worst thing in the world. The guys I went with weren't much different from me, so we went to some little club with a dirt floor and drank a little and saw some kind of exotic dancers, but we got back safe and fairly sober.

My best buddy was Paul Yarcho from Lincoln, Illinois. One night Paul and I got an overnight liberty, so we went to downtown San Diego and drank draft beer with raw eggs and decided we'd get tattoos. He wanted me to go first, so I paid my $6 and picked out a big Marine emblem for my arm. When I was finished, Paul wouldn't get his done. I was really pissed that he wouldn't live up to the deal we'd made. He walked out of the tattoo parlor and I tried to shove him back in. I tried to punch him, too, but after a couple of off-target haymakers, we were back at the bar for a nightcap. I've never regretted the tattoo. Ever since I left the service, it has triggered many conversations with fellow Marines who spot it.

My dad came out to San Diego to see me for three or four days just before we shipped overseas. It wasn't his idea, and he was reluctant to make the trip, but my mother insisted that he go. We did a little sightseeing and I showed him around the base, told him about our training, and introduced him to some of my friends. In the back of both our minds, we were thinking it could be our last time together, but we didn't say anything like that out loud. I was still too young to realize it, but many of the traits that I was developing and that would make me a good Marine came from him. Work hard. Get the job done. Stand up straight. Look people in the eye. Give a firm handshake. Don't pick a fight, but stand up for yourself when you have to. Even now, when I notice guys slouching a little, I want to say, "Stand up straight," and when somebody mumbles I want to say, "Speak up!"

As we got set to go overseas, Gunner Hadrian Libertore from Cleveland—he would be called Warrant Officer now—gave one of those classic Marine pep talks, and we were ready to go. He got us fired up, and there was no question on our part, just, "Get out of the way, let me at 'em." I was only afraid of one thing. We were scheduled for a physical exam before we shipped out, and I worried that after all this training, for some reason I wouldn't pass the physical and I'd get left behind. I passed, and I became a good, gung-ho Marine.

On April 26, 1944, the battalion, consisting of about eight hundred men, sailed to Maui to prepare for its first battle. At Oceanside, the men had trained on a few prototype tanks. The full complement of seventy-five armored amphibious vehicles awaited them at Maui, but with no guns and no protective steel plating. In a few short weeks the tanks were made ready and mounted with 75-mm howitzers. Preparation and training time was much shorter than battalion commanders would have liked, and several tanks were lost in training accidents. In late May, the battalion sailed from Maui aboard nineteen ships called LSTs— the official designation was "Landing Ship, Tank"—which carried in their holds the seventy remaining tanks. Slowly, they made their way to Eniwetok in the Marshall Islands and from there to the island of Saipan, a Japanese stronghold in the Marianas.

A little over 14 miles long and 6 miles wide, Saipan was a mass of ravines, crevasses and dead-end gullies covered over by jungle. The 1,500-foot Mount Tapotchau provided a view of most of the island. More than twenty-nine thousand Japanese military were on the island, and the Japanese held the top of the mountain for the first ten days of the battle. Saipan was surrounded by coral reefs, and the heaviest U.S. losses occurred on the first day of battle as the Marines fought to get over the reefs and onto the landing beaches on the southwest side of the island. On the morning of June 15, 1944, the battalion's LSTs arrayed themselves about four thousand yards off the landing beaches.

We didn't sleep much the night before the Saipan invasion, and we were up early. The Navy had started bombarding the island with the battleships' big guns. They lit up the sky with each salvo, and it seemed that the entire island was taking hits. We wondered whether there would be enough Japs left to offer any resistance. We would soon find out.

At daylight we got the order to go below, load into our tanks, and start the engines. We all worried that we'd be overcome by carbon monoxide before we got out of the hold of the LST. Fortunately, we were near the head of the line. I remember the excitement as the LST lowered its big ramp out in front and we drove our tank down the ramp and into the water. The nose of our tank dipped down into the ocean, and for just a second my heart skipped a beat, but the pontooned sides of the tank did the trick and we bobbed up like a huge cork.

In order to make an amphibious tank light enough to float, the armor welded on the outside wasn't more than a quarter-inch thick, which meant it could withstand nothing more than small arms fire. The tank had a 250-horsepower airplane engine that could operate at about 7 miles an hour in water and 15 miles an hour on land. The tracks had deep grousers or cleats that were cupped to move the water; unfortunately, they tended to get bogged down in sand and soft soil. There were separate controls for the two sides so you could change direction, but it wasn't easy to maneuver against the tide.

We had a 75-mm howitzer, a 50-caliber machine gun in the turret, and a 30-caliber machine gun mounted on a swivel gun port directly in front of me. I was in the cab next to the driver, Steve Semon. He and I each had a periscope to see with once we closed our hatches. Behind us was a metal wall with an opening in it, and behind the wall were three others: our tank commander, Sgt. Wallace Johnson; Bill Hoover, who operated the 75-mm howitzer; and an ammunition loader.

We were maybe a half-mile off the coral reef and a mile from the beach itself, and all the tanks lined up in what was supposed to be a straight line, although it never was. While we waited for the signal to go, Steve and I had the hatches open and our seats up, and we looked up and down the line at all our tanks. It was an impressive sight. I'll never forget the feeling—excited, proud, cocky, with a sense of wonder at what lay ahead, but very little fear (that would come later). Sergeant Johnson got the signal over his radio and passed it along on the intercom: "Let's go." The adrenaline was pumping as Steve and I lowered our seats, closed our hatches, and put up our periscopes. Steve looked at me and winked, and off we went.

It took us quite a while to reach the coral reef. We had little experience operating in the water. The tide was shifting, and the reef itself was very uneven so part of the time the tank would be floating and part of the time bouncing off the reef. That made our line even more irregular. Then as soon as we got over the reef, we were in range of the Japanese, and they started shooting. I started seeing these puffs of water all around us, and it took a second to realize what was causing them. Then we heard small arms fire hitting our tank, and the reality sank in: There were people on that island who wanted us dead. They were dug in on the beach, and there was mortar and artillery fire from many inland positions, too. Steve and I looked at each other like, "Oh, boy, now we're in for it." All of a sudden some kind of shot hit my periscope topside and shattered the glass. I flinched, as if it hit me in the eye. I quickly wheeled the periscope down, showed it to Steve and then dropped it into the big pile of 30-caliber ammunition on the floor. About the time I got the replacement periscope up and started wondering what we'd do if that one got hit, I realized that when the shot hit the first one and I flinched, I also peed in my pants. I could feel it, warm and running down my leg. There wasn't a thing I could do about it, and I had bigger things to think about. (A few years later in a college creative writing course, I wrote about having the piss scared out of me. I got an A.)

Mortars kept hitting the water all around us, and Steve was zigzagging to try to avoid getting hit. Other drivers were doing the same, and once in a while through my periscope I'd get a glimpse of another tank on a crooked course. The shooting continued all the way to the beach, but we made it to shore without getting hit by anything solid enough to hurt us. We rolled out of the water and up onto land, managing to avoid land mines. The objective was to establish a beachhead, to clear out the enemy as we moved inland several hundred yards, and to hold our position until the waves of infantry behind us got ashore.

Because of heavy enemy firepower, many amphibious tanks never reached the beach. Those that did found rough going because of obstacles, equipment failure, and continuous shelling. Some crews found themselves isolated in the jungle undergrowth and in danger of being cut off from the beach by Japanese infantry.

As we crossed the beach and began to move inland, we saw a little shack in some bushes off to our right, and Sergeant Johnson told me to shoot into it. I got off a short burst and followed it with a longer one. I could see the tracers just kind of falling off and dropping, and for just a moment, it went through my head that my machine gun wasn't shooting right, that the damn bullets weren't going fast enough to get where they were supposed to go! As we kept moving inland, the trees and shrubs got thicker. We couldn't see any Japanese, but we could hear mortar fire and every so often something would land pretty close. We just kept shooting into anything that looked like it might be a shelter for the enemy.

We went in almost to the airstrip, a few hundred yards inland, and then we got bogged down. There was a large unexploded Navy shell ahead of us, and in trying to maneuver around it, we hit a big shell hole and bottomed out. Steve burned out the clutch trying to get out. As we sat there trying to figure out what to do, a couple of mortars

hit close by, so Sergeant Johnson decided we'd better get out and
work our way back to the beach on foot. We were trained that if we
had to abandon a tank we were to put a grenade in the breech of the
machine gun and pull the pin so the enemy couldn't use it if it fell
into their hands. I got out a grenade and was looking for the best
place to set it. When I looked around and saw that the whole crew
was gone, I thought, "Screw this." I stuck the grenade back in my
belt, slithered out of my hatch and onto the ground, and found several of my crew mates taking cover in another shell hole, maybe 6 or
7 feet deep. I joined them.

We were outside the tank, caught between our guys and the
enemy. We didn't know that nobody was following us until we got
out and found ourselves alone. It sounded like most of our tanks
were pinned down by mortar fire on the beach. Japanese mortars
kept whistling over our heads. Most of them were headed toward the
beach area, but we never knew when one would come our way. We
also had no idea how long we'd be stuck there. We were there at
least a couple of hours, though it seemed like forever. We had used
up all the water in our canteens a long time ago, and we had never
been so thirsty. Somebody mentioned that we left a five-gallon can of
water in our tank, about twenty yards away, but nobody volunteered
to go after it. After another long while, Bill Hoover scrambled out of
the hole and sprinted to the tank, and came dragging the can of
water back to our hole. We would have voted him the Congressional
Medal of Honor right then and there.

More time went by, and we heard somebody running toward us.
Sergeant Johnson scrambled up to the top of the hole and began
waving. It was a Marine infantryman who had gotten separated from
his squad. That was good news because it meant our forces were on
the move. So a while later, we were momentarily happy to hear the
sound of a tank grinding away . . . until we realized it didn't sound
like one of ours.

Sergeant Johnson climbed to the top of the hole again, and this
time he hurried back down. "Jap tank" was all he said. The tank kept
moving closer to us until we could see the 37-mm turret gun and the
big red "Rising Sun" on the side of the tank. I remember thinking,
"Where in hell does he think he's going?" About then, the tank
stopped just short of our hole and I wondered, "What do we do

now?" Sergeant Johnson told us to throw our grenades and try to get them under the tank. They teach you to pull the pin, release the handle, hesitate a couple of seconds, and then lob the grenade overhand, kind of like a hook shot, to get distance. I should have used a short-armed snap throw—like turning a double play—for accuracy, because my hook shot went wide, clipped a palm tree branch and fell well short of the target.

We ducked and all the grenades seemed to go off at once, with a huge explosion. The concussion blew my helmet off and blew sand and smoke everywhere, including into my eyes. When I finally could see a little, I climbed out of the hole and started running—no helmet, no rifle, no idea where I was going. I ran until I came to an old Japanese artillery piece, and I thought, "Shit, this is the wrong way," so I turned and found a little path, and somehow this time I was going the right way, toward the beach. Then I looked back and there was the Jap tank coming after me. All I could think was, "Damn, I've gotta go faster." I started zigzagging back and forth in case the tank tried to shoot at me, still running as fast as I could. Guys on the beach were waving me in, yelling, "Come on, come on!" I made it to the beach and dove over a small sand dune for cover, and I looked back just in time to see one of our tanks make a direct hit, which knocked the Japanese tank on its side. I watched it catch fire, and that was the end of that particular adventure! I must have run full-out at least three hundred yards. A few years later, when I made my Triple A debut with the Los Angeles Angels, the sports writers loved to tell about how I had used my speed to outrun a Jap tank during the war. That was my first six or seven hours of combat.

The rest of the day is mostly a blur. There was a series of happy reunions with all of the other guys from my tank. Many of the other tanks had taken direct hits from big artillery or had run into enemy soldiers firing from all sides, including from treetops. There were a lot of injuries and too many dead. I got a new helmet and carbine, and I joined in with whatever needed to be done.

I remember clearly the moment I saw my first dead Marine. He was a young lieutenant who had only made it a few steps onto the beach, his helmet still on, not a mark on him, looking like he was just sleeping, but clearly dead. I remember every detail, even his wristwatch. When I close my eyes, I can still see his face and how young he looked. Years later, there was an American League umpire that looked a lot like him, and whenever I saw that umpire, I remembered that young face. The lieutenant wasn't the only dead Marine I saw, but he was the one I'll never forget.

Sometime during the day I noticed some blood on my pants, just above the knee. When I finally checked it out, I found that I had a gash under my left knee, three or four inches long. It was nothing compared to what I saw around me. By nightfall, I was more tired than I had ever been in my life. I slept in another one of our company's tanks, oblivious to the sporadic mortar fire and grateful to be alive.

The 2nd Armored Amphibian Battalion lost twenty-six men on the first day of the battle for Saipan—more than during the entire thirty-six-day battle for Iwo Jima a year later. Terwilliger's "D" Company, which was positioned on the right, or southernmost, flank of the battalion assault force at the south end of the island, was among those receiving the heaviest fire and suffering the heaviest casualties, including eight dead and thirty wounded that first day.

In one of those first couple of days, I was moving up the beach with some other guys from my company when we came under fire. We started running. My buddy Paul Yarcho was hit in the hand, and a couple of others were hurt, too. I didn't know it at the time, but during the attack a U.S. Coast Guard photographer was taking pictures. He caught the exact moment when a couple of guys fell, and he caught me right at the center of the picture. I was amazed to see it when I opened the Sunday magazine section of the *Chicago Tribune* in 1950, and it has turned up several more times since then. (It looked like me but I had to convince myself. The young man in the photo had rolled-up sleeves and carried two canteens, and I was the only guy I knew who did either of those things.)

Eventually we got our tank back, and one day we were on the beach but outside the tank when the Japanese made a counterattack. It was one of those Banzai attacks where they made a lot of noise with horns and anything else they had, and it would either scare us off or be a suicide mission for them. As they came down the beach,

Wayne Terwilliger and other Marines from his company came under Japanese sniper fire as they moved across the beach during the U.S. invasion of Saipan in June 1944. Terwilliger is facing the camera near the center of the photo. *Life* magazine used the photo in its *Picture History of World War II* published in 1950, and the U.S. Postal Service used it in 1999 as the background for a sheet of stamps commemorating the 1940s.
U.S. Coast Guard photograph

the infantry and artillery were fighting them. We jumped into foxholes, but our tanks were parked nearby and I thought we should get into them in case the attack reached us. The guys in charge said, "Just sit tight." It was nerve-wracking, but sure enough, the attack was stopped before it got to us.

For the rest of the time on Saipan, our unit provided support for the infantry. The Japanese started sneaking off one end of the island and coming around to attack some positions from behind, so we were sent to guard the end of the island, positioned out in shallow water, to prevent that from happening. One night we were on duty and John Schrader was taking his turn on the 50-caliber machine gun on the turret. A couple of us were sleeping underneath the machine gun when he opened fire. I was startled awake and I just froze. I looked out where the tracers were going. He was firing toward the water, and I couldn't see a damn thing out there so I thought he'd gotten excited and shot at something that wasn't there. At dawn, we went to look, and there was a Japanese soldier that he'd hit several times. The soldier had a number of grenades, and he had waded out into the water to approach us from behind. That was right around my nineteenth birthday.

It took twenty-six days of fighting—until July 9, 1944—to get the island secured, and even after that other units were engaged in cleanup operations. We stayed on to prepare for the assaults on Tinian and Iwo Jima.

One day four or five of us decided to walk over to a nearby town to see what was left there. We had to walk very carefully to avoid land mines. The Japanese had rounded up the civilians who lived on Saipan and either killed them or held them in prison camps, so the town was abandoned. It had taken a lot of fire and it was a mess, but one small building near the edge of town was still pretty much intact, and we went in. There were papers and books scattered everywhere. There were also lots of condoms and sexual stuff, so we guessed it was a whorehouse. We had been told not to take household goods from the homes of civilians, but we figured it would be okay to look around in this place, and anyway, there was nothing of value. We had to be very careful—we looked under everything before we lifted it in case it was booby-trapped. I noticed a colorful silk cloth with some kind of design. At first I thought it was some sort of flag, but then I saw that the design included a woman and man entangled, with a blanket or cloth around them—you could tell it was a sexual thing. It was beautiful—the colors, especially—and I was pretty pleased as I stuck it in my pocket. The other guys picked up some magazines and a trinket or two, but there really wasn't much left. I had that cloth hidden in my tent for a long time. Then one day I looked and it was gone. Somebody must have known about it and taken it. So that was the end of my only wartime souvenir.

On July 24, 1944, the 2nd Armored Amphibian Battalion began the nine-day battle for Tinian, an island about 3 miles off Saipan. The Japanese had taken advantage of Tinian's flat land-

Company D Marines on Saipan. Back row: Twig's friends Paul Yarcho, John Sleconich and Marion Bozarth. Front: Twig and Sgt. Edmond Norton. They were part of the 2nd Armored Amphibian Battalion, created to lead the assault on key islands in the South Pacific. They fought at Saipan, Tinian, and Iwo Jima, and were preparing for new battles when the war ended. When we posted this photo on www.wayneterwilliger.com, we received a moving letter from a son of John Sleconich, whose family had never seen this photo. *Wayne Terwilliger personal collection*

scape to build three airfields. The United States would expand those fields and fly thousands of B-29 missions from Tinian. The atomic bombs dropped on Hiroshima and Nagasaki in August of 1945 were flown from Tinian.

The Japanese were expecting an invasion at the southwest part of Tinian, and we carried out some diversionary maneuvers there. And, while the Japanese were busy with that, we got 15,000 Marine infantrymen ashore on the northeast part of the island. There was a big counterattack during the night, which turned out to be the only major battle the Japanese put up.

We developed a hole in the pontoon of our tank during the assault, and we couldn't navigate so we kept going around in circles in the water. We crawled out and sat on top of the tank and waited for a PT boat to pick us up and take us to an LST. Eventually we got ashore. One of our guys stayed on the tank and he was still in the turret when the tank sank. It went down 25 or 30 feet into the water before he came bobbing up in his life jacket and was rescued.

Our battalion spent about a week helping out in the fight to take control of Tinian. After that we went back to Saipan and spent about six months getting ready for the next operation, which turned out to be Iwo Jima.

When I entered the Marines, I pretty much figured that baseball was over until I got back to college. But other Marines liked the game, too, so once we had some time on our hands, we cleared some space for a makeshift baseball field. It was nothing fancy. The ground was pretty rough. It was next to the 2nd Marine Division cemetery, and we dug foxholes nearby in case of an air raid. One day a bomber came over in the middle of a game and we all took off for the foxholes. But that kind of interruption was rare, and baseball was a great outlet for a bunch of young guys between battles. Before long, we realized we were pretty good, too.

We borrowed some gear from other units at first, and eventually we acquired some of our own. Some major league teams sent balls and bats and other gear to service units during the war, and that may be how we got our equipment. Shoes weren't part of the deal. We played wearing our combat boots—what we called boondockers—so we didn't steal many bases! Our games started out as casual fun, but we quickly made some real competition of it. The four companies in our battalion played each other, and then we formed a 2nd Armored Amphibian Battalion team, which went out and played five teams from other units of the 2nd Marine Division around the island. Every team had at least a couple of very good players, and one or two of these had been in the major leagues, although they weren't well known. I played shortstop, as I had in high school. I was getting terrific experience, especially for somebody who hadn't played a single game at the college level yet. Our battalion team won twenty-eight straight games, went undefeated, and became the champions of

The 2nd Armored Amphibian Battalion's team went 28-0 and became champs of the 2nd Marine Division league, which they had been invited to join although the battalion was not part of the division. Front row, from left: Al Barnosky, Robert Robbins, Jim Hartman, Edwin "Skee" Kochmanski, Twig, Dick Jones. Second row: Shannon Proctor, Tom Foster, Walter Singletary, Hal Harrison, Bill Spencer, Bill Zack. Third row: Lt. Silas Clatterbuck, Lt. John Crawley, Lt. Albin "Doc" Galuszka, Col. Francis Cooper, Capt. George Warnke, Lt. Walter Storm.
U.S.M.C. photo, September 1945

the division. The officers threw a huge party for us. Several of us were chosen to go to Guam for an all-star game. I was an alternate and didn't get to play, but at least I got a week of R and R on Guam. Our best player—Donald "Rip" Koenig, a second baseman who could play just about any infield position—was so good that the Pacific Fleet got him transferred from our battalion up to their team on Oahu after Iwo Jima.

During all of this time, I was writing regularly to my girlfriend, Mary Jane Locke. I'd had very little time for girls in high school, but Mary Jane and I had started dating after graduation. While I was in the Marines, she served with the WAVES in Texas. I made up my mind that I would marry her when we both got home. We had not slept together, and I knew we wouldn't until we were married. That wasn't all that unusual at the time, but sometimes I felt like the only virgin in the Marine Corps. The longer I was in service, the more I'd hear guys telling stories. They made sex sound pretty interesting, and they had me thinking that it would be terrible if I got killed in combat before I had ever gone to bed with a woman. While we were in Hawaii, I went with some guy to a massage parlor, figuring I was going to get laid. After all, I had heard all about massage parlors. But the one we went to turned out to be a legitimate *massage* parlor. The gal doing the rubbing was attractive, and I enjoyed it, but I didn't say anything and she didn't say anything and that was all there was to it.

It was a fact of life that after the battles were over, after all the fear and excitement, we were a bunch of mostly young, horny guys sitting around in our tents. Supposedly they put saltpeter in the food to tame "the urge," but if they did, I'd have to say it didn't work. So guys would be sneaking off, maybe going to the john, to take care of things. Finally the guys in our tent decided it was kind of silly, and inconvenient, to have to sneak around. We decided to have a regular time every Friday evening when everybody could take care of business—30 minutes of quiet time, no talking and no questions asked. If you wanted, you could just lie in your bunk and think about your mother's apple pie and that was fine, too. Guys were probably doing this all over the world during the war, but I don't know whether anybody else had it organized like we did.

Iwo Jima is about 660 nautical miles from Tokyo, and it was about midway on the B-29 bombing route from Saipan to Tokyo. The United States wanted Iwo Jima as a base for its planned air attacks on Japan, and because it was a keystone of the Japanese defense system. Mount Suribachi, a 550-foot extinct volcano, stands at the southern tip of Iwo Jima, whose name means "sulphur island." The north part of the island is rough and rocky, while the area around Suribachi is covered with ash.

The Japanese general defending the island built hundreds of strong battle positions, which would be defended to the death. Artillery, rockets, and mortars placed on high ground at the north and south ends of the island defended a narrow, low-ground isthmus connecting Suribachi to the rest of the island. Deep underground tunnels protected Japanese troops from U.S. bombing and shelling before the invasion. Natural underground caves connected by tunnels provided multiple entrances and exits for many firing positions. In addition, the entire island was heavily mined, and every square foot was covered by the fire-power of weapons ranging from rifles to rockets.

At 8:30 a.m. on February 19, 1945, the amphibious tanks of the 2nd Battalion headed for six landing beaches on Iwo Jima. A few were hit and damaged on the way in, but there was surprisingly little shooting compared with the landing at Saipan, and there were no enemy troops to be cleared off the beach. But as the amphibious tanks entered the beaches, they encountered soft volcanic ash, which wind and surf had formed into embankments, or terraces. The tanks could get no footing in the ash, and they stalled trying to climb the terraces and move inland. Behind them, infantry poured onto the beaches and then had nowhere to go. That is when the Japanese began firing in earnest. It continued, intense and relentless, for twenty-four hours, and the battle continued for thirty-six days.

Our battalion was on the left flank of the landing force at Iwo Jima, and we landed near the southern end of the island, right next to Mount Suribachi. The water was pretty deep all the way to shore, so we didn't get bounced around like we had on the reefs at Saipan. But as we got onto the beach, there was all this ash, nothing but ash, and the tanks couldn't get any traction to get up the embankment. After a lot of tries, our tank finally took hold—I can hear it grinding yet—and with that we climbed up the bank to the next level. I think we were the first—and maybe the only—tank to get up there. Steve Semon must have been a great driver, because he got us far inland on both Saipan and Iwo Jima when others didn't get beyond the beach.

As soon as we reached higher ground, we could see mortars and stuff coming in at us. I managed to look back down to where the infantry was coming in behind us, in Higgins boats or rubber ducks, and they were getting blown right out of the water. It was bad.

Before long we got orders to get the amphibious tanks back off the island because the Japs were using our tanks to sight in on. We went back into the water and sat just off the island, shooting in toward Mount Suribachi to provide support for the infantry working in that area. The Japanese had a lot of gun emplacements on high ground, including some huge guns in caves on the mountain. We stayed out there the whole first day and into the evening, shooting toward the volcano. We drifted around as it got darker and darker, and the water got rougher and rougher, and we started trying to find an LST to take us aboard.

They had made some modifications on the tanks that weren't helping us in this situation. Because the periscopes hadn't worked or had gotten broken all the time, they took them out and cut a seven-inch by two-inch hole in front of each of us so we could peer out. They also patched a little more armor on the sides of the tanks, but that made us heavier so we were sitting lower in the water. As we bobbed around in the choppy waves, water was coming through the new holes, enough that it was puddling on the floor. Worse, as it came in it was hitting the transmission, right between the driver and the radioman, and steam was coming up at us. We were sick to our stomachs from the waves and the steam and the smell, and we were wondering whether we were ever going to get picked up or whether enough water would come in that it would sink the tank and we would drown out there. But finally an LST came along. They dropped the plank and we rolled aboard and had hot coffee and stayed until morning. Then we got back in our tank and went to the island again. Some other tanks got picked up the same way, and a few went back on shore after dark, but a few unlucky ones bounced around in the water all night.

At the end of day one, twenty-two of the battalion's amphibious tanks—about a third of the tanks they had arrived with—were no longer operating, having been damaged or destroyed by enemy fire.

We spent a big part of the second day carrying wounded guys to Higgins boats that transported them out to hospital ships. As we went back and forth with the stretchers, the footing on the beach was rough, and I worried about tripping and dropping somebody. Eventually some paths were cut through the embankments so the tanks could make it up there, and a couple of units took control of the southern tip of the island. We climbed into our tank and joined them, and for several days we helped provide support while the infantry fought to gain control of Mount Suribachi. We were not far from the mountain and we were looking right at it most of the time. Every so often, there would be shooting or another mortar attack from the Japanese, and we would return fire. On the fifth day, antipersonnel mortars were coming in at us when somebody said, "Hey look, there's a flag on the mountain." And there it was—the American flag flying on Iwo Jima. It was a *great* feeling to see that flag and to know that our troops finally controlled the mountain.

Iwo Jima was declared secured on March 16, 1945. The battalion was on Maui preparing to invade Japan when, after the bombing of Hiroshima and Nagasaki, Japan surrendered on August 15.

In spring 1945, after a couple of months on Iwo Jima, our battalion was sent back to Maui to train to invade Japan. We understood that we were headed there for an invasion similar to the three we had already carried out, except bigger. We knew that bombing was a big part of the plans; we had taken Saipan to give our side an airstrip for taking off and Iwo as a stopping place on the way back. On Saipan we had met some of the guys who flew the B-29s and nobody was saying much; it was all very secret. It was obvious that something very big was coming up, but we didn't know about the Big One until we heard about Hiroshima and Nagasaki after the fact.

I was playing baseball at a naval air station in Hawaii when we heard that Japan had surrendered. It took a while to sink in, but when it did, I was just so glad that it was *over*. A few weeks later, I was on board the battleship USS *Colorado,* headed for California and beginning to dream about the comforts of home. Big mistake. We went through a huge storm that was as frightening as anything I had experienced in combat. The *Colorado* was enormous, but this storm kicked up walls of water higher than the top of the ship and when they crashed down on the decks they easily could have washed somebody overboard. As I got tossed around below decks, I thought, "I never should have complained about bobbing around in that tank off Iwo Jima."

One of the first things I remember once I got back to the United States was looking into a mirror and realizing that my teeth were a solid gray. Everybody's teeth were a little gray, and they told us it was from drinking out of canteens. I drank a *lot* of water, and I was the only guy I knew who carried two canteens. But I hadn't looked into many mirrors while I was overseas, so I didn't know that my own teeth were darker than anyone else's. It took a while to get them back to their natural color.

Our battalion was deactivated on November 30, and I was discharged from the Marines in Chicago on December 5, 1945. I hitchhiked home to Charlotte; a guy in a semi picked me up and took me most of the way. I was a good Marine, nothing more. I never did anything especially brave or out of the ordinary, but I was gung-ho, and when I got an order, I followed it. I'm more proud of my Marine service than of anything else I've done before or since.

5

"Primitive Savagery," or Flying with Angels

Des Moines . . . L.A.
Hot Dog! Hooray!
Moving up . . . more pay . . .
I'm on my way . . .
. . . I hope!

I returned from the Marines a lot more mature and focused than before. Mary Jane and I were married in February 1946, and thanks to the GI Bill I was able to start back at Western Michigan for the spring term. We lived in a campus trailer park for returning servicemen, and Mary Jane got a job as secretary to the athletic director. The baseball program had a good reputation and major league scouts came around on a fairly regular basis, so I knew there was a chance I could get noticed, but in the meantime I began to prepare for other possibilities. I had in mind that I would probably become a high school teacher and coach, but I was thinking about journalism, too, and I thought I might go to the University of Missouri after I finished at Western Michigan. Meanwhile, I did a much better job of selecting courses so I wouldn't repeat the Fall of Western Civilization.

Returning servicemen were automatically eligible for athletics, and in my first year I played three sports. As an end on the freshman football team, I recovered a fumble against Michigan State, caught a long pass between a couple of prisoners when we played Ionia Reformatory, and managed to stay injury-free.

I didn't plan to play varsity basketball, so I joined an intramural team for fun. One day I noticed that the varsity coach, Buck Read, was watching. When we finished, he asked me to come out for the varsity team, the Broncos. I was a little surprised when I made the club and became a starting guard. Coach Read told me, "I noticed you because of your quickness on the court. I saw you go around your man and just leave him standing there while you went in for a lay-up." I was quick, but mostly I used it on defense, which was my strong point. I had an especially good defensive game against Indiana State—got some steals, made some good passes, and added a few points to our winning total. In the locker room after the game, somebody said the other team's coach was asking to see me. He had a very sincere manner; he looked me in the eye and told me he just wanted to tell me that I had played a great game. It meant a lot, because it was pretty unusual for a coach to seek out a player on the opposing team to pay him a compliment. A year or two later, that coach left Indiana State for UCLA, where he spent twenty-seven years building a dynasty. His name was John Wooden. Besides being the "winningest" coach in basketball history, he has a reputation as a great motivator, and I understand why. His gesture was a class act and it confirmed for me that coaching could be about something more than just winning and losing. It could be about character.

Playing baseball in the Marines had made me a lot more confident than I was coming out of high school. I started out playing shortstop, but I began to feel that second base might be a more natural spot for me. I went to the coach and explained that I didn't think my arm was really strong enough for the longer throw from short to first. I was making most of the plays but not every one, and I thought I could do better at second. Fortunately, the coach agreed. I became good at it. I could get to the ball, make a quick pivot and get rid of the ball in a hurry, and that meant I could turn double plays. Meanwhile, I was batting .350—no home runs but a pretty good mix of singles, doubles and triples against some decent college-level pitching. We played a tough schedule, and in 1948, my third and final season, we went 16-5 and just missed first place in the Mid-American Conference.

The highlight of my college baseball career was in 1948 when we beat our big rival Michigan State. As I recall, we beat their pitcher Robin Roberts, later of Phillies fame, twice in one year by identical

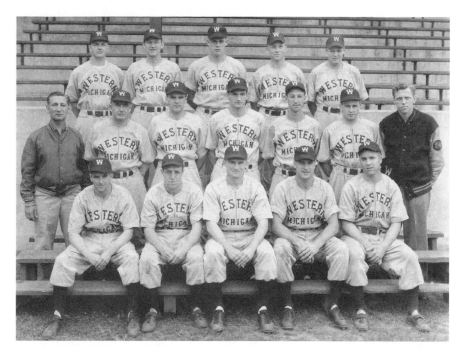

The Western Michigan Broncos went 16-5 in 1948, Twig's final season, and they beat both of their in-state rivals—Michigan and Michigan State—twice. Front row, from left: Bob Pollard, Joe Cooper, Ted Plaza, Don Groggel, Walt Young. Second row: trainer Ed Gabel, coach Charles Maher, captain Dick Groggel, George Duditch, Twig, assistant coach Ivan Fleser, manager Walt Dmytryshyn. Third row: Carlton Coss, Bill Kowalski, Don Boven, Gene Schlukebir, Gordon Bowdell.
Photo courtesy of WMU Archives and Regional History Collections

scores of 9-1. When I hit against him with the Cubs, he took a little revenge. I got a sign to hit on a 3-0 count, and I fouled it off. He was an established star, and I'm sure it bothered him to have me swinging on 3-0, so with the next pitch, he hit me in the rear end. When I celebrated my fiftieth year in baseball, Roberts sent a note reminding me that our college team hadn't treated him very well. Then he said, "Congratulations on getting older. The alternative sucks, I hear."

In the summers during college, I played semi-pro ball for the House of David team in Benton Harbor, about 50 miles from Kalamazoo.

The House of David, a religious sect located in Benton Harbor, Michigan, sponsored a series of semi-professional baseball teams from 1915 until the late 1940s. Initially, teams were made up of members of the sect, who wore long hair and beards and lived communally, abstaining from liquor, tobacco, sex, and shaving. Occasionally a professional player would become a "ringer," hiding under a long false beard. House of David teams are credited with such innovations as the "pepper game" and night baseball. By the mid-1940s, the group was sponsoring teams of players who were not members and did not masquerade as members.

We played at a ballpark right on the House of David grounds. The first summer, I tried hitchhiking to every game. It wasn't a very reliable form of transportation, so the team's owner, Tate Edgell, loaned me his big Chrysler for the summer. What a treat! The second year, I stayed with a couple of other collegians in a makeshift apartment on the House of David grounds. We trimmed a few trees during the day and played baseball two or three evenings and Sunday afternoons. We were paid $15 a day. To maintain our college eligibility, the money was supposedly for the tree-trimming. A couple of guys played under different last names just to be safe, but Edgell assured me that everything would be fine, so I just used Terwilliger. My dad's bar was closed on Sundays, so those summers were the best opportunity he ever had to watch me play. My folks would drive the 100 miles from Charlotte, pack a picnic lunch, and make a day of it.

Our team was called the House of David in '46; the next year for some reason we became the Benton Harbor Buds. We were in the Michigan-Indiana league, and our big rival was St. Joseph. While Benton Harbor was a working-class town, St. Joe was a rich town with a lot of summer visitors. It was our favorite place to play because they had a fancy new ballpark, big crowds, and a good team. Their owner, a guy named Walter Tiscornia, made the ballpark a real showplace, the best in the league. It even had a ball-server—the umpire would walk over and push a button, and a ball would come up out of the ground into a little basket.

Tiscornia built up his team by bringing in a few ex-major leaguers like Roy Henshaw, a former Tigers pitcher, and Benny McCoy, a bonus baby second baseman for Detroit and Philadelphia. Their first-base coach, a guy called Long John Tucker, had been a star first baseman with the House of David for years. They were an all-around strong team and in '46 they won the National Baseball Congress World Series. So it was fun to play St. Joe, and it was always a big deal to beat them.

For great competition and crowds, though, you couldn't beat our Sunday afternoon exhibition games against barnstorming teams from the Negro Leagues. In the 1920s the House of David had teams that barnstormed around different parts of the country to make money and to gain attention for their beliefs. In the '30s they began to play against teams from the Negro Leagues, and they often toured with them—either one of the official teams or a traveling team assembled just for that purpose. These games were a big attraction in Benton Harbor, where a lot of the residents were blacks who had moved up from the South to work in the town's factories. The team I was on didn't barnstorm, but we hosted as many teams as we could schedule—traveling squads from teams like the Kansas City Monarchs, the Homestead Grays, and the Indianapolis Clowns.

In 1946 only Jackie Robinson had left the Negro Leagues for a major league organization; he was playing for the Dodgers' minor league club in Montreal. Larry Doby, Monte Irvin, Satchel Paige, Dan Bankhead, and others I would later play against in the majors were all still with their Negro League teams, along with Josh Gibson, Cool Papa Bell, Buck Leonard, Buck O'Neil, and so many others. The traveling exhibition squads that we played may have been made up of lesser-known guys, but they weren't pushovers by any means. They had talent, and they played the kind of baseball I like—aggressive base running, the hit-and-run, always trying to make something happen. Our games against them were exciting. We won our share, but we had to play well. It was great experience.

Unfortunately, most of us didn't know a lot about the Negro Leagues at the time, so even though they had some of the all-time great players, we didn't know many of their names. I wish now that I had rosters for the teams I played against so I could see exactly who was there. I do remember that Dan Bankhead pitched against us in '46 or '47, and he was tough. He was being called "the next Satchel Paige"—he was about fifteen years younger than Paige, who was forty by then. In August of 1947, a few months after Jackie Robinson made history as the first black player in the majors, Bankhead also joined the Dodgers and became the first black pitcher. He was a reliever with the Dodgers in 1951 when I joined them, but he wasn't pitching as well as I had seen him at Benton Harbor, and '51 was his last season in the majors.

All of the Negro Leagues teams knew how to entertain a crowd. I particularly remember one of them doing infield practice with an imaginary baseball, tossing and catching and jumping for a ball that wasn't there. They had it down pat—you could *see* that nonexistent ball travel around the field. The crowd loved it, and we did, too. We tried to work up a routine like that, but it's tough to do, and we never got it right.

The Benton Harbor Buds suffered a severe blow when it was announced that Wayne Terwilliger, brilliant fielding second sacker and able hitter, had signed a Chicago Cub contract. . . . Wayne participated in nine games this year, hit .347, made 24 put outs and 25 assists, and committed only one error.
—Benton Harbor (Michigan) News-Palladium, *June 1948*

My first big professional break came in 1948, just after classes ended at Western Michigan. I had only a few courses left, so I wasn't going to be playing college baseball anymore. A few scouts had come around to talk to me, including the White Sox, Saint Louis Browns, and Red Sox, but nobody offered anything worth considering. I planned to spend the summer playing for Benton Harbor again, and then I'd finish my degree. Nine games into our season, the Chicago Cubs sent Tony Lucadello—the scout who signed more major leaguers than any other—to ask me to work out at Wrigley Field. I had just agreed to go when I also heard from a Detroit Tigers' scout who had seen me play at college. As much as I loved the Tigers, I wasn't too impressed with his offer, and besides, I had already promised the Cubs I'd try out. Frankly, I was happy to be talking to the Cubs because I knew that with some of their players getting older, they would need infielders before long.

They paid my way to Chicago and put me up at a hotel. I was so excited. I worked out one day, stayed overnight, and worked out again the next day, taking batting practice and fielding ground balls. Phil Cavarretta, their long-time first baseman, was throwing batting practice, and they had me take a few swings. I hit a couple of balls pretty well, although nothing spectacular. Then Milt Stock, one of the coaches, hit me a bunch of hot grounders, and I was gobbling them up; he couldn't hit one by me. I could tell that people were watching, and I knew I was doing well, making an impression with my glove. It was a good tryout, and it was pretty consistent with how my career would go—good fielding and so-so hitting. After I showered, they called me into the front office to talk to Harold George, the assistant farm director, about signing.

"We'd like to give you a chance," Mr. George said. "We'll send you to Des Moines." The Des Moines Bruins were the Cubs' Single A club in the Western League. Now that I was getting this opportunity, I was determined to make the most of it. "I'd be happy to spend this season at Des Moines," I told him, "but I need to ask for one thing. I'm twenty-two years old, and I have a lot more experience than some of the young guys you're signing. I've been playing semi-pro ball, and I played on a team in the Marines that won twenty-eight straight games. So I'll play the rest of this season in A-ball, but I want the opportunity to go to spring training with your Triple A club next year." Mr. George agreed to that, and I signed for $450 a month plus a signing bonus, which brought my total pay for 1948 to $4,000.

Just before I was to go to Des Moines, they sent me instead on a long, hot train ride to Macon, Georgia. But that was a mistake; when I got there, they didn't have any room on their roster. I watched two ballgames and never put on a uniform. A couple of phone calls later, I got back on the train and went to Des Moines, where I discovered that the club was in first place—and that they had a second baseman named Red Treadway, who was leading the league in hitting at .323. I could see that I was going to spend a fair amount of time on the bench. The team had quite a few solid players who were on their way up. Outfielder Bob Borkowski, infielder Randy "Handsome Ransom" Jackson, and catcher Carl "Swats" Sawatski, who led the league with twenty-nine home runs, all would be with the Cubs a couple of years later. So would I, but that didn't seem very likely as I sat and watched the others play.

I got my first professional RBI—with my head—with Des Moines. We were playing in Denver. The bases were loaded and the count went to three and two. I wasn't a good breaking ball hitter, and the pitcher kept throwing me breaking balls and I just kept fouling them off. Finally, he threw a fastball right at my head. I was still waiting for it to break when it hit me just behind my left ear. I went down in a daze. When I opened my eyes, I looked up to see my manager— Stan Hack, the old Cubs All-Star third baseman—standing over me with a big cud of tobacco in his cheek. For a brief moment I was more concerned about the juice collecting in the corner of his mouth than with the pain in my head. Eventually, I got up and went to first base, trying to run, but not very gracefully. The next hitter, Bob Borkowski, tripled to right center field, and I had to run the bases. I thought I was doing a good job until I got into the dugout and the guys told me that on my way from third I ran outside the baseline, staggered, and just barely made it home. Somebody told me to go back to the hotel and lie down, which I learned later is probably the worst thing you can do with a head injury. But that's what I did, and I survived. I might be the only guy ever to have knocked in his first run with his head.

I got into eighteen games that season, and hit a whopping .196. I had never hit that poorly in my life, but sitting on the bench most of the time didn't help. We each got a $100 bonus for winning the pennant, but I couldn't take much satisfaction in it. I went home disappointed, but knowing that in a few months I was going to spring training with the Los Angeles Angels in the Pacific Coast League.

Terwilliger, in particular, has [Angels Manager Bill] Kelly eating his meals with his fingers crossed. . . . "He's our second baseman until somebody better comes along. And if he should flop under fire, I can use Mickey Burnett or Albie Glossop."
—Los Angeles Times, *March 29, 1949, the day before the season opener*

Even my dad was excited about my first spring training. He knew an old-time wood-worker in Olivet, 10 miles from Charlotte. He asked the guy to make me a bat. I was skeptical at first, but when I took my first few swings, I was impressed. It was heavier and had a bigger handle than I was used to, but it was well balanced and it looked "real." I used it in spring training and at the start of the regular season. It had some iron in it, as we liked to say. But I must have looked like the original country-boy rookie when I stepped off the train in Fullerton, California, glove and bat in hand.

> *A double dip on Sundays*
> *No games 'til Tuesday nights*
> *Mondays can be fun days*
> *Stay out, enjoy the sights*

A betting man would have had to figure that if anybody from the '48 Des Moines Cubs was going to play second base for the Angels, it would be Red Treadway, with his .300 average. But by the end of spring training in March 1949, I had gone from sitting on the bench in A ball to a starting position in the Triple A Pacific Coast League (PCL).

The PCL was a thriving organization that was still hoping to become the country's third major league. Because of the favorable weather in places like San Diego, Sacramento, Seattle, Portland, and Los Angeles, the PCL played a longer season than the majors, and players were compensated accordingly. And the schedule was great. Traveling teams usually stayed for most of a week. Typically, we'd open a series on a Tuesday night and close it with a doubleheader on Sunday. We'd have Monday off, and then start another series on Tuesday. There were players who could have been in the majors but preferred the PCL because of the money, the climate, and the schedule. Many of the 1949 PCL managers had major league experience. San Diego's Bucky Harris had led the Yankees to a World Series championship in 1947. Charlie Dressen, who had been one of Harris's coaches, was managing the Oakland Oaks. The Angels' manager, Bill Kelly, didn't have their major league credentials, but he was a good baseball man *and* he gave me a chance to play.

The PCL had a new rule that every team must have at least three rookies. Besides that, Bill Kelly (and his bosses in Chicago) had decided it was time to bring some youth onto his club, so he was willing to take a look at me. Still, I suspect that he and everybody

Young MGM star Esther Williams threw out the first pitch of the Los
Angeles Angles' 1949 season, winding up with such enthusiasm that her
sunglasses flew out of her pocket. Twig made his Triple A debut that day.
Los Angeles Times Collection, UCLA Library, Department of Special Collections

else in the organization figured that when the season began I would
be back in A ball, or maybe Double A if I was lucky. How could you
blame them? Most players came to the PCL with a fair amount of
professional experience. I had played eighteen games with Des
Moines and hit .196. But in training camp I went at it the only way I
knew, and that was to bust my butt every day. Kelly seemed to
appreciate that. I also had help from things beyond my control.

About a week before our season started, the previous year's second baseman, Cubs veteran Don Johnson, was called back to the major league team. Then Mickey Burnett and Al Glossop, also veteran infielders, developed sore arms. So Bill Kelly took a deep breath and put me into the starting lineup for opening day along with a couple of other rookies. Later he told reporters he could see that I was fast, had good hands, and knew "instinctively" what to do. All those hours of make-believe fielding as a kid helped.

We opened Wednesday, March 30, against the Seattle Rainiers, and we had more than 20,000 fans at old Wrigley Field in Los Angeles. It was a great ballpark with a double-decker grandstand built to look pretty much like Chicago's Wrigley Field, except there was a narrow twelve-story office tower right at the entrance. Several baseball movies had been shot there, including *Pride of the Yankees* in 1942. *Damn Yankees* was one of many others made after I played there. The grandstand held a little over 20,000, and we filled it a few times, but attendance was up and down, as I learned on the second day of the season, when only 2,000 fans showed up. There were a lot of show business people in the opening-day crowd, and Esther Williams came to throw out the first ball. She was always one of my favorite actresses, and now she was standing in our dugout, right next to me, in a skirt and jacket and high heels. She sure smelled good! She was wearing sunglasses, which she put into her pocket when she went out to the mound. She used such an enthusiastic windup and delivery that the sunglasses flew out of her pocket when she threw the ball.

It wasn't quite the same as Wrigley Field in Chicago, but with the big crowd and all the opening-day festivities, it sure seemed like the big leagues to me. Then I went hitless in three times at bat, and Kelly took me out for a pinch-hitter. I was devastated. Kelly could see I was upset, and at the end of the inning he came over and said, "You're still my second baseman." That made me feel a lot better, and when he paid me a compliment in the next day's newspaper, using the words "intelligence" and "determination," I felt better yet.

I doubt that would have counted for much if I hadn't started hitting, but the day after the opener I took off on the best hitting streak of my life. Somebody was injured, so Kelly juggled the batting lineup and moved me from eighth to second. I'll never know whether that

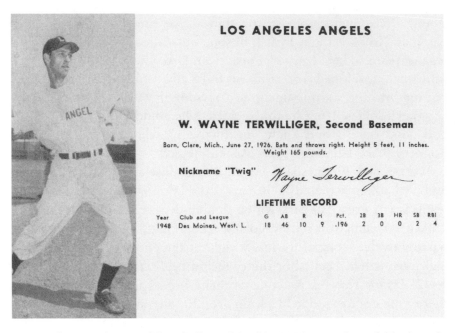

LOS ANGELES ANGELS

W. WAYNE TERWILLIGER, Second Baseman

Born, Clare, Mich., June 27, 1926. Bats and throws right. Height 5 feet, 11 inches. Weight 165 pounds.

Nickname "Twig" *Wayne Terwilliger*

LIFETIME RECORD

Year	Club and League	G	AB	R	H	Pct.	2B	3B	HR	SB	RBI
1948	Des Moines, West. L.	18	46	10	9	.196	2	0	0	2	4

Twig's first professional baseball card is this 1949 team-issued black-and-white card, measuring nearly five by seven inches. No number appears on the card, but we have seen it listed as #27. In 1949 it was extremely rare for a minor league team to issue baseball cards. *Nancy Peterson personal collection*

had something to do with it, but I hit two doubles in our second game, and I hit safely in the next seventeen straight games. At the end of the opening six-game series with Seattle, I was hitting .370, I had 13 put-outs and 20 assists, I had participated in 6 double plays, and I hadn't yet made an error. By April 16, my .390 average put me in a tie for third-best in the league and I led in doubles with 10. I kept on hitting, and a week later my average stood at .412. I was having the time of my life. On top of that, we were winning, and although it didn't last, for a while in April we were leading the league.

Wayne connected for a double and a single in addition to his home run to bring his batting average up to a healthy .398. [He] has hit safely in 20 of 22 games [and] has either started or been the vital pivot in a dozen double plays.
—Al Bine, Los Angeles Examiner, *reprinted in* Kalamazoo (Michigan) Gazette, *April 21, 1949*

Because I played in Los Angeles, I got what for me was an amazing amount of press coverage. The city had two morning and two evening papers—the *Times* and the *Mirror,* which I thought of as our "home" newspapers, and the *Herald* and the *Examiner,* which seemed more oriented toward our big rivals, the Hollywood Stars. Before the season, the writers were speculating about all the rookies, and since I was the one with the least experience they wrote about how little I had played in '48 and how I had once used my speed "to get away from a Jap tank that was in pursuit." After the second game, they started focusing on my play. The *Los Angeles Times'* Al Wolf wrote that I "performed like a grizzled vet." A few days later, Ray Canton of the *Mirror* called me "one bright spot in the Los Angeles camp." Every game was written up in detail, and since I was getting at least a hit per day I was always mentioned in the coverage. I saw my name in the out-of-town papers, too, like the *Oakland Tribune* and the *San Francisco Examiner.* The *Sporting News* included me in an item about the PCL's rookies—"the best crop in years." Along with the game coverage, the papers sometimes ran action shots, and through the summer eight or ten of those shots involved me sliding into base or making a defensive play. I had made the papers at college and at Benton Harbor, but this was a *lot* of attention for a small-town boy!

The attention didn't stop with game coverage. In late April, a San Francisco reporter wrote that if Billy Martin of the independent Oakland Oaks was worth $200,000, as was being speculated, then I might be worth that much, too. Because I said I planned to be a sports writer some day, the *Mirror* ran a page of publicity shots of me pounding out a story on an old manual typewriter, checking news on the teletype, editing at the copy desk, and working in the composing room.

I enjoyed all this, but I should have recognized that my success at the plate was just an especially good streak. I wasn't really a .400 hitter, and on April 23 when my average slipped below that point I shouldn't have been so disappointed. I started thinking that I *had* to get my average back up there, and I put a lot of pressure on myself. I was keeping track of my average every day, and I began to think in terms of how many base hits I needed in every game to keep my average up. Any day that I only went one-for-four I was very

Twig slides safely into third against the San Francisco Seals infielder Reno Cheso (#7) in the first game of a doubleheader in May 1949. The Angels won the game 10-6, then lost the second game 6-1.
Los Angeles Times Collection, UCLA Library, Department of Special Collections

unhappy. I lost confidence. Like the golfer who replaces his new ball with an old one when he has to hit over some water, I went to the plate expecting the worst, and sometimes that's what I got. I benched my homemade bat and started experimenting with different models. I changed my stance this way and that. Off-speed stuff and breaking balls were giving me the most trouble. My average kept slipping, and by mid-July it went below .300. I began to realize that I wasn't helping myself, but once you start focusing on a slump, it's almost impossible to change your thinking until the slump is over. It was something I would experience many times during my career.

Eventually I told myself to forget about hitting .400 and just ease back to something more appropriate for me. Something must have clicked, because in late July I started hitting with a little more power and regularity again. It all seemed to come together in Hollywood one night. Ray Canton of the *Mirror* devoted most of his coverage of our July 20 game against the Hollywood Stars to me, and he really got carried away: "The athlete with the primitive savagery of a young beast broke the deadlock to drive home two runs in the seventh . . . then in the ninth [he] poled a smashing home run over the left field fence with two aboard to clinch the game."

I took some flak in the clubhouse over that, but the attention was flattering and obviously Mr. Canton was one of my biggest supporters. He called me "the finest defensive second sacker in the Pacific Coast league today" and "the man who should become the major leagues' greatest second baseman by 1952." As it turned out, I did have a good year in 1952, but I spent most of it with St. Paul in the American Association and hit my career-best .312. Sorry, Ray.

A couple of months into the season, I was talking one day with our veteran shortstop, Bill Schuster, about money. He asked how much I was making, and when I told him $450 a month, he said, "You gotta make more than that—go in and talk to the boss." I wasn't sure I could pull it off, so he said, "I'll go with you." We went in together, he did all the talking, and I got a raise to $650 a month. Bill was definitely one of my favorite teammates. He had played some for the Cubs but spent most of his career in the minors. He turned thirty-seven that summer, but he could still move pretty well and he played the game hard. He was also a character. He liked to have some fun and he was known for his antics. One day he hit the ball back to the pitcher. With no hesitation, he ran directly to third instead of first. The fans loved it. The umpires put up with it, and the manager just shook his head. Another day, Bill successfully pulled the old "hidden ball" trick against Sacramento, talking to a base runner and then tagging him as he stepped off the bag. He earned a standing ovation from the home crowd. I have a photo of the two of us each holding up a bottle of milk for some dairy promotion. As we posed, he kept up a steady patter for the photographers and anyone else within earshot. As a finale, he chug-a-lugged the entire bottle.

Dom Dallesandro, a former Cubs outfielder, and Hank Wyse, a pitcher with the Cubs and Phillies, were big names on our team. Another veteran, Pat Seerey, joined us during the season. A roly-poly outfielder who had played mostly with Cleveland, Seerey was only twenty-six, but his major league career was over. He had come up during the war years and had a big swing—it was either hit 'em a long way or strike out. In 1948 with the White Sox, he hit four home runs in a single game. He also led the American League in strikeouts

Among Twig's first-time experiences as a rookie with the Los Angeles Angels was being called on to pose for promotional photos. During a dairy promotion, veteran shortstop "Broadway" Bill Schuster kept the rookie laughing throughout the photo shoot. As a finale, Schuster chugged the milk. *Wayne Terwilliger personal collection*

three straight years. Seerey might have stayed around longer if he had kept himself in better shape. Some baseball people said that he ate his way out of the game.

My best friend and roommate was Bob Kelly, no relation to the manager. Bob was a twenty-year-old rookie with a good curve ball. Bob was in the regular rotation, and I think he won about as many as he lost that year. I remember a game in late April when he and Oakland's ace, Frank Nelson, got hooked up in a pitchers' duel that was scoreless for eleven innings until I singled in the winning run in the bottom of the twelfth. (It wasn't all that unusual that they both went all the way. Starting pitchers worked a lot longer in those days unless they were really getting knocked around.) Bob was excited about his performance and I was excited about my game-winning hit, so we got the ball that I had hit and cut it in half so we'd each have a souvenir.

Terwilliger . . . does everything that baseball men look for in a prospect. He's fast and has a strong arm. He has a fine sense of balance on double-play and a natural smoothness while going to his right or left to field ground balls. He never looks awkward.
—Ray Canton, Los Angeles Mirror, *July 27, 1949*

By mid-July we were losing more than we were winning, and we dropped into last place. The Angels had won a dozen PCL titles, the most recent in '43 and '47, so there was some grumbling about our poor showing.

It seemed to me that the strongest team in the league was the San Diego Padres. Their ball club included Max West, who had just come down from seven seasons in the majors; Luke Easter, one of the great players of the Negro Leagues; and Orestes "Minnie" Minoso, a future Hall-of-Famer who was just starting his U.S. career after playing in Cuba. They drew good crowds even on the road; a double-header against them at Wrigley Field one weekend drew a more-than-capacity crowd of 23,000.

As good as the Padres were, the Hollywood Stars soon took over first place and stayed there. The Stars and Angels had a traditional cross-town rivalry, and some of our games got pretty heated. The Stars drew even more show business people than we did; they were owned by a group that included Gene Autry, George Burns and Gracie Allen, Gary Cooper, Bing Crosby, Cecil B. DeMille, George Raft, and Barbara Stanwyk. Fans could almost always count on seeing a few of the star-owners and their families or friends at home games. Their seating was close to the playing field; it was about 30 feet from home plate to the first row of seats. One day early in the season, I was leading off for the Angels at Gilmore Field and I heard somebody yell, "Hit one for me, kid." I looked over, and there was Hollywood "tough guy" George Raft. I had no trouble recognizing him; he had made sixty movies by then, including six that came out in 1949 alone! He'd been in the baseball news, too. Leo Durocher was suspended as the Dodgers' manager for the 1947 season for hanging around with Raft and his gambling pals. So here was George

Raft in person, watching me play and shouting encouragement! I hit the first pitch off a former Red Sox right-hander named Pinky Woods over the left-field fence. As I crossed the plate and headed for the dugout, I took a peek in Raft's direction. He was clapping his hands and laughing, and he called out, "Atta boy, kid!" Maybe he was betting that the Angels would beat his Stars, who knows? For whatever reason, George Raft was cheering for me. I couldn't wait to tell Mary Jane and my folks.

I was selected to play in the PCL All-Star game at Seattle, which was another thrill. I got a double, scored a run, and took part in a timely double play. Our South team beat the North 5-3.

By late July I was still playing regularly, fielding well, and hitting around .280. The Angels were in last place, but I was a professional baseball player gaining experience, and life was good. I figured that after the season, I would go home and finish up the last few courses I needed at Western Michigan, and then get some kind of job until it was time to come back to the Angels. Then out of the blue, Bill Kelly called me in to tell me I was going to Chicago. He said Emil Verban—a five-time National League all-star who had joined the Cubs a year earlier—was hurt, so they needed another body. They had long been out of the pennant race, and they figured this was a good time to take a look at me.

When the call came, Mary Jane and I were about to have dinner with my Marine tank-mate Bill Hoover and his wife, Flo. In rapid succession, I cancelled dinner, called my parents with the news, packed up my stuff, and talked the club into paying for Mary Jane's plane ticket to Chicago along with my own. On Sunday, July 31, I played in a double-header to conclude an eight-game series against Sacramento, and on Monday we got on the plane. I was on my way to the majors.

6

Stan Musial
Knows My Name!

Stan's the "Man," I'm the "Rook,"
Something we all know.
How about the time he took
Just to say hello!
. . . Now that's class.

I'll never know whether it was a good thing or a bad thing that the Cubs brought me up so fast. I had spent most of 1948 sitting on the bench in Des Moines, and now they were moving me up after exactly four months with the Angels. There's a good chance that I would have benefited from a little more time facing the pitchers of the Pacific Coast League, building experience and confidence at the plate, but you don't get to make those calls for yourself. The call came, and I answered it. This was what I'd been dreaming about and working for all along, and I was going to do everything I could to show that I was ready.

When I arrived in Chicago on the first of August, the Cubs were showing the signs of having spent much of the season in last place. They didn't yet have their reputation for losing; as the Cubs' yearbook pointed out, they had won the National League pennant fifteen times, and no other club had done better than that. They were a team that everybody assumed *should* be winning, and they weren't, which made people unhappy.

There were some injuries on the team, but the team's owner, P.K. Wrigley, was complaining publicly about too many complacent ball-players accepting paychecks and not contributing. In June he replaced long-time manager Charlie Grimm with the veteran player and manager Frankie Frisch. They put Grimm in charge of bringing in new personnel—preferably younger and more motivated. By the time they sent for me, they had made some roster changes, but they had also lost eight straight games and were promising more changes to come. The players were feeling the pressure, and there was a fair amount of grumbling about management. Then to make room for me, the club sent infielder Frank Gustine to Los Angeles just a few days short of his becoming a ten-year-man and qualifying for a bump in his pension. The players were mad, and the team's business manager told the Chicago *Daily News,* "It's none of the players' business." The fact that I had so little experience might have added insult to injury, but if anybody resented me personally, I wasn't aware of it.

First you meet the manager, for whose autograph you battled wildly when a kid, and moments later a pitcher, whose signature is one of your prize possessions. The individuals, of course, are Frankie Frisch, Cubs boss, and Dutch Leonard. "I gotta get down to earth before I can play," said Twig.
—Bud Shively, Benton Harbor News-Palladium, *August 1949*

I reported to the Cubs on Tuesday, August 2, and began to meet my new teammates. Frankie Frisch was still pretty new to the Cubs but he had lots of experience as a manager, dating back to the early 1930s when the young phenom known as "The Fordham Flash" was player-manager of the Saint Louis Cardinals. He led the wild and woolly Gas House Gang to the pennant and the World Series championship over my beloved Tigers. Long-time Cubs favorite Phil Cavarretta, a competitive and hustling first baseman, led Chicago in World Series play against the victorious Tigers in 1935 (at age ten I'd listened to every game) and again in 1945 (I was in the Marines and I followed it from Maui). He was the team captain, and he was a natural leader in the clubhouse and on the field. Outfielder Andy Pafko, another Cubs favorite and as talented as they come, was enjoying his third consecutive All-Star season. Hank Sauer, a big power hitter, had joined the team earlier in the season after several years with Cincinnati. The pitchers included Johnny Schmitz, who had an amazing curveball, and knuckle-baller Emil John "Dutch" Leonard, whose autograph I had gotten in 1939 when I was fourteen and he was winning twenty games for the Senators. Pitcher Doyle Lade and catcher Smoky Burgess had started the season with me in Los Angeles Catcher Mickey Owen was just back in baseball after being banned for his participation in the Mexican League in 1946. Infielders, besides Cavarretta, included Gene Mauch, Bob Ramazzotti, and shortstop Roy Smalley, who became my roommate on the road. I was excited to be joining these guys, and a little nervous. Then I realized who we were playing.

The Giants were in town. I looked out on the field and saw Johnny Mize, Bill Rigney, Sid Gordon, Willard Marshall, Whitey Lockman—I was in awe. Those guys had real star power for me, and the idea of going up against them was overwhelming. It's a good thing Frankie Frisch sat me on the bench the first few days, because I would have been too excited and starstruck to play well.

On Saturday, August 6, we were leading the Boston Braves 10-0, and late in the game Frisch sent me in to bat in place of Gene Mauch. I struck out on three straight pitches. Johnny Antonelli, the Braves' left-handed bonus baby, threw me three fastballs; I swung at all three and never touched a single one. Twenty years later, Ted Williams told me that his first time at bat in pro ball, he took three pitches right down the middle and couldn't manage to swing at any of them. He told me he waited a long time for his second at-bat. I got mine the very next day. With Boston leading 11-0, I entered the game and got my first major league hit, off Bill Voiselle. He was a pretty good pitcher and had been part of the Braves' pennant-winning season in '48, although if you remember the saying "Spahn and Sain and pray for rain"—supposedly the Braves' formula for success—Voiselle was one of the starters they hoped would be rained out. (He wore his address on his uniform: Ninety-Six, the name of his hometown in South Carolina.) I drew a walk and hit two singles against him that day. The first was a little bloop to right field—nothing dramatic, but it was my first major league hit. Nobody told me that when you get your first base hit in the big leagues, you usually get the ball, and nobody tossed it to me, so that's one memento I don't have.

A couple of days later, I got another bloop single, this time against Pittsburgh. When I got to first base, Johnny Hopp congratulated me.

1949 OFFICIAL PROGRAM 10¢

WAYNE
TERWILLIGER

CHICAGO CUBS · WRIGLEY FIELD

The Cubs official scorecard carried Twig's photo on the cover for a series
with the Philadelphia Phillies on September 21 and 22, 1949.

Nancy Peterson personal collection

I said, "Well, thanks, but it wasn't much of a hit," and Johnny answered, "Son, you take that hit. You'll be glad to take it no matter how long you've been around." His advice made an impression on me: Be glad for a hit and don't worry about what it looks like.

My first major league start came on Wednesday, August 10, against Pittsburgh. On the few occasions that I had played before then, I was excited, but there hadn't been time to get nervous because I just ran out there when Frisch put me in. This time I had a day to think about it, and I was pretty keyed up. It showed. My reactions were slow, my timing was off, and at one point I bobbled an easy grounder for an error. By the next day, I settled down some. I managed two singles and a walk. I made several plays in the field including a back-handed running grab of catcher Phil Masi's ground ball, which I threw to first to kill a rally. Maybe I could play in this league.

> *You . . . will be reading about a baseball player named Wayne Terwilliger. . . . Suffice it to say that he's the best young second base prospect since [Billy] Herman came up. . . . "As an old second sacker I'll have to admit he looks pretty good out there," grinned [Frankie] Frisch.*
> —*Edgar Munzel,* Chicago Sun-Times, *August 12, 1949*

On August 15 the Saint Louis Cardinals came to Wrigley Field. Again, I found myself looking over the other team to see who I'd be playing against. I saw Red Schoendienst at second and Enos Slaughter in the outfield, but the one I couldn't take my eyes off of was Stan Musial out there in left. He was one of my all-time heroes and pretty much at the top of his game. In the second or third inning, I was running out to second from the third base dugout, and Musial was coming in from left field. We crossed paths at the pitcher's mound, and he said, "Hi, Wayne, how's it going?" My mind went blank. I blurted out, "Uh, hi, Stan," or something like that, but all I could think was, "Stan Musial knows my name!" I was so distracted it's a good thing nobody hit anything to me that inning. Later, I thought, now that's a class guy. When I started managing, I decided to follow his example. I'd spot some kid that I liked on the other team. I'd find out his name and then make sure to cross paths with him so I could say, "Hi, Jim, how're you doing?"

My biggest claim to fame for 1949 is this: I became one of only four rookies since 1900 to get eight or more consecutive hits. The Dodgers' Babe Herman had nine consecutive hits in 1926; Ted Williams, Glenn Wright, and I each had eight (Williams in 1939 with Boston and Wright, a shortstop, in 1924 with Pittsburgh). It was a thrill—and it still is—to have my name in the record books in the same category as Ted Williams, and I hoped it was a sign of what I could do at this level. My streak began on August 18, in my ninth major league game, with a triple and a single in my final two at-bats against Pittsburgh's Jim Walsh. The next day at Cincinnati, I went three for three against Herman Wehmeier. A day later I had a double and two singles off the veteran lefty Johnny Vander Meer (who had made his reputation by throwing two consecutive no-hitters in 1938) and reliever Ewell Blackwell before closer Bud Lively struck me out in the ninth. Frankly, the eighth hit surprised me. I hit a shot right at Ted Kluszewski, the Reds' big first baseman, and I thought, shoot, he's got it; my streak is over. But it went right between his legs and kept on going. I was on base, but I was sure they would rule it an error. I peeked up at the scoreboard and couldn't believe they ruled it a hit. The Cincinnati scorer was being generous to Klu rather than to me; he led the league in fielding that year. But it's in the books, and as Johnny Hopp advised me, I'll take it. (The *Sporting News* wrote it up this way in their synopsis of the game: "Rhinelanders collected 16 hits off three Bruin moundsmen, while Cubs tagged trio of Cincy hurlers for nine, including three by Terwilliger, who ran string of bingles to eight in row before drawing collar from Lively in ninth.") My hitting streak was only two short of the National League record at the time, and I hadn't yet played a dozen games in the majors. Things were looking good.

Somewhere around that time I went down to a Chicago Pontiac dealer to buy our first car. In the window was a '49 Pontiac with gray body, red hubcaps, and white sidewalls. It was a beauty, and I bought it literally right out of the window. That was my only big purchase; like other players, I was going to have to work during the off-season to make ends meet. I began to settle into a pretty quiet life in Chicago. All our games were day games, and afterwards I'd go and fish off Montrose Pier. I got to be a regular. I'd take a six-pack and plop myself down, and once in a while a guy would come over to ask how the game went. The old-timers used to throw an anchor out and run a trawl line down with a bunch of hooks and connect it onto a bell. They'd sit there until the bell rang, and then they would disconnect the line from the bell and jerk it and pull the trawl line all the way up and they'd have fish on it. I learned how to do that, and I loved it. Those quiet early evenings were a perfect balance to the excitement of playing big-league baseball.

Wayne Terwilliger, the sprightly rookie who has taken over at second base in the absence of the injured Emil Verban, blasted a three-run homer, his first in the major leagues, in the third. . . .
—*Joseph M. Sheehan,* The New York Times, *August 24, 1949*

My first major league home run was another big event, and it happened August 23 in a pretty memorable game. It was my first time playing at the Polo Grounds, and in the third inning, with Mickey Owen and Bob Ramazzotti on base, I hit a pitch off Dave Koslo into the upper deck in left field, just inside the foul pole. It put us ahead 3-0, and I was feeling pretty proud of myself. But in the fifth, I messed up what was supposed to be a bunt for a squeeze play. We had runners at first and third. For some reason, when the pitch came I made a half-assed bunt attempt but didn't touch the ball. The runner at third had already taken off and he was trapped for a few seconds, but the third baseman dropped the catcher's throw, so the runner got back safely. Meanwhile, I had moved so little that the umpire ruled it a ball, and that brought Leo Durocher charging out of the dugout to complain loud and long until he got tossed from the game. Before the inning was over both runners had scored, so my mistake hadn't cost us, but it was embarrassing. I was happy to get my first home run at the Polo Grounds, which became one of my favorite places to play, pleased that it came in a winning game, and proud to get it off Koslo, who had the best ERA in either league that year.

Two weeks later I hit a three-run shot at Wrigley Field off Pittsburgh's Bob Chesnes as part of an eight-run inning. I remember it vividly, because I had fouled off a couple of pitches trying to sacrifice our two base runners along. By the seventh-inning stretch, we had a downpour and the game ended in an 11-7 win. My folks were there, which made the second home run even more special than the first.

I hurt my arm in the first game of a Labor Day double header so I missed a few games. But I was anxious to play—and Frisch needed me, because we had an awful lot of injured guys. By the time the season ended on October 2, I had played in thirty-six games. My hitting had cooled down; I ended the season with a .223 average—not great by any means, but not too bad for a starstruck rookie. The Chicago papers were more cautious about me than the L.A. papers had been—after all, the Cubs were in last place and I was pretty green. Still, one of them quoted catcher Mickey Owen as saying "Terwilliger is going to be the National League's best second baseman one of these days."

For a youngster with only one year of professional experience, the 23-year-old product of Western Michigan College is doing a remarkable job. In the 13-game stretch, he erred only once on 69 chances. That boot was in the first tilt he started, [then] he handled 63 chances without a miscue.
—Edgar Munzel, Chicago Sun-Times, *August 22, 1949*

If those two months of 1949 had been my whole major league experience, I would have been a little disappointed, but for the rest of my life I would have felt that I had realized my dream. I played with, and against, guys whose names I had known for a long time. I got home runs off a couple of good pitchers, and I proved that I could make the plays. As a child bouncing a ball off the steps, I imagined that I was playing against big-league batters, and now my dream had come true. As proof, I had some newspaper clippings and publicity photos, I had some programs with my name printed in the lineup, I even had the program for a late-September home series against Philadelphia that featured my mug on the cover. If I try real hard, I can imagine myself becoming a high school teacher and coach back in Michigan—maybe doing some broadcasting and managing my dad's bar on the side—talking to folks and saying, "Oh, yes, I played in the majors." I could have looked through my mementos sometimes, and it would have been a pleasant memory. When Mike Max described my career as "a cuppa coffee," he would have been accu-

The baseball is still sailing through the infield as Twig slides home in a 1950
preseason exhibition game against Cleveland at Wrigley Field.
Los Angeles Times Collection, UCLA Library, Department of Special Collections

rate. Luckily for me, my baseball career didn't end there, and I didn't
go back to Michigan to live off my memories—I just kept on making
new ones.

> *The bulldog spirit of the Frisch kids never has been more con-*
> *vincingly demonstrated than in the case of Terwilliger. . . .*
> *"How can you keep the kid out of there?" said Frisch, his eyes*
> *fairly sparkling with admiration. "That's the kind of moxie I*
> *like. If he wants to play, he'll play."*
> —*Edgar Munzel,* Chicago Sun-Times, *April 24, 1950*

The Cubs were serious about bringing in younger players, and all
through spring training in 1950 the papers were full of talk about
Frankie Frisch's energetic team of "kids." As a former second baseman himself, Frankie seemed to take an interest in me; he taught me
some of the finer points of the "keystone" sack. But I wasn't sure I'd
be starting again, so I treated every practice like it was a tight game.
Eventually, Frankie let it be known that he was planning to start four
rookies: first baseman Preston Ward, third baseman Bill Serena, outfielder Carmen Mauro, and me. Filling out the infield was Roy Smalley, just beginning his third season at shortstop. We played a hustling

Twig tags out Wally Westlake of the Pittsburgh Pirates, foiling his attempt to steal second base during a preseason game in March 1950.
Los Angeles Times Collection, UCLA Library, Department of Special Collections

style of baseball that Frankie liked to compare with his old Gas House Gang. We were on our way to a 23-10 record in spring training, and hopes were high as we headed toward the season opener in Cincinnati.

On Sunday, April 16, we had our last two exhibition games against the White Sox in Chicago. In the first game, Gordon Goldsberry hit a slow roller to my right. I had to scramble to pick it up and then twist around to make an off-balance throw. In the process, I spiked myself along the inside of my left leg, just above the knee. I made the play, and then I noticed that I was bleeding some. I was going to shake it off and go back to my position until I looked down and saw blood running down my leg and soaking my uniform, stocking, and shoe. They took me out of the game, and when I looked, I found that the gash was about three inches long and about a half-inch deep, and it wouldn't stop bleeding. Pretty soon somebody said, "We're taking you to the hospital for stitches." Oh, great. I didn't want to go to any hospital. "Can't you just fix me up here?" I said. But off I went, and a doctor put in five stitches to close it up. When he was done, he said, "Stay off it for a couple days, and don't try to play for five days, maybe a week." This was Sunday, and the season opener was Tuesday. I pictured Emil Verban, whose injury had brought me to Chicago, getting to start the season instead of me. We were leaving for Cincinnati in a few hours. It was awkward getting around but I got my stuff together and got on the train.

We arrived in Cincinnati in the wee hours Monday morning and checked into our hotel. As I headed for my room, Frankie told me to stay there and rest my leg instead of going to the ballpark for our two-hour workout. I nodded, but I got on the bus at 10:15 along with everybody else, and we all went off to Crosley Field. Coach Roy "Hard Rock" Johnson, whose name suited him perfectly, was hitting grounders for infield practice, and he usually gave everybody a pretty good workout. This day he said, "Hey, Twig, I'll just hit them right at you so you don't have to move from side to side a lot." "Nope," I told him, "just hit them the way you always do." The leg hurt like the devil, but I figured I could rest it later. I heard Frisch tell a reporter that he wasn't sure how well I could get around and didn't want me to tear open the stitches. I went to him and said, "Frank, I can play." He said, "Okay, I'll put you in the lineup, but I'll keep an eye on you and if I think you need to come out, I don't want any argument." I played the whole game, made five fielding plays, and went 2-for-5 at the plate including beating out a bunt. We won the game 9-6, and I had pretty well established myself as the starting second baseman for the season.

The one thing Frankie was still concerned about was my hitting. Because I was a decent base runner, he wanted me to be the leadoff hitter. He had worked with me some on my batting, and he asked Wid Mathews to help. Wid was a former Brooklyn coach who had just taken over Charlie Grimm's responsibilities for player development. Mathews looked at my wide stance and decided that it was okay but I was too far back in the box, limiting my reach on outside pitches. Frisch had always told me to stay back, but Mathews told me to step forward about six inches. I almost hated to admit that it worked. About a month into the season, I was hitting .290. My average leveled off to .242 by the end of the year, but I continued hitting with more power.

I hit ten home runs in 1950, which turned out to be almost half of my career total. I got four during May, a couple in July, a pair four days apart in August, and another pair in back-to-back games in September. They came off some pretty good pitchers. For example the

1950 Bowman, #114. Twig's first major league card. Although Twig was born in 1925, he gave his birth date as June 27, 1926. All of his cards through 1958 used the incorrect date.

Nancy Peterson personal collection

Giants' Larry Jansen won nineteen games that season and struck out six guys in the All-Star game. The Phillies' Curt Simmons, another post-war "bonus baby," was having his first great season, going 17-8. A two-run shot came off the Giants' Dave Koslo, who had given up my first major league home run the previous year, and again it happened at the Polo Grounds. Best of all, against the Dodgers on July 30, I hit a solo into the left-center-field stands in the fourth inning off big Don Newcombe, who pitched his tenth complete game of the year that day. Newcombe had been a rookie sensation in 1949, and he was even better in 1950. When they created the Cy Young Award in 1956, they gave the first one to Newcombe for winning twenty-seven games that year.

Second basemen get themselves into all sorts of twisting and turning and jumping positions that make interesting action shots. I have a lot of old newspaper photos in which I was leaping for a catch or twisting for a double play or tagging somebody out. In other shots I was the one getting tagged out or sliding into base and pushing up dust all around me. In May 1950 the *Chicago Tribune* ran a photo of Alvin Dark sliding into me feet-first at second, trying to break up a double play. With it, they ran a small photo taken an instant later where I'm in the air with my legs flying in different directions, and I've just released the ball. Several months later, a magazine ran that second photo as the opening to a feature story which suggested that people who like ballet might like to watch baseball for its balletlike moves. And in 1951 the same photo turned up in an ad in *Life* magazine. The ad showed a couple enjoying their new seventeen-inch

Jackie Robinson runs out from under his cap in a failed attempt to make it to second, in a Cubs-Dodgers game May 6, 1950. Twig (#21) completes a double play, shortstop Roy Smalley (#39) to Terwilliger to first baseman Preston Ward. *Wayne Terwilliger personal collection*

television set, "new styling, new power . . . proven in millions of homes," and that photo is on the screen. I didn't get a fee, but I didn't care.

I still enjoy looking at those old photos, partly because the action is so intense and partly because the opposing players were like my own private Hall of Fame. I page through my scrapbooks and see a picture of myself grabbing for second base while Pee Wee Reese sprawls in the dirt, having just missed tagging me out; or me stepping on second just ahead of a sliding Ralph Kiner; or me sliding into third as Billy Cox jumps to take a too-high throw from Roy Campanella. Or, on the other hand, caught in midair with my foot a few inches from first base as Gil Hodges, with his toe firmly on the bag, stretches to his full length and grabs a throw to put me out. When I look at them, I can picture the kind of day it was, how the game was going, how the action played out.

Terwilliger is quick to learn, and a fellow who profits by his mistakes. He won't make the same ones twice. . . . He has nerve and intelligence, and although he won't be in professional ball two years until this coming August, he is ready now to "take charge" of the infield.
—Clifford Bloodgood, Baseball Magazine, *June 1950*

As the season went on, I started getting attention for my on-field chatter. It was pretty natural for me to call out encouragement to my teammates in the field, to help keep up the enthusiasm, or point out something that we needed to focus on. My sharp voice seemed to carry, so people heard me and started to call me a "holler guy." Frankie Frisch encouraged me to keep it up; he thought it could unify our infield. One day Frankie told a reporter that even though this was Roy Smalley's third year at shortstop and I was just breaking in, I would "make a better player out of him" by helping to "keep him on his toes." I wondered how Smalley, my friend and roommate, would take that.

He didn't mind at all. Roy had already shown that he was an outstanding shortstop, and in 1950 he was having the best season of his career. He played in every single game and had a big year at the plate with 21 homers and 85 runs batted in. Roy Smalley Jr. played several years for the Minnesota Twins. When I got to the Twins as a coach in 1986, Roy Junior was back as a designated hitter, and we were both with the team that won the 1987 World Series.

Late in the season there was a Terwilliger Day at Wrigley Field. The Junior Chamber of Commerce in Charlotte booked a special excursion train and brought 300 fans from Charlotte and half a dozen other towns for a Sunday game and special ceremony. Everybody had paid $10 for the trip. The train left Charlotte at 7:30 in the morning, and they had expected to be back home at 10 p.m., but because we were playing a make-up double header they didn't get home until well after midnight. Before the first game, my parents came onto the field and all the players of both teams gathered around. Mary Jane watched from box seats with her parents, brother, and grandfather, who all came out on the train, and my sister, Mary Lou, was there with her husband. The president of

Twig slides safely into third as the Dodgers' Billy Cox leaps for the high throw from catcher Roy Campanella at Ebbets Field in May 1950. "You have to be thinking every minute about how you're going to get to the next base," Twig says about base running. *Wayne Terwilliger personal collection*

the Jaycees presented me with some gifts from my hometown, and in the process he let the big Chicago crowd know about some of Charlotte's businesses and attractions. Then they had my high school coach, Malcolm Gobel, present me with a nice watch from one of the stores on Main Street in Charlotte. After that, Phil Cavarretta gave me a very fancy silver coffee service from the team. Finally, I took the microphone to thank the Charlotte businessmen for organizing the day, to thank everyone for the gifts, and to thank all the Michigan people—especially my parents and my former coach—for their support. I was a little embarrassed by the whole thing—I had barely made it to the majors and I didn't think I was doing well enough to have a "day," but it meant a lot to me that Coach Gobel and my parents could be there on the field, and I wanted to be sure they knew it. I went hitless that day, but I had a long sac fly and some good defensive plays—and we won both games—so the hometown fans had something to cheer about. The community was pleased with the chance to put Charlotte into the spotlight; the *Charlotte Republican* called it "probably the greatest bit of community publicity" since "Charlotte's spectacular accomplishment in leading the nation in the sale of war savings stamps back in World War I."

[The Cubs] had two on with none out in the first, on a walk to Terwilliger and the first of three singles by Hank Edwards, but Terwilliger wandered too far off second on a line drive to center by Preston Ward and was an easy double-play victim.
—Joseph M. Sheehan, The New York Times, May 18, 1950

The thing about being praised for your play in the media is that when you screw up everybody knows that, too. It wasn't like today, where television can bring us every detail of a player's personal life, but it was embarrassing to know that people all over the country might know about an error or a base-running mistake. Take, for example, a mid-May game at the Polo Grounds. I made a nice tag on Alvin Dark during a run-down play, and the next day the *New York Times* ran a big photo of it. But here's what else happened. First, I made an error that allowed Monte Irvin to get on base, and he scored on a Bobby Thomson inside-the-park home run. After that, I got on base but took too big a lead at second and got doubled off. Then we made what we thought was a great double play, but the umpire didn't see it that way. And with the Giants leading in the eighth inning, I got a leadoff double and scored a couple of plays later in what we hoped was a rally, but the rally died. So, on top of everything else, I was learning that there are plenty of ups and downs in the game.

I wish I could say that before long I learned to take things in stride, or at least to separate the on-field competition from the rest of my life, but I didn't. Too often, I allowed myself to be a horse's ass when things went wrong at the plate or on the field. I would go storming out of the clubhouse and head for my car, and too bad for any fans that wanted to come up and talk. I clearly remember one day when we were playing at home, I hit a home run in the bottom of the ninth inning to tie the game. That was exciting, but we couldn't score again and we lost the game in extra innings. The home run was

Twig, leading the National League in stolen bases, cleans his spikes and chats with teammate Hank Sauer, leading the league in RBIs, in this June 1950 photo. Twig finished the season sixth in the National League, with thirteen steals. *Wayne Terwilliger personal collection*

my only hit of the game, so I was down on myself—if I'd gotten another hit earlier and knocked in some runs, maybe we'd have won. As I came out of the runway and was walking to my car, a little kid yelled to me for my autograph. I shook my head no, and the mother said "Can't you just stop and sign this little boy's program?" He didn't care that I only had one hit, he was probably really excited—here's a guy who hit a home run. I just kept walking, and they followed me down the sidewalk to my car. I could have stopped and signed the thing and been done with it, but the longer I went and the more they followed me, the more pissed-off I got. Finally I said, "Look, I'm not signing any autographs. Good-bye." I heard her sputter something but I just closed my car door and drove away. It was terrible, but that's what I did. Well, she turned me in to the front office, and I heard about it from the Cubs. I was wrong and I knew it, and I still regret it. Occasionally my parents came from Michigan to see a game and we'd have dinner afterwards. But if I had a bad game I'd just shut down and not talk to them. It especially wasn't a nice way to treat my mother, my faithful number-one fan. I did the same to Mary Jane, who also didn't deserve it.

Terwilliger's an old pro already. He plays ball like we used to in the old Gas House Gang in St. Louis.
—Manager Frankie Frisch, quoted in the Chicago Cubs News, *May 27, 1950*

The Cubs held their spring training on California's Catalina Island, and that seemed like the height of luxury to me in 1950 and 1951. The club wasn't allowed to start training before the first of March, but the team went out a week or two early to start conditioning. We hiked up into the mountains every day to get our legs in shape; when we got back there would be a huge arrangement of shrimp cocktail and fruit. I thought, "So this is spring training in the big leagues!" Even when we got down to business, Catalina was a nice place to be.

Chuck Connors—later to be TV's *Rifleman,* although he wasn't an actor yet—was at spring training in 1951, and we got to be friends. He was 6-foot-6 and thirty years old, and he had played some professional basketball with the Boston Celtics before spending several years in the Dodgers organization. He'd had exactly one at-bat with the big-league team, in 1949, and he was hoping to do a little more with the Cubs. Chuck and I hit it off right away. He loved the sound of the name "Terwilliger" and he said it often, for no reason, just "Terwilliger." Again we had a week or two before the actual start of training camp when our only job was to hike up into the mountains and back.

One day, Chuck and I decided to go horseback riding to see a little more of the island. Neither of us had ridden before—if he had, it certainly didn't show in his riding style. I remember him sitting on the horse with his long legs just hanging down on either side like he didn't quite know what to do with them. We went up into the mountains and stopped to let the horses rest and graze a while. When we decided to get going again, I reached to take the reins and the bit came out of my horse's mouth and slid to the side. The horse rolled its eyes toward me and I thought, "Uh-oh, I'm in trouble now." I threw my arms around the horse's neck and held on, and the horse took off down a narrow part of the trail. It carried me a few hundred feet until we came to a point where the horse either had to jump over the edge or stop. Fortunately, it stopped. I could hear Chuck laughing the whole time.

Chuck was a very bright, outgoing, and talented guy, always quoting from literature or reciting verse or being entertaining in some way for whoever was around, and I really enjoyed his company. He would recite "Casey at the Bat" at the drop of a hat. The team's owner, "Mister Wrigley" to us, had a ranch on Catalina, and he invited the players there for a day of relaxation. Chuck easily became the center of attention, and the climax was when he recited "Casey" with more than the usual dramatic turns.

He and I went out to dinner one evening at the nicest restaurant in Avalon, the city on the island. It was a weekend, and the place was packed. We were eating our salads when Chuck leaned forward and said to me, "You know, in a classy place like this, people expect everything to be nice and polite. If they heard something rude or crude, they would just tell themselves they must have imagined it." I didn't know where he was going with this. "I bet I could yell out the word 'shit' nice and loud, and hardly anybody would even look up. If we just looked around like we didn't know who said it either, everybody would just go back to their dinners and their polite conversations as if nothing had happened." I begged him not to try it. He said, "Just keep on eating your salad, and when I say it, look around for a second or two and then go right back to eating." There was no way to stop this experiment, so I buried my head in my salad. Out came the word, "Shit," louder and clearer than I had expected. I couldn't bring myself to look at anybody, so I just kept my head down, but Chuck was looking this way and that, as if he was wondering where the sound came from. Sure enough, people who had looked in our direction started looking elsewhere. He went back to eating, and everybody else did too. I was choking on my lettuce, but Chuck had proved his point.

Kevin Joseph Aloysius "Chuck" Connors had grown up in Brooklyn, and his childhood dream was to be a member of the Brooklyn Dodgers. When they finally called him up in '49, he sat on the bench because he was a first baseman playing behind Gil Hodges, who was having a terrific season. In his one time at bat, Chuck grounded into a double play to end a losing game. I'm sure that experience helped add drama to his delivery of "Casey at the Bat." In 1950 he played in Montreal, the Dodgers' Triple A club. They traded him to the Cubs, who brought him to spring training and then sent him to Los Angeles, where he got off to a great start with the Angels. He was playing well, and his showy personality—which he used on the field as well as off—was a big hit with the Angels fans. I was hoping we'd be teammates, but the Cubs didn't call him up to Chicago until just after they traded me away.

Chuck told me that after baseball he wanted to be in the movies, and he seemed to be preparing for that and other possibilities. He had a business card that said, "Kevin (Chuck) Connors, affiliate Brooklyn Dodgers Baseball Club: recitations, after-dinner speaker, home recordings for any occasion, free-lance writing." He also sold insurance; maybe he had another card for that. He played in sixty-six games for the Cubs in 1951, and then he went back to the Angels—cart-wheeling around the bases, among other things, to the great enjoyment of the crowd. He was supposed to be subject to the major league draft, but he was making good money in the PCL and he wanted to stay in California, so he became the first player ever to refuse to take part. His action forced the major leagues to increase the amounts they offered minor-league players.

I lost track of Chuck until one day in about 1954 I saw that he was in a war picture with Virginia Mayo and Burt Lancaster where, if I remember correctly, he dove a fighter plane into the smokestack of a Japanese battleship. Before long, of course, he became a big TV star with *The Rifleman*, and eventually he did more than seventy movies and six or seven TV series. I saw him a couple of times after that. He

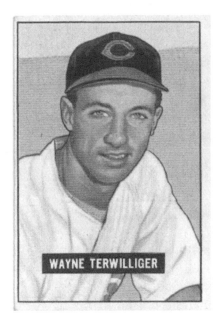
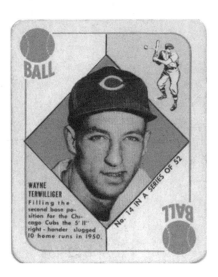

In 1951 Twig had two cards: Bowman, #175, on the left, and Topps, #14 red back, on the right. The first year of Topps baseball cards featured a game in which each card was labeled a strike, single, foul out, etc. Topps and Bowman competed for exclusive player contracts until Topps bought Bowman in 1956, ending the conflict. *Nancy Peterson personal collection*

came, wearing his Rifleman costume, to an old-timers' game at Yankee Stadium in 1980 or so. He was still smart and funny, and he still loved to be the center of attention. About ten years later, I saw him at a reunion of former Dodgers players in Brooklyn. He was about seventy by then, and he brought a woman who was about thirty-five and a real knockout. This time, he drank quite a bit during the various activities, and we'd have to get his attention and direct him when it was time to go to the next event. I could see that he had been living a hard life and that his health was failing, and not long after that he died.

Twig looks just like Gehringer did when the Tiger great first broke into baseball.
—Pittsburgh Pirates coach Milt Stock, quoted in the 1951 Cubs yearbook

In 1951 I was playing every day, but not as well as I knew I could. Over the first fifty games I only managed to hit .214. Wid Matthews told me I should concentrate on being a more effective leadoff man. "Your job is to get on base any way you can," he said. "Don't think about trying to hit home runs." I was proud of the fact that I had hit ten homers the year before. "Nope, you gotta get out of that way of thinking," he said. "Use a lighter bat and go to right field more." I did start using a lighter bat, but the truth is I didn't know how to go to right field and nobody could tell me. Years later, when I was in the minors and was experimenting on my own, I finally figured out how to do it.

On June 15, the deadline day for trades, the Dodgers were in town to play us. Mary Jane and I were at home in the morning and I was sitting on the john with the radio going when I heard that there was a big trade today, four Cubs for four Dodgers. Then they named the Cubs who were leaving: Andy Pafko, Johnny Schmitz, Rube Walker, and Wayne Terwilliger. I couldn't believe it. I yelled to my wife, "Did you hear that?" She said, very quietly, "Yes, I did." I had not heard a word from the Cubs. Their excuse later on was that they couldn't get hold of me. But we had a phone and we were home, so I have to think they didn't try.

Even though I was going from a last-place club to a first-place club, being traded was a kick in the ass. I took it personally. I had played well for the Cubs the year before; didn't I deserve more time to work out my hitting problems? They had brought me up fast, and now I thought they were giving up on me awfully fast. The trade wasn't really about me, though. The key to the trade was that Brooklyn wanted Johnnie Schmitz and Andy Pafko. The Cubs got four utility players—pitcher Joe Hatten, catcher Bruce Edwards, outfielder Gene Hermanski, and infielder Eddie Miksis. I'm not sure anybody ever knew how the rest of us figured in.

As a kid, the Tigers were "my team." As a pro player, the Cubs had become "my team." Now they were sending me on my way, and there wasn't a thing I could do about it. So I went to the ballpark and got my stuff out of our clubhouse, walked to the visitors' clubhouse, and put on my new uniform.

7
Playing in Jackie's Shoes

Not here that long,
and already gone.
Last to first . . .
it could be worse!

When I tell the story of my sudden trade to the Dodgers, people ask whether I had to turn around and play against the Cubs that very day. Several of the traded players were in the game, but I wasn't. For some reason the Dodgers played a guy named Jackie Robinson at second base that day, and nearly every day after that. Jackie was so competitive that no matter what kinds of aches and pains he was having, he wanted to play. Every few days I went in to relieve him, and when he had hemorrhoid surgery I got promoted to starter—for four days. I wasn't used to sitting on the bench, and I never did learn to like it. On the plus side, though, I got to watch Jackie Robinson play for three and a half months, I was part of a team that was leading the league by thirteen and a half games on August 11, and when that lead disappeared, I was present at one of the most famous moments in the history of baseball. Through it all, I had the privilege of associating with all the legendary Dodger players of that time.

What a lineup the Dodgers had. At second base, Jackie Robinson, 1947 Rookie of the Year in spite of death threats and hostilities of every sort, who was very quiet off the field but full of competitive energy in the game. At shortstop, Pee Wee Reese, a smooth player and one of the nicest men I ever met. At first base, the great Gil Hodges, so soft-spoken and friendly that you'd never suspect he was a big power-hitting ex-Marine. He had giant meat hooks for hands; the day we met and shook hands mine just disappeared in his. Reese used to say, "Gil doesn't need to wear a glove; he only does it to be fashionable." Billy Cox had great moves at third—Casey Stengel once said of him, "That ain't a third baseman, that's a f—ing acrobat!" Roy Campanella, one of the greatest catchers ever, made everything look easy; on foul balls he'd run to the spot where the ball was going to come down without even having to look at it. I saw him get hit in the left ear by Cubs pitcher Turk Lown; he went down and there was blood coming from his ear and his nose, and I don't think he even missed a game. Carl Furillo, a classic tough-talking New York Italian, was known for playing right field at Ebbets just about perfectly. There were a lot of singles hit off that right-field fence because he knew exactly how every ball would bounce and with his great arm he'd get it back to the infield in a hurry. The great power hitter Duke Snider was in center, and Cal Abrams and Don Thompson alternated in left. The Dodgers had fabulous pitchers, too, including Preacher Roe, Don Newcombe, Carl Erskine (Oisk, as they called him in Brooklyn), and Clem Labine. All that talent on one ball club—they should have won the pennant that year, and of course they almost did.

When I talk about my other teams, I usually say "we," but when I talk about the Dodgers, I often say "they." I admired the Dodgers and I felt privileged to come along for the ride, but I never really felt like one of them. They were an established ball club with a lot of veterans—on their way to being legends—while I had only been in the big leagues a couple of years and hadn't established what kind of career I would have. After Frankie Frisch had been so friendly and helpful, I was a little surprised that Dodgers manager Charlie Dressen was just the opposite. I soon learned that he hardly spoke to any of his bench players no matter how long they had been around. On the other hand, the Dodger players—especially Jackie Robinson and Pee Wee Reese—went out of their way to be nice.

I joined the team at the start of a two-week road trip, and by the time we got to Brooklyn, Mary Jane had gotten us an apartment in Bay Ridge. We had a game the next day, and I asked somebody for directions to Ebbets Field, but I managed to take the wrong train and get lost. I came running in just before batting practice. I don't know which I hated more—coming in late for my first home game with my new team or getting lost on my first day living in The Big City. Word of my mistake got around to the other players, and most of them razzed me about it. But after the game, Pee Wee came up to me and said, "Listen, until you get established here and know how to get to the ballpark, I'll pick you up. I'll pick you up tomorrow." I said, "Oh, no, you don't have to do that, Pee Wee." He just said, "Tell me where you live." So the next day, Pee Wee Reese picked me up in a black Cadillac and drove me to the ballpark.

From the first moment I met Pee Wee, I felt that I could talk to him. One day I asked him for some advice. I had played that day, and I'd had a hell of a time catching the ball. I didn't make any errors, but I had struggled, laying back when I should have charged the ball, just making every grounder tougher than it really was. I started thinking, geez, don't hit the ball to me; I can't catch it. I was pissed off about not playing well, but what really bothered me was not wanting the ball to come my way. I went to Pee Wee and asked him, "Have you ever played in a game where you just didn't want the ball hit to you?" He chuckled a while and then said, "Sure. Every infielder you talk to, if he's honest with you, will tell you there are days like that." I don't know whether it really happened to him, but he was nice enough to say it, and it made me feel better.

I didn't know what to expect from Jackie; word was that he kept pretty much to himself, and I could see right away that it was true. So, when he did reach out to me, it meant a *lot*. For example, one day I made a backhand play behind second and a quick throw to first to get the runner. It was a fairly ordinary play, but it's one I'll never forget because Jackie made a point of coming over to me to say, "Nice play, Twig, I never could have made that play." Each time he went out of his way to say something like that showed me that there was more to him than people usually saw. He would have made the play, and I knew it.

For my money, Robinson and Reese were one of the all-time great middle infield combinations, and working with them was a highlight of my career. I worked out with them every day, and when I did get called upon to play—usually in Jackie's place—I was always

conscious of whose shoes I was filling. It was no easy task. By the end
of the season Jackie led the team in batting average, doubles (tied
with Campanella), and stolen bases, among other things, and he and
Hodges posted fielding averages of .992.

What Jackie and Pee Wee had in common was that they were both
great competitors. Their playing styles were very different from one
another. Pee Wee was smooth in everything he did—catching,
throwing, running, hitting. He had no wasted motion, and it all
looked effortless. Jackie had an aggressive style that wasn't as
smooth—he had more body movement when he ran, for example—
so instead of everything looking easy, you could see more of the
energy he was putting into his running and his pivots and his throws.
He had good hands and good moves, and he was an expert base runner. He could drive pitchers crazy with his ability to take huge leads
and get back to the bag safely, and he was just about the best I ever
saw at being able to get out of run-downs—you *might* get him with a
dozen throws and some luck.

My first appearance in a Dodger uniform was at Ebbets Field
against the Giants. Like Yankee Stadium and the Polo Grounds,
Ebbets was a very exciting place to play, and it drew a lot of politi-
cians and celebrities. When the time came for my first home appearance, the Dodgers were not only playing our archrivals, but the game
was tied and I went in to play third base—which I hadn't played
since high school. Charlie Dressen had pinch-hit for third baseman
Billy Cox, and he needed to replace him in the field. Charlie had
barely even nodded to me in weeks, but now he came over and
asked, "Have you ever played third?" If he had asked under different
circumstances, I might have told him the truth. But this was a game
situation and I wanted to play, and I knew better than to say no. So,
there I was playing out of my usual position, teamed with Jackie
Robinson and Pee Wee Reese and Gil Hodges, at Ebbets Field,
against the Giants, in a tie game. Late in the game, the Giants got a
man on first base and Willie Mays came to the plate. It was Willie's
rookie season, and by this time, he had gotten over his slow start and
was hitting everything in sight. I was thinking, "It's a bunt situation
but surely Willie Mays won't bunt. Or will he?" I didn't know. I
looked at the dugout for some help on how to play him—get back,
or come in a little, or whatever—but nobody there gave me any help

Twig fires to first to complete the double play after retiring Phil Rizzuto (#10) in the Mayor's Trophy exhibition game at Yankee Stadium in June 1951. It was Twig's first start as a Dodger. *Wayne Terwilliger personal collection*

at all. So, I played kind of halfway in, and Mays hit a one-hop shot right at me. One hop and bang, it hit my glove before I could think. My knees were shaking as I went to throw to Robinson at second base and it seemed like it was slow motion. Slooooow motion—I can still feel that. I was trying to make sure I made a good throw, so I kind of eased it over there. It was a half-assed throw and a little high, but Jackie reached up and grabbed it and turned a double play. *Terwilliger to Robinson to Hodges.* I hung Jackie out to dry with the high toss, but it was as important a defensive play as I ever made.

After we won the game on a squeeze play by Preacher Roe in the last of the ninth, I apologized to Jackie for the bad throw, and he just said, "Hey, it was fine." So I was over the hump.

My first Dodger start was in the Mayor's Trophy game, a charity exhibition at Yankee Stadium in front of 70,000 people. Quite a few celebrities turned out—I remember that bandleader Skitch Henderson and his wife, the very attractive actress Faye Emerson, were in box seats right next to our dugout. Because I knew I was starting, I had time to get nervous before the game, but once we started to play I got the jitters under control and began to enjoy myself. Gil Hodges was taking the day off so Jackie moved over to first and I played second. I got a single, and better yet I turned two double plays. The box score read *Bridges* (Rocky, playing at third base that day), *Terwilliger and Robinson*, and also *Reese, Terwilliger and Robinson*. (Some guys named McDougald, Rizzuto and Mize also made a double play in that game.) It took the edge off the fun when we lost the game in the bottom of the ninth, and I had to keep reminding myself that at least this game didn't count in the standings. We also played in the annual Hall of Fame game at Cooperstown in July, a huge event with old-time baseball celebrities everywhere. I went into the game for Jackie and contributed to our win over the Philadelphia Athletics with a double play and a ground-rule double in the ninth.

The most memorable hit of my brief time with the Dodgers was a game-winning pinch single at Ebbets Field. We had the bases loaded in the bottom of the ninth against Saint Louis, and Harry Brecheen was pitching for the Cardinals. Charlie Dressen called me over and asked, "Can you hit this guy?" I would have said yes anyway, but it happened to be true that as a Cub, I'd had some luck against Brecheen. He put me in, and I hit a soft line drive to center field, a clean base hit to win the game. The newspaper ran a photo of me coming off the field, with Jackie Robinson and Pee Wee Reese extending their hands to shake mine. I have a framed copy of that photo; it's my favorite picture of my entire baseball career. Robinson and Reese shaking *my* hand!

Jackie was in his fifth season in the major leagues. I had read stories about what he went through as the first black major leaguer, and I knew that he never showed his anger, as difficult as that must have been. It's not surprising that he was a little reserved and guarded,

Jackie Robinson (#42) and Pee Wee Reese (#1) congratulate teammate Wayne Terwilliger after his line-drive pinch single brought Robinson home for a ninth-inning win against the Saint Louis Cardinals at Ebbets Field July 21, 1951. The game was tied and the bases loaded when Twig entered the game in place of outfielder Don Thompson to face the Cardinals' Harry Brecheen. The photo is a favorite memento of Twig's career.
Barney Stein Photo Collection LLC

and there was a bit of an edge to him. He was polite, he was never unfriendly, but he never seemed to relax. I had the sense that he was always alert to what might be said or what might happen. By 1951 he had established himself as a talented and valuable ball player. I'm sure he still met up with some prejudice, but I never saw it on the ball field.

At the end of the season, Jackie made one of the greatest plays ever made in baseball, in terms of tough plays under tough pressure. Brooklyn had led the league all year, sometimes by more than a dozen games. But in August the Giants—thanks in large part to Willie Mays—started on a sixteen-game winning streak, and they just kept closing the gap until on Friday, September 28, we were tied. On Saturday we both won and we were still tied. On Sunday, September 30, the last day of the season, the Giants won their afternoon game. Now we had to win our night game at Philadelphia to force a play-off. We tied the game in the eighth inning, and it was still tied in the bottom of the twelfth. Philadelphia had the bases loaded with two out. Eddie Waitkus hit a line shot toward center field and Robinson made a headlong dive, caught the ball back-handed in the air and banged down on the ground, hitting his stomach hard. But he held on to the ball, the inning was over, and we were still alive. Jackie lay there a few seconds with the wind knocked out of him. In that few seconds, coach Cookie Lavagetto came down to the end of the bench and said, "You better go loosen up a little, in case Jackie has to come out." I just looked at him and said, "Are you kidding?" I knew Jackie wouldn't come out of the game, and there was no way I wanted to replace him in a game this important. Pretty soon Jackie got up, took a deep breath, and walked slowly off the field. I let out a huge sigh of relief. In the fourteenth inning, he hit the game-winning home run off my old college foe Robin Roberts.

The win set up the three-game play-off series for the National League pennant. The Giants won the first game 3-1 at Ebbets Field, and the Dodgers won 10-0 at the Polo Grounds. Game 3 was also at the Polo Grounds, and we went into the bottom of the ninth with a 4-1 lead. Three outs and we'd be on our way to the World Series. I was sitting on the bat trunk watching. The Giants' Alvin Dark and Don Mueller each singled off Don Newcombe. Whitey Lockman doubled, scoring Dark and sending Mueller to third base. Charlie Dressen brought in Ralph Branca to face the next hitter, Bobby Thomson, who wasn't having a good day—he had made a costly base-running mistake and a couple of our guys had reached base on hits that could easily have been ruled errors on Thomson. If the Giants lost, Thomson was pretty likely to get the blame.

While Branca threw his warm-up pitches I started thinking about how much fun it was going to be to take part in a World Series, even from the bench, and how nice it would be to get the bonus money, which I figured would be about $5,000. I sure could use that money, especially with our first baby due in a few months. Branca's first pitch was up and in; it just caught the corner for strike one. Branca threw another fastball, a little higher and a little more inside. Thomson got around on it and hit it on a line toward the stands in left field. I had to lean forward in order to watch the flight of the ball, and I fell right off the bat trunk and onto my knees as I followed it. When I saw Andy Pafko turn around to watch it sail over his shoulder, I realized it was gone. It didn't hit me that the game was over until I looked back toward the infield and saw the Giants in a wild celebration. I just stayed there on my knees. I was one of the last guys to leave the dugout.

The clubhouse after the game was quiet. These were class guys, and they handled it well, but it hurt and everybody felt it. Owner Walter O'Malley came in and tried to offer us some encouragement. He told us not to take this too much to heart, that we should be proud of the great season we'd had and we should go home and enjoy the off-season. Then he noticed that Billy Cox was putting on a pair of black silk under-shorts, and he said, "No wonder we lost, look at the color of Billy's shorts." He was trying to lighten the mood and get us to laugh, but nobody did.

Thomson's home run came to be called "The Shot Heard 'Round the World," and I imagine just about everybody has heard a recording of the Giants' radio announcer making the call: "There's a long drive . . . it's gonna be . . . I believe . . . The Giants win the pennant! The Giants win the pennant! The Giants win the pennant!" It was an amazing finish, but I had no idea people would still be talking about it fifty years later. In 2001 I was interviewed for a big fifty-year anniversary newspaper story. The reporter said the *Wall Street Journal* was reporting they had confirmed what was long suspected: that the Giants stole signs all season. Bobby Thomson was reported as saying that although they did steal signs that year, he was not clued in on the home run pitch. When I played with the Giants in '55, they were stealing signs—pretty creatively, too—but not every batter wanted them, and I believe Bobby Thomson when he says he didn't.

Since I only played every three or four days that season, I spent a fair amount of time sitting with the other bench players who were also being ignored by Charlie Dressen. About the only thing Dressen ever said to us on a regular basis was that he wanted us to be bench jockeys—to get on some of the opposing players when they were at bat. Well, chattering to my teammates on the field came naturally to

Wearing Dodger blue, Twig was part of a legendary team and present at one of the most famous moments in the history of baseball, "The Shot Heard 'Round the World." *Wayne Terwilliger personal collection*

me, but getting on opposing batters didn't. I would try to think of things to say, but not much sounded clever to me, so I pretty much quit trying. I said it was because my voice didn't carry very well out of the dugout. The truth is that being a bench jockey is about the only thing in baseball I couldn't get enthusiastic about. Some guys cracked up laughing, and some weren't very original in what they said. Dick Williams, a rookie left fielder, was a great bench jockey because his voice was loud and clear and because he could always come up with clever things to say. The rest of us were an appreciative audience, egging him on and laughing loudly for the batter's benefit.

One of the guys we could always get to was Wally Westlake, an outfielder with the Pittsburgh Pirates who was a pretty good hitter, but not at Ebbets Field. Just before the pitcher delivered the ball, Williams would call out, "Fast ball, Wally," or "What are you looking for, Wally?" or "Here comes a curve, Wally." We could see Westlake get rattled, and since we knew we could get to him, Williams did it every time he came to bat. Every time. It was pretty funny to see Westlake get frustrated, swing at bad pitches, take good ones, and all the time he would be one-eying our bench. Others were affected, too, but nobody else like our number-one target.

Umpires got the treatment, and one I especially remember is Frank Dascoli. On a road trip some of the Dodger players were checking out hotel windows and saw Dascoli inside a room. I have no idea whether they actually saw him doing something embarrassing, but they had him *believing* they saw something. One day at Ebbets Field he was struggling behind the plate, and the guys started calling out, "Next time pull the shades, Frank," and "Shades down, please." It was obviously getting to him. I don't know why he didn't clear the bench, unless he didn't want to write in his report what was said to him that caused him to kick somebody out of the game.

Rocky Bridges got into games about as often as I did, so we sat on the bench together and sometimes we'd hang out together. Rocky wasn't good at bench chatter, because his mouth was always full of tobacco juice that came running out when he talked. But, he was a naturally funny guy who kept our entire team laughing much of the time. He was a rookie infielder just turning twenty-five, but he looked and acted like he came straight out of Babe Ruth's time: Rocky had a bit of a gut, his shirttails were always coming out, and he always had a huge wad of tobacco in his cheek and juice running down from the corners of his mouth. He had a Texas accent and kind of a "poor hayseed" sense of humor that played well among the Dodger regulars—so much so that Pee Wee Reese started rooming with him on the road. He was a great storyteller, and I'd find myself kind of staring, watching the tobacco juice as I listened to him. He saw every movie that ever came out—during the day he'd go to as many as he could squeeze in before he had to be at the park—and he loved every one of them. I went with him sometimes, because it was so interesting to hear him talk about the movie afterward. He would recall the story in great detail, and then embroider on it, adding his own humor.

Rocky loved it when other players had a sense of humor, and he told me stories about pranks Don Newcombe had pulled before I arrived on the team. Don gave the appearance of being a quiet guy, but he had great wit, and one of his favorite targets was Leo Durocher, who by then was the manager of the "enemy" Giants. Rocky told me, for example, that during a Dodger-Giant game early in the season, Newcombe had a clock swinging on a chain visible in the dugout, referring to the rumor that Durocher had once stolen Babe Ruth's watch. I remember Newcombe taunting Durocher in another way. Our shower room at Ebbets backed right up to the visitors' shower, and you could hear some sound through the wall. I can still hear "Newk" pounding on the wall after we beat the Giants in a couple of close games in July, yelling, "Eat your heart out, Leo, eat your heart out." We all knew Durocher couldn't help but hear him.

In 2001 there was a fifty-year reunion of players involved in the 1951 play-off game. It was a very classy affair in New York. They invited every living member of both teams and put us up in a brand-new hotel near Times Square. Rocky Bridges looked the same as always: the tobacco juice, the gut, the shirttails. Newcombe looked great, and Al Corwin looked so good I'd swear he had a facelift. Duke Snider, Clem Labine, Alvin Dark, Wes Westrum, and so many others . . . it was great to see them. We all talked about how much we felt the absence of the greats who have passed away, including Hodges, Robinson, Reese, and Cox—the whole Dodger infield—plus

Twig slides in safely while the ball bounces out of the glove of Boston Braves third baseman Bob Elliott, who takes off chasing it. "You've got to be aggressive," Twig says. "There's always a chance the fielder will mishandle the ball." Twig had advanced from first on a single by Dodgers pitcher Ralph Branca in August 1951. *Wayne Terwilliger personal collection*

1952 Topps #7, Brooklyn Dodgers. A near-mint version of this card sold at auction for more than $1,300 in 2002, presumably to a collector seeking the full 1951 Dodgers team set.

Nancy Peterson personal collection

Furillo and Campanella. The Yankees played host and some of the great old Yanks were there as well. Of course Ralph Branca and Bobby Thomson were the centers of attention, and anybody who was covering the event for the media had to ask the two of them how "the shot" had changed their lives. Even though one of them was the hero and one was the victim, it gave them something in common—from the minute it happened, they both have been known for that one play.

The main event of the reunion was a huge dinner, with all the Dodgers and Giants players at a huge head table. Mayor Rudy Giuliani was the main speaker, and it was just a couple of weeks after the attacks on the World Trade Center, so there was a strong sense of New York pride in all the remarks. People also talked a lot about the good old days when the Dodgers and Giants were still New York teams, but it was all too obvious that the teams have moved on and that many of the players have left us.

At some point before dinner, a woman came up to me and said, "You're going to get an award." I looked around at who was there and I said, "You must have the wrong guy," and forgot about it. I was sitting next to Rocky Bridges when somebody called my name, and I whispered, "What is this about?" Rocky said, "Don't worry about it, just go up and get it." I realized everybody was waiting, so I hurried to the podium. They gave me a very classy plaque that said "Dodger Hall of Fame." I said, "Well, this is very unexpected, but if Rocky got one, I guess it's alright to accept it." When I sat back down I said, "Hey, I hope you know I didn't mean anything bad." He just laughed. Anyway, it was quite a celebration, all because of the home run that abruptly ended our season in '51.

In the spring of 1952, I went to the Dodgers' training camp at Vero Beach, Florida, and then back to Brooklyn to start the season, but they had a lot of infielders and I knew somebody was going to have to go. They still had Hodges, Reese, Robinson, and Cox as starters, and they had Bobby Morgan and Rocky Bridges and me as utility infielders. (I never did like that word "utility"—it made me feel like an extra piece of hardware.) I wasn't surprised when Buzzie Bavasi called me into the office one day and said I was going to the Dodgers' Double A team, the Fort Worth Cats. At the last second he called me at home and said, "We want you in Triple A, so make it Saint Paul instead." We got into the car with Marcie Lee, who had made her debut in January, and drove from New York to Minnesota. (I did eventually get to Fort Worth, but not until fifty-one years later, when the Cats were reinvented as an independent ball club, and I became their manager.) I didn't mind leaving the Dodgers because I wanted to play more, and before long I was playing pretty regularly with the Saint Paul Saints. I had a good season both defensively and at the plate, and my batting average for the season—thanks to a bang-up last game—was good enough to get me back into the majors.

We played at old Lexington Park, at University and Lexington Avenues in Saint Paul. It was a pretty basic baseball park, but it had a lot of history. Charles Comiskey built it for his Saints in 1897; three years later that team moved to Chicago and eventually became the White Sox. A new Saints franchise joined a new league called the American Association and in 1952 it was still going strong. Babe Ruth had once played at Lexington Park in an exhibition game, and several other Hall of Famers played there, either with the Saints or against them.

In a March 1952 publicity photo, third baseman Billy Cox stakes out his position during spring training at Vero Beach, Florida, as Twig, Bobby Morgan, and Rocky Bridges look on. With a surplus of Dodgers infielders, "No Vacancy" turned out to be the case for Twig. He was in spring training with Brooklyn but spent the season with the Dodgers' Triple A team, the Saint Paul Saints of the American Association. *Bettmann/CORBIS*

By '52 Lexington Park was definitely showing its age. The clubhouse was the smallest I ever saw in organized baseball. Left field was short because it ran up against the back wall of an indoor roller-skating rink; when you hit the ball onto the roof of the rink, you had a home run. The other memorable feature of Lexington Park: rats as big as rabbits. Our clubhouse was right next to the right-field stands, and the bullpen was in front of them. I went down there to warm up the pitcher a few times when I wasn't playing. The first time I did that, I said to one of my teammates, "Look at all those rabbits running around under the stands." He said, "Hey, buddy, look again; those are no rabbits." Sure enough, they were rats, and they were *huge*.

We had a pretty good team, including three outfielders who became big names: Gino Cimoli, a future All-Star; Sandy Amoros, who played on some of the great Dodgers teams; and Bill Sharman, who was an emerging basketball star. Bill Sharman had just started playing with the Boston Celtics, and I was surprised that they would let him play baseball. I guess it didn't hurt him, because he was an All-Star all through the '50s and they won a lot of championships. He was a decent baseball player, although he could shoot much better than he could hit. What surprised me was that he was slow. I couldn't believe it the first time I saw him run. He was a flat-footed runner, clop, clop, clop, to first base. I thought, wow, this is the great Bill Sharman? But his basketball specialty was free throws, so I guess he didn't need speed.

The Saints and the Minneapolis Millers were cross-town rivals, and the two teams played several times during the season. On holidays—Decoration Day, Fourth of July, and Labor Day—we played double-headers, starting at one park in the morning and moving to the other in the afternoon. The rivalry went all the way back to the Civil War, and the crowds really turned out. Since the Saints were the Dodgers' Triple A club and the Millers were the Giants', it was a little like the rivalry I'd experienced in New York. I heard that over the years there had been plenty of brawls on the field, and sometimes even among fans. We felt the rivalry, too, but in those days you put your energy into the play, not into a brawl. At one point during the season, I was hit in the head with a pitch that was pretty obviously intentional. When I finally could get up and walk off the field, my teammate Jack Cassini went in to run for me. On the first pitch to the next hitter, Jack took off for second base. He went roaring in with his spikes high, and he practically undressed Daryl Spencer, covering the bag for the Millers. The ball went one way, Spencer's glove went another, and when the dust had settled Spencer was leaving the field with torn pants and a limp. There was no brawl, it was just one tough play following another and the matter was settled.

Jack Cassini was our regular second baseman, and the fact that he was having an especially good year with the bat kept me from playing as much as I should have. I was hitting just under .300 most of the season, which wasn't bad at all. I did better toward the end of the season, and in the last game I went three for three and boosted my average to .312, the highest of my career. It was good enough that the Washington Senators bought my contract from the Dodgers in the off-season, and I was on my way to spring training at Orlando.

8

"Isn't That Terwilliger Playing Grand Ball?"

I liked Ike
and he liked me,
back in 1953,
he told "Mr. G."

The 1953 season was the best of my big-league career. I played well defensively, got some memorable hits, contributed to a fair number of wins, got a compliment from the President of the United States, and got a private one-on-one batting lesson from the world's greatest hitter. What more could a guy hope for?

As usual, I had to earn a spot on the team. This time it was the Washington Senators—officially the Nationals at that time, but they'll always be the Senators to me. Bucky Harris, Washington's "boy wonder" player-manager back in the '20s, was back managing the Senators. He had seen me play in 1949 in the Pacific Coast League when he managed at San Diego. In '53 he was looking for a second baseman who could hit a little better than Floyd Baker and Mel Hoderlein had done the year before, and when he saw that I hit .312 in Saint Paul, he asked the club to purchase my contract from the Dodgers. He told the *Sporting News*, "a .300 batting average in any league looks good to me." I had a lot of competition, though; Bucky was looking at six or seven potential second basemen. Then just before camp opened, he narrowed the field to me, Hoderlein, and a rookie named Leroy Dietzel.

I always loved spring training. Yes, there was pressure to make the team, but I didn't feel it the way I did during the season. In camp, it was never a problem to be enthusiastic and to hustle all the time. Why walk when I could run? Besides, I was happy to go from cold and snowy Michigan to warm and sunny Florida—the Senators trained at Orlando—and as we drove into the state I loved the smell of oranges in the air. Mary Jane and I rented a little house with grapefruit trees in the yard, and I got busy. I knew that Harris liked Leroy Dietzel; this was the third time he brought him to Orlando. Both previous times, though, Dietzel went back to the Chattanooga club, and two years in a row, he fractured his leg playing there. Dietzel was giving it his best effort, but the leg hadn't healed properly. Meanwhile, I was busting my butt every chance I got, and in the last few exhibition games I helped my chances with some extra-base hits. Harris decided to use Hoderlein as a utility player, and by the end of spring training, I had another starting spot.

Every team had its special traditions, and in Washington it was exciting to open the season by having the President throw out the first ball. The players all bunched together on the field, and President Eisenhower tossed the ball in among us. Whoever caught it had a nice souvenir. I never came close.

Nobody on that team was what you'd call a big name, but we had a solid infield with Eddie Yost at third, Pete Runnels at short, and Mickey Vernon at first. Our star pitcher was Bob Porterfield, who won 22 games and lost 10, with 9 shutouts and 24 complete games. I started out with a bang; a week into the season, I was hitting .360, the highest average on our team and tenth in the American League. "I always did think the Cubs brought him up too fast," Bucky told a reporter. "He may just be finding himself this season." I hoped he was right.

Playing in the American League meant that I was seeing a new set of ballparks and going up against a whole new set of players—again, some of them rising stars and some of them childhood heroes of mine. A couple of weeks into the season, I watched Mickey Mantle smash the longest home run ever hit in Griffith Stadium, and maybe any stadium; it cleared the left-field bleachers and traveled about 565 feet. What a shot! I can still see it. At first, it looked like a real high fly to left center field. It kept going up, almost in slow motion, and I

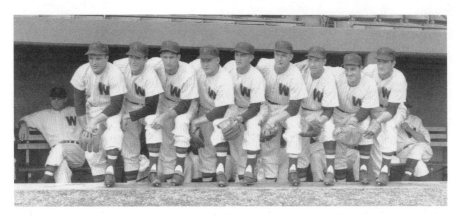

Opening day Senators' lineup in 1953—Twig's best season as a player—
included, from left, Eddie Yost, Jim Busby, Mickey Vernon, Jackie Jensen,
Pete Runnels, Ken Wood, Wayne Terwilliger, Mickey Grasso, and pitcher
Bob Porterfield, whose 22 wins made '53 his own best season.
Wayne Terwilliger personal collection

thought, geez, he really hit it high in the air. Then it kind of leveled
off and started going out, and I turned to watch it disappear way out
in left—and Griffith Stadium's left field is a road trip; it's way out
there. The ball hit the side of the scoreboard in left center field and
ricocheted out. The next day they had a big photo in the paper, with
dotted lines showing the path of the ball. In the picture, I'm standing
at second base, probably shaking my head. Yankee pitcher Bob
Kuzava supposedly said you could have cut that hit into fifteen singles. He should have said 150!

> *In addition to solving the second base troubles of the Senators,*
> *[Terwilliger] has been the solution to a weak spot in their batting*
> *order—second place. Terwilliger . . . the other day single-handedly*
> *won a game with a perfect hit-and-run swat. . . . "That's the kind*
> *of hit-and-run production I like to see our guys make," said Harris.*
> —*Shirley Povich,* The Sporting News, *June 17, 1953*

I got a home run off Whitey Ford at Yankee Stadium, one of only
thirteen he gave up that season. He probably didn't throw more than
half a dozen hanging sliders in his career, but I got one of them and
hit it hard enough that it snuck over the left field wall near the foul

line, probably a whopping 310 feet or so. Whitey was on top of his game; when he pitched, the Yankees won. So when a wiry second baseman with skinny wrists got a home run off him, I bet it bothered Whitey and Yogi Berra, too, but I had to laugh. I had said to Mickey Vernon before the game, "I'm not swinging the bat very well, so I'm going to try something different today." I opened up my batting stance and went into more of a crouch. I used my "Whitey Ford batting stance" for a couple more games but I didn't have the same success, so I moved on to trying something else.

I also got a game-winning hit off Satchel Paige, who was then a relief pitcher for the Saint Louis Browns. The record books say Paige turned forty-seven years old that summer, and he may have been even older than that. His career in the Negro Leagues began in 1926, before I was a year old. He had pitched against barnstorming major-leaguers like Babe Ruth, Rogers Hornsby, and Bob Feller, and many of them said he was the best pitcher they'd ever seen. Bill Veeck signed him, first for the Cleveland Indians in 1948 and then for the Browns. They put a big easy chair in the bullpen, and Satchel sat there with his feet propped up until he was ready to get loose. I faced him twice in one day. My first time up, I hit a line drive to the center fielder, who caught it for an out. The game was tied when I came up in the top of the tenth. Eddie Yost singled and then stole second, and I hit a little bloop single to right that drove him in for what turned out to be a 3-2 win. I still have the *Washington Post* headline that somebody saved for me: "Terwilliger Single in Tenth Beats Paige." That was a real highlight in my career. After that season Paige went back to the Kansas City Monarchs and then played in the minor leagues. In 1965 he played one final major-league game with the Kansas City Athletics and pitched three shutout innings against the Red Sox. He was at least fifty-nine years old by then. You gotta love a guy like that.

Two days after my hit off Paige, I hit a grand-slam home run. We were playing the White Sox at old Comiskey Park, and in the second inning we had the bases loaded with two outs when I came up against a pitcher named Saul Rogovin. I hit a high fly that carried surprisingly well. It bounced off the top of the left-field wall and back into the bleachers and put us ahead in the game. It was a stormy night, with lots of thunder and lightning that started in the distance

"Safe!" says umpire Joe Paparella as Twig gets a fingertip on first base despite the best efforts of White Sox first baseman Ferris Fain. Twig eventually scored in the 7-3 Chicago victory at Griffith Stadium May 17, 1953. *Wayne Terwilliger personal collection*

and kept coming closer. I held my breath hoping that the rain would hold off. We finished the game without getting wet, and my bases-loaded blast went into the books. Back home in Washington, they were playing the annual Congressional game at Griffith Stadium. President Eisenhower, who was a baseball fan and a big Senators fan, was sitting with our owner, Clark Griffith. At some point, they announced the Senators' win and my grand slam. According to the *Washington Post*, "all eyes turned to Ike and Griffith." Griffith said to the President, "Isn't that wonderful?" Ike replied, "And isn't that Terwilliger playing grand ball?"

Ted Williams used to say that hitting is 90 percent from the neck up, and I proved that against Yankee left-hander Eddie Lopat. Eddie had a strange motion; he'd throw his shoulder and his head at you, and then here comes the ball. The first time I ever faced him, I saw the ball well, I got three hits, and I hit the ball hard every time. After the game, the other guys told me they were surprised that I was able to hit so well against him and his off-speed pitches. I didn't say much, because I didn't want them to know that I thought they were

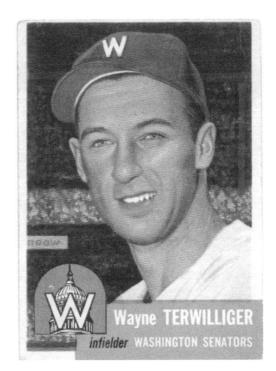

1953 Topps, #159. Washington's 1953 and 1954 cards used the designation "Senators" although the official team name was "Nationals" through 1955.

Nancy Peterson personal collection

just fastballs that didn't have much on them. I found out Lopat had a whole lot of "junk" pitches that came at you at different speeds and from different motions, and he mixed them up to keep hitters off-stride. After that, instead of just swinging the bat, I started worrying about the pitch, and I don't think I ever got another hit off him. So once again, when I just relaxed and let my instincts work, I did just fine. As soon as I started *thinking* about it, things didn't go so well.

> *Not the least factor in the Senators' surprising surge into the first division has been their talent for making double plays, a skill at which they are leading the American League. . . . "Wayne Terwilliger has made our infield," says [Manager Bucky] Harris. . . . There's nobody I'd rather see make good than Terwilliger."*
> —Shirley Povich, Sporting News, *June 17, 1953*

Some time in July my hitting began to slow down a little. I still had good days, but they weren't coming often enough. We didn't have a hitting coach, and there wasn't anybody who could help me. So

Photographer Don Wingfield worked for the *Sporting News* and took publicity shots for several teams. He took this photo of Twig for the Senators in 1953. *Wayne Terwilliger personal collection*

Clark Griffith decided he would do it himself. He called me into his office one morning—I still remember the plush carpeting—and started talking about my stance. I had an unusually wide stance, which I liked because I felt balanced and comfortable. He picked up a bat and held it up over his shoulder and spread his feet way out to imitate me, and then he said, "Young man, the only man who could hit with a stance like this is Joe DiMaggio." I thought, "This guy is eighty-four years old, and he was a pitcher, so what does he know about a batting stance?" but of course I listened politely. Then he told me he was going to ask the Red Sox permission to have Ted Williams talk with me, to see if he could give me some advice. I realized that Griffith wasn't criticizing me, he was taking an interest because he wanted to help me do better. And I was going to spend a little time with Ted Williams! Griffith wouldn't have needed to ask permission because Ted was always ready to talk about hitting, but I guess it was a courtesy, owner-to-owner.

Ted was just back in baseball after serving as a Marine fighter pilot in Korea for a year, and everybody in the country was watching his progress day by day. The Marines deactivated him on July 28 and he was back with the Red Sox the next day. He worked out and took batting practice for a week or so, then pinch-hit in a few games, and then played partial games while he worked his way back into form. The Red Sox came to Washington three weeks after Ted's return, and I think he made his first start against us. He hit two sharp line drives over my head at second, and two more over Mickey Vernon at first. They were four of those sinking line drives that he often hit, except that one of them didn't sink until it went over the wall. It was a typical Ted Williams exhibition!

The next day just before the game, Ted came over to where I was and said, "Wayne, Mr. Griffith wanted me to talk to you. I don't know what I can do to help you, but what problem are you having?" I told him about Mr. Griffith's comment on my wide stance and Ted said, "Okay, show me." We went over how I placed my feet, how I gripped the bat, how I held it before the pitch. Ted said, "I don't see anything wrong, but you should try different things if you're not comfortable." I told him that I *was* comfortable with my stance. Then he asked me to show him my swing, and he had me repeat it several times. Finally, he said, "Well, the only thing I could tell you is to lay your bat on your shoulder and wait a little longer to swing." Then he asked what kind of pitch I looked for, and I thought, *Oh, boy, whatever I answer is going to make him throw up his hands and walk away.* I took a deep breath and told him that I looked for a fastball until I had two strikes on me. He asked why. I said because I couldn't hit a curve ball. Ted said, "Not bad thinking." I was surprised, and also relieved. Years later when we worked together, I came to understand that my answer was pretty much the same as Ted's approach to hitting, which was "get a good pitch to hit," and with two strikes you have to deal with whatever the pitcher throws you.

I know Ted would have talked longer about the mental part of hitting, but we each had to get ready for the game. So I had about twenty-five minutes with him, which was more than I had ever expected but less than I would have liked. I felt almost cheated—in the back of my mind I was thinking maybe if we'd had more time, he would have said the magic words that would turn me into a .300

Twig's intensity shows as he forces Boston Red Sox centerfielder Tom Umphlett (#38) and throws to first for the double play. Boston won the game 4-3; it was the first of a doubleheader played May 30, 1953.
Wayne Terwilliger personal collection

hitter. I did try what Ted suggested. I laid the bat on my shoulder, waited a little longer on the pitch, and got three hits that night. None of them was hit very well, but it was still three hits, so I had to try it another night. It didn't work as well the second time, or the time after that, and it wasn't comfortable for me so eventually I dropped it. Ted had said to try different things, so every time I had a bad day

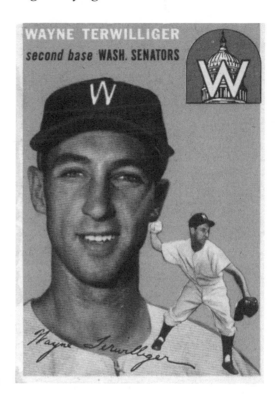

1954 Topps, #73.
Nancy Peterson personal collection

at the plate, I experimented the next day with some new stance, some little adjustment, anything I could think of. But he had also said to go with what was comfortable. My natural stance was comfortable, and my swing was good and quick. I believe now that what I really needed to do was to stay with it.

Yogi Berra also gave me some batting advice without meaning to. I fouled off a pitch one day while he was catching, and he said, "Look out, you're almost stepping on me with your back foot." I thought about it for a minute and realized that he was right. Instead of planting my foot, I took a little step just before the pitch. So I was careful not to do that, and on the next pitch I got a hit. I eventually scored an easy run, and as I crossed the plate he said, "I ain't going to say no more to you."

While my hitting was cooling down, Mickey Vernon's was picking up steam. Mickey had been playing first base for Washington since 1939—except for two seasons in the Navy and two in Cleveland—and he was a real favorite with everyone including President Eisenhower. In '53 he had a great season at the plate, as did Al Rosen of the Cleveland Indians. On the last day of the season, Mickey was leading the league in doubles and Rosen was leading in home runs and RBIs, and their averages were .003 apart—Mickey at .336 and Rosen at .333. That day, Cleveland was playing at home and we were at home against the Philadelphia Athletics. We—and our fans— were keeping track of what Rosen was doing. The press box would say, "Rosen got a base hit," or "Rosen beat out a bunt," and we'd say, "He's bunting? Are they trying to give him the title?" As the evening went on, we were more and more interested in that contest.

Sometime in the eighth inning, we heard that Cleveland's game was over; Rosen had gone 3-for-5 and ended up with an average of .336. Mickey had already gone 2-for-4, putting him at .337. If he didn't bat again, he had the American League batting championship. If he came up and didn't get a hit, he would lose. So the guys ahead of him in the lineup started making sure that wouldn't happen. In the bottom of the eighth, we had two out and Mickey Grasso came to the plate. Almost accidentally, he hit a line drive to left for a base hit. The first-base coach said, "Keep on going," so Grasso ran, as slow as he could without being too obvious, and I think he even stumbled going around first. But the left fielder bobbled the ball, so Mickey had no choice but to go into second standing up. We were behind in the game, but it didn't mean anything in the standings, and if we rallied, Vernon would have to come up. So Grasso took a big lead off second and managed to get picked off, and the eighth inning was over. In the bottom of the ninth, outfielder Kite Thomas led off with a single. He, too, kept going to second at something less than his usual pace, and they got him. Next up was Eddie Yost, who was known for having a good eye and not going after bad pitches; he popped up, swinging at a ball that was almost over his head. That brought Pete Runnels to the plate, with Vernon on deck. Pete struck out, the game was over, and Mickey had the batting title with a .337 average. In spite of losing the game, we really celebrated that night.

I played almost every game that season. I hit .252 with 4 home runs and 46 RBIs—not an MVP year but a pretty solid one for a second baseman. I did get some big hits when Bob Porterfield pitched. He won 22 games in '53 and I always seemed to do well with him on the mound. We ended the season in fifth place with 76 wins and 76

Leaping over Cleveland Indians outfielder Dave Philley after the forceout, Twig whips the ball to first to complete a double play in June 1954.
Wayne Terwilliger personal collection

losses, a pretty good year for the Senators. They would finish above .500 only one more time, in 1969 when Ted Williams was the new manager and I was third-base coach. It never happened again; three years after that, the team moved to Texas.

> *Twig is the best I've ever seen at getting rid of the ball rapidly— he can cut loose quicker than Bobby Doerr, Joe Gordon, Charley Gehringer, Tony Lazzeri or any of the other great second base-men I've seen.*
> *—Washington coach and long-time major league player Heinie Manush, quoted in the* Washington, D.C., Evening Star, *date unknown*

Like a lot of other ballplayers I had to work in the off-season to support my family. In the fall of 1953, I went back to working for a

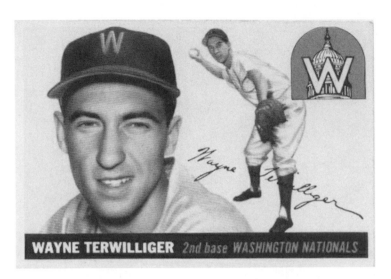

1955 Topps, #34. *Nancy Peterson personal collection*

paper company in Kalamazoo doing odd jobs in the mill, including sweeping up at the end of each day. We lived in a little cabin on a lake nearby, and I did some basketball officiating, which gave me another paycheck and helped keep me in shape. Some time after the first of the year, as I started to think about spring training again, I got a contract in the mail from Clark Griffith himself. It was for $8,000—the same amount I had made in 1953. I sent it back with a letter that said that I'd had a good season and I was quitting smoking, which would help my performance, and I expected to get a raise. He sent it back. I sent it back again and said I had contributed to the team's good year and deserved a raise. Some time went by. Spring training was getting closer, and I had no contract. This was well before free agency, so I either signed with the Senators or I didn't play. Finally, just before training was about to start, a contract arrived for $8,500. I was so relieved I couldn't wait to sign it and get it back into the mailbox. So after my best season, I ended up with a $500 raise.

As it turned out, in 1954 I didn't do enough to earn even that. I didn't quit smoking, either.

Things started going sour during spring training. I didn't play as much as I thought I should have and I couldn't understand why. George Myatt, our third-base coach, kept telling me, "Bucky knows what you can do; he wants to see the other guys." I wasn't sure about that explanation, but I did play a few games near the end, and I did start the season as the regular second baseman. Unfortunately, I really stunk it up with the bat. I got off to a slow start and never recovered. Except for a series in Philadelphia when I hit home runs in three consecutive games, the whole 1954 season was a year to forget.

The low point happened late in the season when I was really struggling at the plate. I had been batting eighth every game. One day at batting practice I started into the cage in the eight-spot when Mickey McDermott, that day's starting pitcher, headed in at the same time. He said, "I'm batting eighth today, see ya." I thought he was joking. I said, "Yeah, bullshit, get out of the way." McDermott stayed in the cage and said something else, but he was doing it in a joking way. He had appeared at a nightclub as a singer and comedian; he was always talking and clowning around, so I still didn't know he meant it. But pretty soon I'd had enough, so I said, "Get out of the way so I can hit," and I gave him a little shove. He pushed back. We got into a shoving match until somebody said, "Hey, Twig, he's hitting eighth and you're ninth. Look at the lineup." The lineup had been posted late, and I hadn't seen it, but they were right. So I had to back off and walk out of the cage. I was embarrassed, and I was mad. I never forgave Bucky Harris for that incident. I thought about it again when I started managing—why would a manager do that to a player who is struggling? He should have talked to me. I know he wanted to shake things up, but to put me down below the pitcher without even talking to me was really horseshit.

I kept on struggling; the harder I tried, the worse things got. Late in the season I wasn't starting every day, and I ended up hitting .208, the lowest of my career. We won ten fewer games than we had the year before, and I couldn't help feeling it was partly my fault, because I hadn't contributed like I had in '53.

Bucky Harris didn't return for the '55 season, and neither did I. But I would always remember Griffith Stadium as a place I really liked. We didn't draw huge crowds, but they were enthusiastic, and it was a great old ballpark with a great playing field; the dirt was always dark and true.

9

"Get on the Bus, You're Coming with Us"

New York and back,
Game's out of whack
Can't play much better
Now a bench-sitter.

In 1951, when the Giants won the pennant, I played for the Dodgers. So it only makes sense that in 1955, when the Dodgers won the pennant, I played for the Giants.

Charlie Dressen replaced Bucky Harris as manager of the Senators after the '54 season. Given the poor year I'd just had, and my experience with Charlie in Brooklyn in '51, I knew right away I wasn't going to be playing for Washington in 1955. They sold me to the Giants, who optioned me to their Triple A team, the Minneapolis Millers, back in the American Association where I had played with Saint Paul in '52.

I was happy to get a fresh start. The Millers were a very talented and experienced team; many of the players were on their way to the major leagues, or like me, had been there and would get back again. Among the thirty-seven guys who played for Minneapolis that season, twenty-four had at least some time in the majors, and quite a few had significant careers—pitchers Al Worthington and Ralph Branca; shortstop Eddie Bressoud; infielder Billy Gardner; catcher Carl Sawatski, and outfielder Ron Northey, to name a few. Our manager was Bill Rigney, a Giants infielder not so many years before.

He'd always been a gung-ho player; as a manager he was always pumped up and always had a lot to say.

We came together well as a team, and we played with a lot of confidence. I remember a game where Louisville scored seven runs—six of them unearned—in the second inning. We didn't panic and we didn't get upset, we just made up our minds that we would hold them defensively and score some runs. Everybody pitched in. We got nine runs that night, and we all made sure we played tough defense. I scored a couple of runs and made a game-saving catch where I threw myself at the ball, caught it, and landed hard on my stomach. Bill Rigney said it was as good a play as he'd ever seen, and Ralph Branca said it reminded him of the catch Jackie Robinson made at Philadelphia in the last game of the 1951 season to force the play-off game with the Giants. I was playing good baseball, and it felt good to be appreciated.

We played at Nicollet Park, an odd and ancient place that was in its last season. The park had a lot of history, and the playing surface was pretty good, especially the infield. But it was built in the 1890s and it was definitely showing its age; they hadn't made any improvements in quite a while because they were building a new stadium in the suburbs. Bob Casey, the Millers' public address guy (later the long-time Minnesota Twins announcer), used to say that every time a foul ball hit Nicollet Park's tin roof, all the toilets would flush. The clubhouse floor sagged, and in the middle of the locker room was a big pot-bellied stove, which we needed at the start of the season because it was plenty cold. We opened at home in late April right after a big snowstorm, and although most of the snow had melted, there were still banks of it against the fence in the outfield. Early in the game, a ball was hit down the short right field line and into a snow bank. I went out to take the relay, and I had to wait while the right fielder—a guy named George Wilson, who was quite a practical joker—rooted around in the snow trying to find the ball. Finally he came up and fired in a perfect one-hopper—a snowball that hit the ground and splattered about 6 feet in front of me.

I was hitting .303 in late June when the Giants came to town for an exhibition game against us. Their second baseman, Davey Williams, had back problems, which had gotten worse in April when Jackie Robinson took him out of a double play with a hard slide.

Williams was still hurting, and there were rumors that the Giants might take me with them when they left. I was having such a good time with the Millers that I didn't think about leaving. So I was surprised after the game when Manager Leo Durocher said, "Get on the bus, you're coming with us." I left my wife and daughter in Minneapolis (they went back to Michigan) and finished the road trip with the Giants. To make room for me on the team, they left behind Monte Irvin, the future Hall-of-Fame outfielder who hadn't been getting much playing time. I don't know what I'd have done the rest of the season in Minneapolis, but Monte hit .344 with fourteen home runs. The Millers won both the American Association pennant and the Junior World Series, the championship of minor-league baseball.

The 29-year-old Terwilliger, brought up from Minneapolis, has been with the Cubs, the Dodgers and the Senators. . . . Tonight Wayne was a busy boy, handling seven assists and one putout faultlessly.
—*Roscoe McGowen,* New York Times, *June 25, 1955*

I was having a lot of fun playing in Minneapolis and I hated to leave, but I was glad for the chance to be back and playing every day in the majors. Some of the New York sports writers were pretty skeptical, along the lines of "What does Leo want with a guy who was rejected by the Cubs, the Dodgers and the Senators?" It helped that I started my Giants career with a big play in my first game.

Ruben Gomez was pitching a 1-0 shutout for the Giants against the Cardinals in Saint Louis, and in the bottom of the ninth we got two pinch-hitters out, both on ground balls to second. Stan Musial was due up, and Durocher had the infield shift way over to the right, leaving the left side pretty much open. Musial took the challenge and lined a single into left center, and then Bill Virdon hit another single. With those two on base, Red Schoendienst hit a hard grounder just over the bag at second. I backhanded it and flipped it to Alvin Dark for the force-out to end the game. It was one of the memorable plays of my career. For one thing, it gave Leo Durocher a way to say in his post-game interview that he thought I could help the team. For another, saving Gomez's shutout made me a friend of the pitchers

Giants' manager Leo Durocher was all smiles after bringing Twig up from the Minneapolis Millers in June 1955. On his first day in a Giants uniform, Twig made a ninth-inning forceout play to preserve a win against the Saint Louis Cardinals. *Wayne Terwilliger personal collection*

for the rest of the season. Most important, though, when I made that play everything fell into place. I couldn't wait for the ball to be hit my way. Things went right for me for the rest of the season, and I ended up tied with Red Schoendienst for the best fielding percentage in the league at .985. I had 70 double plays in 78 games, a pace that would have put me at the top of the list if I had played a full season. If that play in Saint Louis had been tougher and I hadn't come up with the ball, who knows how the rest of the year might have gone.

> *In 1955 when I was 11, at the only major league game my dad and I ever attended together, Wayne's game-ending play behind second preserved a 1-0 Giants victory over the Cardinals in St. Louis. . . . In 2000, I met him at a morning game for kids in St. Paul. I couldn't help but think of my long-deceased dad while I visited with Twig. I made a wonderful connection with a truly great memory from my childhood.*
> —James McKinnis, Austin, Texas, e-mail, September 3, 2003

In 1998 when I was coaching with the Saint Paul Saints, I got a letter from a man who was at that game as a boy of eleven. He talked about his memories, including that play. A couple of years later, he came through town on a tour of ballparks and we visited at Midway Stadium. Later he created a painting for me, based on an old action shot. It's really interesting to find people with such clear memories of some of those games, and to hear about how much baseball, or even a particular game or play, has meant to them.

My new teammates were mostly the same guys who won the pennant for New York in '54 and then just walked all over Cleveland in the World Series. But instead of leading the league, we were struggling to stay somewhere around third place, which is where we ended up. Third place didn't seem so bad to me after being with the Cubs and Senators, but it was a letdown for the others, so the feeling around the clubhouse was a little flat. Even Durocher didn't show the kind of intensity I had expected, he mostly sat back and watched us play. On the other hand, he talked to me more than a lot of managers had—he'd mention something he wanted me to work on or something I could have done better on a particular play, and I liked that. He didn't try to change my game, which I also appreciated.

The Giants had a lot of guys who played hard; among my favorites were Alvin Dark, Whitey Lockman, Dusty Rhodes, and of course Willie Mays. Turning double plays with Al Dark at short was a snap because he had a great feathery touch that made his throws easy to handle. I lockered next to Dusty Rhodes, a pinch hitter and part-time outfielder who was one of the heroes of the '54 World Series. He had a locker full of photos of himself, and at the end of the season I took one home for my dad's bar—Dusty after one of his big Series games, with a cigar in his mouth and a cocky grin on his face, signed "To Twig and the Dearborn Bar." Pop thought it was great, and it hung in the bar for twenty years.

Willie Mays was simply the greatest player I've ever seen. He could do everything. He was a great base runner, a good hitter for average, and a power hitter on top of that. And of course, he was a great outfielder with a tremendous arm. He made plays in the outfield like nobody else. I had played against him in '51, his rookie season, and I saw him go from a struggling kid to Rookie of the Year; he had a lot to do with the Giants' huge comeback to win the pennant and the Series. In 1954, his first year back after military service, he was the league MVP. That was the year he made the spectacular World Series catch that still sets the standard for outfield play—the one you've seen replayed again and again, where he runs full-speed toward the fence, catches Vic Wertz's long drive with his back to the infield, then whirls around and fires it in so fast that the two base-runners can't advance. He said that another play later in that game was even more difficult, but "The Catch" is the one that caught everyone's attention. In '55, the year we were teammates, he led the league in home runs and triples, stole twenty-four bases, and was always making great plays in the outfield. I loved being able to watch him play every day. He loved the game, and he brought energy and enthusiasm to the clubhouse in spite of the fact that we weren't winning as much as the Giants usually did.

The rivalry between the Dodgers and the Giants was still pretty intense, and when we played each other, you could feel it. You didn't have bench-clearing brawls, or umpires inserting themselves into the action, either. One day Don Newcombe hit Whitey Lockman with a pitch. Lockman just shrugged, picked up the ball, and threw it back—*to* Newcombe, not at him. Lockman didn't charge the mound, and the ump didn't run out to get between the batter and the pitcher; things just went on. In the next half-inning, Jackie Robinson came up with Sal Maglie pitching for the Giants, and Jackie had to use his hand to deflect the ball away from his face. That's all there was to it; it was over. The pitchers were quick to protect their batters, so it didn't matter whether the first time was an accident or on purpose, you knew there would be a response. But you took it and moved on.

There had always been a lot of talk about the Giants stealing signs, possibly with a telescope. Other teams tried to protect themselves by giving multiple signs to try to confuse them. When I was with the Cubs, we used multiple signs all the time, even when nobody was on second. One time we had pitcher Bob Rush signaling the pitches *to the catcher,* wiping his shirt or adjusting his cap or scratching his ear to let him know what was coming. Meanwhile, the catcher was putting down fingers just for show. I don't know what the Giants did other years, but in 1955 they had a pretty elaborate system set up at the Polo Grounds, and it did involve a telescope. Joe Amalfitano, a reserve infielder with a keen eye for numbers and patterns, would exchange his seat in the dugout for one in owner Horace Stoneham's office, high above the fence in dead center field. Joe had paper and pencil and a telescope strong enough to detect life on Mars, zeroed in right between the catcher's legs. Because of the multiple signs and wipe-offs and such, it sometimes took Joe two or three innings to figure out the signs, but he was good and he always got them. When he was sure, he would buzz the Giants' dugout and the bullpen, which was just to the right of center field. When the buzzer went off in the dugout somebody would say, "He's got 'em." One of the pitchers, Don Liddle, would move into plain sight in the bullpen and sit with one leg crossed over the other. When Amalfitano buzzed once for a fastball, Liddle would hold his foot still or swing it up and down once. On two buzzes for a breaking pitch, Liddle would nonchalantly swing his foot twice.

Not every hitter wanted the signs. Some said it interfered with their concentration. Some, knowing that signals can get crossed up, didn't want to take the chance. I never took them because I had too many things to think about as it was. Gail Harris, a backup first baseman, was so obvious about looking for signs that he would take half a step out of the batter's box and peer toward the bullpen to get a better view—the other players finally banned him from getting signs so he wouldn't give away the secret. The players talked about a game where Pittsburgh pitcher Vernon Law shut them out even though they knew every pitch that was coming, so the system wasn't foolproof. Even if you knew what was coming, you still had to hit it.

I had a little trouble with my own hitting during my first month or so with the Giants, and my average was running below .200. I knew I couldn't continue that way, so as usual I started experimenting. The answer came to me the hard way—after I got hit in the head with a pitch that knocked me flat. The beaning happened at a night game in Cincinnati; Johnny Klippstein was pitching, and I never saw the ball coming. We had started wearing batting helmets a few years earlier. The ball hit the helmet just above my left eye, the helmet broke, and it gave me a big knot above my eye. They sent me to the hospital and took X-rays, and as the joke goes, they found nothing. In other words no skull fracture, but enough bruising and swelling and headaches to keep me out of about ten games. I had been beaned twice before with no batting helmet, and this time *with* a helmet I was hurt worse than before.

While I was recovering, I had plenty of time to think about hitting, and I went over all the advice I had received from Rogers Hornsby, Clark Griffith, Wid Mathews, and of course, Ted Williams. I remembered that Wid Mathews had me standing closer to the plate, which had worked for a while, but this year all it seemed to do was get me hit in the head. I was worried about how that was going to affect me, because when you get beaned, you have that little nagging thought in the back of your mind. Then one day Frankie Frisch—my old Cubs manager who now was a radio announcer for the Giants—came over to talk. He said, "You got hit pretty good. You know what you should do now? Why don't you just back off the plate a little bit more than you usually do, just to help you get back in the swing of things." I thought, "That's pretty good advice." He also suggested that while I was backing off I should use a heavier bat. Sure enough, things picked up. I hit about .290 for the last two months of the season and I finished with an average of .257. I was pretty sure I had

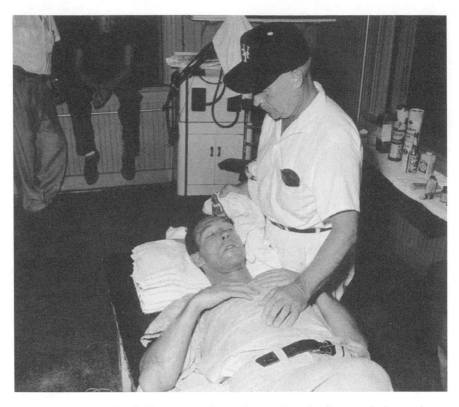

Twig never saw the ball coming, but when it hit the batting helmet above his left eye it broke the helmet, sent him to the hospital, and kept him out of about ten games. *Associated Press*

found myself as a hitter, and I was having an outstanding season in the field, too.

There was something special about playing for a New York ball club, especially because I lived right in Manhattan, at the Henry Hudson Hotel where a lot of celebrities stayed. Martha Raye rehearsed her variety show in the basement of the hotel; she and Rocky Grazziano were around there quite a bit. As I walked around the area, I was always seeing some big-name movie director or boxer or entertainer or politician, which I found exciting. Sometimes other people would recognize me, like the day I was walking past a theater and an usher standing at the door called out, "Hey, Twig, how you gonna do tonight?" There was a bar right next door to the hotel, and I got to be one of the regulars; I made it my own little place to wind down after the game. I'd have a beer and talk to a few people about the game or how the team was doing. Since they were mostly New Yorkers, they had strong opinions, which made lively conversation. When I was ready, I could just walk right next door and I'd be "home" at my hotel. I was starting to feel like a real big-city guy.

The Giants asked me to appear on the radio program "Breakfast at Sardi's," where the host did live interviews with a few celebrities gathered around a table at the restaurant. I was a last-minute substitute for another player who couldn't make it, and I was happy to step in but a little nervous. The other guests were Eartha Kitt, who I was familiar with, and Shirley Yamaguchi, who I hadn't heard of until then, but she was starring with Robert Stack in the movie *House of Bamboo*, which was just coming out. They asked us before the show if we'd like something to drink. Eartha Kitt asked for a martini or something like that, and I thought I'd *really* like a beer to help me relax, but I decided it wouldn't be wise. Once the show got started and the host began asking us questions, my nerves settled down and I really enjoyed it. Afterwards, I was pretty happy with how I had done, and I thought that I had represented the team well. I also did two interviews on live television, which was a fairly big deal in 1955. The actress Laraine Day, who was married to Leo Durocher, had a show on game days, and as part of it she interviewed a Giants player. I was chosen to appear a couple of times. I got to sit on a couch with Laraine Day—who I always liked— and answer questions. And, they paid me $50. I never liked making speeches, but answering questions was a snap.

The Twig has a quiet confidence that he'll be in there when things really count. "I know Rig is trying to get more punch into the batting order and I can't blame him, but I know, too, that he knows the value of a guy who can make the double play."
—Arch Murray, New York Post, *March 3, 1956*

When I was playing college basketball, we once took part in an invitational tournament at Madison Square Garden. We played a hard-fought game in front of seventeen thousand screaming New Yorkers, losing 48-46 to Long Island University, the home-town favorite. The noise was deafening, but I liked being "on stage" for a large crowd, and I loved the way the New York fans got into it. It appealed to the performer in me—the boy who had recited all those nursery rhymes for relatives as a child.

I loved the big, noisy baseball crowds in New York. I loved living there and playing at the Polo Grounds, and I found myself hoping it wasn't true that Horace Stoneham would move the team if he didn't get a new stadium—which didn't appear likely. Unfortunately, I left the Polo Grounds before the Giants did. After the '55 season, Leo Durocher resigned, and Bill Rigney, who had just managed the Minneapolis Millers to the Junior World Series championship, succeeded him. At first I was happy about that; Rigney knew me from the Millers and I thought he liked me. But at spring training in Arizona he was looking at Daryl Spencer and Foster Castleman as possible replacements, and he was acting as if I wasn't even there. During our early exhibition games, I sat on the bench while the others played. It was a lot like spring 1954 all over again, and I had a hard time just sitting around. One day some newspaper reporters came around asking how I felt about getting benched. I knew I had to be careful not to show up the skipper, so I told them no, I wasn't angry and no, I wasn't resentful but also no, I didn't understand why I wasn't getting any playing time. I told them I understood Rigney's concern over the hitting but that I had improved a lot in that department. What I couldn't say was that I didn't think Spencer or Castleman were as good in the field as I was, or much better at the plate, either. Both of them had played with the Giants before. Castleman hit .214 in seven games in 1955; Spencer played most of 1953 and hit .208. How could those stats outweigh the year I had in '55, both at the plate and in the field? Other players seemed to agree with me, and a couple of them went public with their opinions. Wes Westrum and Dusty Rhodes both told a reporter that I had come in and helped the team a lot, that I had solved their problems at second base and helped them finish higher than they would have without me. I didn't know how Rigney would react to being second-guessed in print. He never said a word about it, but for the next several exhibition games, which were the last of the preseason, I started at second. And I hit just about everything in sight. In my first eleven trips to the plate, I got six hits. I started breathing easier, figuring I had just nailed down the starting position.

Photographer Don Wingfield took this publicity photo of Twig for the Giants, probably early in the 1956 season. Note Twig's Marine Corps insignia tattoo. *Wayne Terwilliger personal collection*

Instead, Rigney started the season with Daryl Spencer at second base and Foster Castleman at third and me on the bench. He never explained his decision, and I never understood it. Spencer hit .221 for the season, but he mostly substituted at short after they traded Alvin Dark to Saint Louis and brought in Red Schoendienst to play second. By the time they made that trade, I was long gone. I wasn't

WAYNE TERWILLIGER

second base NEW YORK GIANTS

1956 Topps, #73. The card back notes that Twig "made the fewest errors of any NL 2nd baseman in '55." *Nancy Peterson personal collection*

happy sitting on the bench and I had no way of knowing whether Rigney would ever use me. So I looked around for other possibilities, including winter ball in South America. I found out that professional players with more than a couple of years' experience who were on a big-league roster weren't allowed to play winter ball. But if I was on a minor-league roster I could go. So I figured instead of sitting on the bench here, why not go back to Minneapolis, get some playing time, and then play winter ball and make some money? I talked it over with Rigney, and he didn't try to talk me out of it, so after eighteen at-bats with the Giants in 1956, I went back to the Minneapolis Millers.

As a young Cub Scout in the mid-1950s, I attended a game between our Omaha Cardinals and the Minneapolis Millers. During pre-game warm-ups, one of your throws sailed into the bleachers where it struck a young vendor in the back of the leg. He was on the verge of tears when you ran off the field, jumped over the fence and comforted him. That was the closest we'd come to an actual professional ball player and your kind actions made quite an impression on our group.
—Larry Lehmer, Urbandale, Iowa, letter, June 28, 2005

I hated to leave New York, but by the time I got to Minneapolis, I was glad to be back. In '55 I'd had *almost* as much fun in Minneapolis as in New York. The Millers were a strong team, the fans were terrific, Minnesota was a great place to live, and I knew I'd get to play. I played there in '56 and '57. We continued to have good teams with a mix of up-and-coming young talent and seasoned experience, including guys I played with in New York. I was happy to have Eddie Bressoud, my double-play partner, at short both seasons. In '56 the rest of the infield was Ozzie Virgil at third, and Gail Harris and Bill White at first. Gil Coan and Joey Amalfitano were in the outfield (someone else must have taken over Joey's sign-stealing duties back in New York) along with outfielder Willie Kirkland, who was starting to show his power by hitting thirty-seven home runs. In '57 we had a young guy named Jim Davenport at third and a nineteen-year-old power hitter named Orlando Cepeda at first; both of them were on their way to being rookies with the brand-new San Francisco Giants in '58 (Cepeda would be Rookie of the Year). Davenport and I used to go crappie fishing together, and we got into the habit of coming early to the clubhouse to play gin rummy before the game. Felipe Alou—who also made his debut with the Giants in '58—was in our outfield for a time in '57, and I played with him again in Dominican winter ball. He was a talented player, he had some pop in his bat, and he was smart. Like me, he stayed in the game to coach and manage, and in the same year that I became manager of the Fort Worth Cats at age seventy-seven, he became manager of the San Francisco Giants at sixty-seven.

Carlos Paula "played" right field in '57, meaning he was stationed out there. Hitting was his strong point, and he knew it. He was a big, strong guy, and I decided early in the season that I didn't want to compete with him for any fly balls in short right, so we made a deal. If he had to come in on a fly more than a couple of steps, the ball was mine. He should call out "Tweeg" and get out of the way. It worked out fine, and I think I led all second basemen in the league in putouts that season.

We had some pretty strong pitching both years. Gene Bearden made a big hit with our infielders in '57 when he told a reporter that our Millers infield—Davenport, Bressoud, Cepeda, and me—was the best he'd had behind him since '48 when he won twenty games with Cleveland. Frank Barnes, Jim Constable, Curt Barclay, Max Surkont, and Pete Burnside were real workhorses and won a lot of games for us. Burnside was the kind of guy who would finish—and win—a game on a leg that was broken by a line drive, which is exactly what he did once in the majors. Surkont was intense on the mound and a big joker off the field. One day in Louisville, he was fooling around in the clubhouse and threw some ice water on Orlando Cepeda. He was just joking, but the next thing we knew they were really going at it. Cepeda, who had gotten the nickname "Baby Bull" as a youngster in Puerto Rico, grabbed a bat and was cornering Surkont when Jim Davenport and Foster Castleman tackled him. They saved old Max from a big-league headache, but they got a few bruises of their own, casualties of the "bullfight."

We were playing at the brand-new Metropolitan Stadium in Bloomington. It was a few miles south of old Nicollet Park and quite a change! The Met was a great ballpark, intended for a major league team some day. It had a wonderful playing surface, and the infield was the best I ever played on. It was true and it was manicured, just fast enough that you could get a jump on a ground ball but still not penalize the hitter. The other teams in the league were Denver, Omaha, Toledo, Louisville, Indianapolis, Charleston, and of course our cross-town rival, the Saint Paul Saints. We had great fans and a lot of support from the community; the Minneapolis paper printed the American Association standings *above* those of the National and American Leagues. (The Met got its major league tenant in 1961 when the Washington Senators became the Minnesota Twins, at which point the Millers and the Saints no longer played in the Twin Cities.)

Eddie Stanky became manager of the Millers in 1956 after several seasons managing at Saint Louis. I admired him as a second base-man—I had played against him in '49 when he was with the Braves and in '50 and '51 when he was with the Giants. He was scrappy as the devil; his nickname "The Brat" suited him well. He would slide hard into bases, and if the fielder had the ball there ahead of him, he would go in kicking, hoping to knock the ball out of the fielder's glove. At the plate he didn't move away from inside pitches; he stood firm and was willing to get hit just to get on base. The "experts" said he couldn't hit, couldn't run, and wasn't a good fielder, and yet he was one of the most valuable players the Giants and the Boston Braves ever had. I heard a story that when he was starting out in the minors he got discouraged and asked his mother to send him money so he could come home. She told him she wasn't giving him the money, and if anybody else did, he shouldn't bother coming home because she didn't want any quitters around her.

That "anything to beat you" approach made Eddie a tough manager to play for. He expected everybody to play as hard as he did and, more than most managers, he couldn't stand to lose. He hated anything that sounded like an excuse or anything that looked like you were not hustling, and he let you know it. He didn't want anybody helping the other team, either, even with some little gesture like picking up the catcher's mask after he tossed it off to make a play. I *still* think of Eddie when I see a guy pick up an opponent's mask or bat and hand it to him. I respected him and really enjoyed playing for him.

We had a jukebox in the clubhouse, which surprised me given Eddie's intensity, but I guess he thought the music kept the team energized. It didn't take coins; all you had to do was push the buttons. We liked it, and we had it going a lot of the time. Eddie usually showered with the players, but if we had a bad game we all waited, with the jukebox silent, until Eddie showered and was gone.

After one real disappointing loss at home, we were sitting in front of our lockers waiting, nobody saying a word. Pretty soon he came striding by, bare-ass naked with a shower cap pulled halfway down on his head like always. Nobody said a word. But just as he got past us, the jukebox started blaring Elvis Presley's "Hound Dog." I was in shock. I urged my chair as far into my locker as I could get it, and like everybody else I kept my head down and tried to disappear. A couple of guys started snickering, and with that I was sure Eddie was going to hit the ceiling. But he just kept walking without a word, and pretty soon we heard the shower running. The record was just finishing as he turned off the water and came stomping past us, and again nobody said a word. I took a peek just as Eddie was turning the corner toward his office, and I was pretty sure he hadn't even taken the time to towel off. When he slammed the door behind him, the buzz returned to the locker room and the guys who knew who the culprit was started yelling at him, "Thanks a lot, asshole, we'll hear about that tomorrow." But Stanky never said a word about it. It's possible that after he cooled down and dried off, the slightest hint of a smile might have crossed his face. Our 78-74 record got us into the American Association playoffs, and we finished in fourth place. We were disappointed that we didn't repeat the previous year's first-place finish, but our disappointment was nothing compared with Eddie's. The next season he was gone, replaced by John "Red" Davis.

There probably isn't a better fielding combination in the minors today than Eddie Bressoud and Wayne Terwilliger. They keep on playing sensational ball for the rampaging Minneapolis Millers, but don't get much of a look by teams in the big show who could eliminate their troubles by picking them off.
—*Charles Johnson,* Minneapolis Star, *May 23, 1957*

Red Davis was a player's manager; he mixed right in with the rest of us. After the game, especially if we won, we'd get eight or ten guys around a big table in the locker room and play Crazy Eights. Red would be right in the middle of it, and he'd slap those cards down on the table and make a big deal of it. He enjoyed it as much as we did. Red's wife was more visible than most managers' wives; she came to the ballpark often and she didn't mind being around the players. She always had a lot of flair—she would wear bright clothes and fix her hair in a special way, maybe with a scarf or flower—and the players liked her.

Red knew that a lot of the players had quite a bit of experience and he didn't over-manage; he mostly just let us play. His approach seemed to work: We won 85 games and lost 69, we made the playoffs again and ended up in third place. It worked for me, too. I had a great year in the field and hit .270. Early in the season, my average wasn't that great but I was getting on base more than anybody else so Red moved me from second in the lineup to leadoff. For reasons that once again I can't explain, I immediately started to hit better. Within about ten days I had my average up to .305. I seemed to lay off the bad pitches better than usual, and although I was still moving around in the box and constantly changing my stance or my swing, it all seemed to work. At some point I had an eleven-game streak going until I pulled a thigh muscle and had to sit out a game or two.

Then in the middle of the season, I strained my back somehow. I didn't miss many games, but it bothered me for quite a while. It was still killing me during our annual Fourth of July series against the Saint Paul Saints, but I played anyway, starting one game, and getting a pinch-hit RBI in the tenth inning of another; we beat them both games. In spite of my back, I was playing as well as I ever had defensively, turning a lot of double plays and playing the last seven or eight weeks of the season without an error. As a result, I led the American Association in fielding at second base. I had become a complete player, but I was still in the minors.

I enjoyed those summers in Minnesota. It wasn't the majors, but the baseball was good. I liked the people and the climate, and there was always a lot to do. In August I would take my daughter Marcie to the Minnesota State Fair, where we looked at a few of the farm animals and then headed to the carnival games. I liked the coin toss, where you pitch dimes and try to get them to stay on the glass plates instead of bouncing or sliding off. By the second summer, I figured out that if you put a tiny bit of chewing gum on one side of the coin and rubbed it in, it didn't bounce as high and it had a better chance of staying on the plate. One afternoon Marcie and I went home with an armload of stuffed animals, and a day or two later, we went back—over my wife's objections—to get more prizes for the neighbor kids. The guy running the game told me I was banned. I put up a protest, but it was pretty weak, and before long I gave up and we headed to the merry-go-round. About thirty years later, I would move back to Minnesota and live there for seventeen years—but that's another story.

10

Short Bat and Shower Shoes

First trip overseas
Without a gun or shaky knees.
Came not to fight but just to play.
Muchas gracias . . . Olé!

When I first thought about playing winter ball, it was just a good way to make some money in the off-season. But it was more than that. It was interesting to spend some time outside of our own country, and the baseball—especially in the Dominican Republic—was terrific.

In the fall of 1956, I went to Maracaibo, Venezuela, to play with a team called the Centauros. It was a Venezuelan team, but we had five Americans, mostly affiliated with the Giants, there for the season. Maracaibo is pretty much surrounded by oil derricks and, since it's a port on the Gulf of Venezuela, oil tankers. I knew enough Spanish to order breakfast and a beer—*"un cerveza grande, por favor."* The five American players all stayed together in a big house, along with our families. It was a little cramped with each family living in one air-conditioned bedroom, but we all got along. Everybody pitched in—one week your family did the cooking and the next you did the laundry and then you did the dishes.

The house was within walking distance of the ballpark; the five of us would put on our uniforms at home and walk to the park for the game. Afternoons were so hot that we usually played at ten in the morning. Most people were working, so there weren't a lot of fans.

Many of the fields we played on were skinned diamonds—no grass, just dirt. That took a little getting used to for the Americans, but the Venezuelans had grown up playing on them.

One of the clubs we played was at a town called Cabimas, which had some players from the Dodgers organization. It was maybe 20 or 30 miles as the crow flies, but it was across a narrow part of Lake Maracaibo and we had to go there by ferry. Between the bad smells and the rising and falling of the boat, it wasn't a pleasant way to travel. The most memorable thing about Cabimas was that when you turned the showers on, you not only got water, you got oil. It smelled, and there was enough of it that you couldn't get clean, so you ended up smelling like sweat *and* oil. Then you had to get back on the ferry and ride the waves again. If you weren't seasick on the way over, there was a good chance you would be on the way back. Even so, the baseball was pretty good and it was a lot more fun than working at a Michigan paper mill for the off-season.

Our wives had it a little tougher than we players did; there were children to keep entertained and it wasn't always easy to get around. We were usually home from our games by mid-afternoon, which helped. One of the other families told us about a swimming pool near our house, so we took Marcie there a lot. She was four, and she remembers Maracaibo as the place where she learned to swim. The hardest thing was spending Christmas far from home, and without snow. We got some kind of little tree, but it didn't look much like Michigan! By the time the baseball season was over, we were ready to go home. When we got our final paycheck, we had to go to the bank and wait around for a long time getting it converted to dollars. We had $2,000 or so, and I was afraid it might get stolen, so I put most of it into a baseball sock and tied it around my waist like a money belt for the trip home to Michigan.

The next fall—1957—I got a call from Salty Parker, a long-time baseball man who was working with the Giants. "I'm going to manage a team in the Dominican Republic," he said. "It's a mix of major-leaguers, up-and-comers, and Dominican players. Do you want to play for me?" I had enjoyed Venezuela, so I said yes. But when we first got there, I thought I had made a big mistake. Rafael Trujillo was in power, and you could see that he was running the country with a tight fist. We were living in Santo Domingo, the capital city, and there were soldiers everywhere. We'd walk around doing some sightseeing, and if we wandered anywhere we weren't supposed to be the soldiers would immediately come over and tell us to move on or to put our camera away. Even though we didn't speak a lot of Spanish, we could tell *exactly* what they meant and we moved on, no questions asked. There weren't as many soldiers in other towns where we played, but you still knew that a dictator was running things. But wherever we went, the people treated us very well, and once we got used to the soldiers and the dictator, we had a great time.

Santo Domingo had the country's two original professional base-ball clubs. I played for *Los Leones del Escogido—the Lions of the Chosen One*—and our local rivals were the Tigers of Licey. The two teams played at the same stadium, a beautiful brand-new park. They played up their rivalry through team colors; everything about Escogido was red, and Licey was blue. Trujillo, a big baseball fan, would come to watch us play. We knew when he was arriving because everything came to a stop. He would come in surrounded by soldiers and take his seat in the front row, very close to the field, and once he was settled, people would start to move around again, but very carefully. There were jail cells right under the stands, so if some-body acted up during the game, they didn't have to go far to lock them up. I remember a lot of very enthusiastic cheering, especially when Trujillo wasn't there, but not much rowdy behavior.

The quality of Dominican baseball was very high, and the idea of Americans coming to play winter ball there was just beginning to catch on. There were maybe a dozen of us playing for Escogido, mostly affiliated with the Giants. Some were guys I had played with in Minneapolis, including power hitter Willie Kirkland, Gold Glove first baseman Bill White, and pitcher Max Surkont. Third baseman Ozzie Virgil and outfielder Felipe Alou, who also played on the Millers, were big crowd favorites in Santo Domingo. They had played with Escogido before, and they had both gone into the Giants' minor league system. Ozzie had been called up to New York in September of '56 and played part-time all through '57, making him the first—and at that point the only—Dominican player in the majors. Dominican fans—including the Number One Fan, Trujillo—were excited about him, and I think they knew he was the first of many. When winter ball was over and the 1958 major league season got started, Felipe Alou was an everyday starter, making him the first Dominican to play regularly in the majors. Meanwhile, he was the Escogido MVP and a big factor in our winning the team's third consecutive league championship. He had all the skills—good hands, good hitter—and he played smart. He *is* smart, which is why he has been successful coaching and managing all these years.

A young pitcher named Juan Marichal—the first Dominican Hall-of-Famer—was also on our team. He was nineteen years old and he had been working on his pitches from the time he could pick up a ball. I enjoyed watching him work. It didn't take long to see that he was going to be special. I wasn't surprised by his tremendous success with the Giants all through the 1960s, and I could still see the same form, with the same big leg kick, that he showed with Escogido.

People in Santo Domingo loved their baseball, and whether they were rich or poor they treated players like VIPs. The team's owner, Ramon Embert, owned a cement-block factory; he was very rich and he seemed to like spending money on us. When we won our first game against Licey, he decided to reward us with individual gifts. He sent someone to the clubhouse to ask each of us what we wanted. I didn't have any shower shoes, so that's what I asked for and that's what I got—a pair of shower shoes. Most of the guys asked for a little more than that—extra meal money or a more expensive gift. We started wondering out loud what we should ask for next, but it turned out that the gifts were a one-time thing. Instead, we got invitations. Mr. Embert lived in a beautiful big house, and he had the team there a few times for very fancy food and drinks. When we won the league championship at the end of the season, he threw a party at a restaurant and sent his limousine to pick up the players and wives. I wasn't used to riding in a limo. I remember very clearly how exciting it was getting into that limo with Mary Jane and being driven to the restaurant for this fine banquet.

The fans, mostly *not* wealthy, found other ways to show us their appreciation. They really paid attention to everything we did, and they let us know it. During the time I was playing there, in yet another variation on my stance and swing, I was choking up on the bat. The fans spotted this immediately, and they started calling me "bata corto," or "short bat." Before long I started hearing it on the street, too. People would greet me, or point me out to somebody else, and even if I didn't understand what else they were saying, I'd hear "bata corto." It always made me laugh.

Instead of living with a lot of families as we had in Venezuela, we had an apartment of our own. Mary Jane was pregnant with our second child, so she was happy that we had an English-speaking maid, Olga, who did the shopping, cleaning, and most of the cooking, all for a dollar a day. Olga's rice and beans with chicken were wonderful! We knew the chicken was fresh because Olga would go to the market and barter, come back with a live chicken, and take it out back to wring its neck. Mary Jane and I didn't watch. Marcie, who was five by then, watched sometimes and didn't understand why I wouldn't go along—to her it was just something new and interesting.

We had a small room where Olga could "take five" or even stay overnight if she wanted to, but most of the time she went home, which we discovered later was just a shack. Once in a while she brought her daughter Doris to play with Marcie. The two girls didn't speak much of each other's languages, but they seemed to communicate just fine. We always added to Olga's daily wage, and when we got back to the States we sent her money several times. Her notes to us were censored, but by reading between the lines, we soon realized that she wasn't getting the money.

The down side of living in our own apartment was that there weren't as many people around to talk to all the time, so we had to find ways to entertain ourselves. We got a little TV set, and we would watch whatever was on and try to understand a little of the Spanish. Every once in a while they would show an old American movie, usually a western, in English. It was a real treat. Marcie had learned to swim in Venezuela, and in Santo Domingo she started school. It was a Spanish-speaking school, but some other American children went there, too. The school bus picked her up and delivered her right to our door. It was very convenient for us and quite an adventure for her. I sympathized with my little girl who had to go off to school by herself, on a bus, in a strange place where not everybody spoke English. What gave her trouble, and what she still remembers, is being teased about her saddle shoes. At home, she would have been right in style, but in Santo Domingo she was the only one wearing them. For a little girl, *that's* a problem.

11

Not Quite a Tiger

Oh, to be a Tiger,
A championship to win
Like back in 1935.
Instead, a Senator again . . .
. . . Charleston, that is.

In the spring of 1958, at long last, I became part of the organization that meant so much to me as a kid, the Detroit Tigers. Not that I would actually *be* a Tiger. I was going back to the American Association, this time playing for Charleston, West Virginia, Detroit's Triple A club. I didn't understand why the Giants would trade me, especially after the big year I had for Minneapolis. Oddly enough, when I got to Charleston I found myself playing for a team called "Senators." I never did figure that out.

We had spring training in Lakeland, Florida, not too far from where the Tigers trained, but not nearly as nice. They put us up in a barracks-type building and it felt like boot camp again. The best thing about that spring was the food, which was outstanding. They served it cafeteria style and it was plentiful, and because it was so good and there wasn't much else to do, we spent a lot of time eating. Players with cars lived off the "base," but the rest of us were stranded. Alcohol wasn't allowed, so when we wanted a beer we had to take quite a hike to the nearest bar. There was a lounge with a TV in the main section of the barracks, but almost nobody used it except Schoolboy Rowe, the old Tigers pitcher, who was always in there.

He was in camp as an instructor, but he wasn't in very good health—his ankles were badly swollen and he didn't get around too well. Being the big Tiger fan that I was, I introduced myself to him one evening. He was friendly, but he wasn't up to talking very long.

Maybe because we had so few distractions, we had a good spring training. We left Florida with a good club and we got better as the season went along. Watt Powell Park, on the edge of Charleston, had a good infield and a good background of trees for the hitters. A railroad track ran behind the center field fence, and the trains never seemed to be in a hurry. Bill Norman, our manager, had played with the White Sox briefly in the '30s, and he was a lot like Millers' manager Red Davis: He let us play. No meetings; just play hard. We liked that. We stayed motivated, and he kept us loose. When we'd win a couple of games in a row and he'd hear some of the guys laughing, he would bellow out, "Don't get gay when you're full of shit." We weren't sure what he meant, but we heard it so often that we figured it out: Don't get too cocky when things are going good. In the middle of the season, Bill was called up to manage the Tigers, who were struggling. We were in first place, and I guess the Tiger brass must have figured Bill had something to do with it. We were pulling for him, and when the Tigers won a double header from the Yankees on his first day, I wanted to call him and say, "Remember, Bill, don't get gay when you're full of shit." Then they started losing, and they struggled through the rest of the season. We all decided that he had probably used his favorite saying on the big-leaguers, and they just didn't understand him the way we did.

My Dad and I shared a love of baseball and trips to Watt Powell Park are some of my happiest memories. Wayne Terwilliger . . . would spin his glove as he waited in the field between pitches. My dad told me that he was a great fielder but that I was NOT to pick up THAT habit!
—Allen Jenkins, Orlando, Florida, e-mail, October 13, 2005

To replace "Big Bill" at Charleston, the Tigers brought in a scout named Bill Adair. Like Norman, he kept us focused and let us play, and the approach must have worked because we won the American Association pennant. I found out later that the organization almost

Twig was the American Association's Most Valuable Player in 1958, when he played for the Charleston (West Virginia) Senators. Despite its name, the club was the Triple A affiliate of Twig's childhood favorite, the Detroit Tigers. *Wayne Terwilliger personal collection*

chose me to be player-manager after Norman left. I was having a good year just playing, so I wasn't sorry about their decision. But for the first time, I did start thinking about managing.

By this time in my life, I was a little less hot-headed, but I still had my moments. Early in the season at home, against a right-handed pitcher who was really shutting us down, I hit a home run to tie the game. Then in the ninth, Ron Samford hit another one to win it. Later in the season, we faced the same pitcher on the road, and my first time at bat he threw a fastball behind my head. As I dropped out of the way, the pitch hit my bat for a little popup to the third baseman. That was bad enough. When I got back to the bench, somebody mentioned the home run I had hit off the same pitcher earlier. I hadn't made the connection, but then I realized the s.o.b. was trying to hit me in the head! I'd already been beaned three times, and I'd had enough. The longer I thought about it the more pissed-off I got. As I walked into the box for my next at-bat, I turned to the catcher, big old Walker Cooper, and said, "If you weren't so goddam big I'd take a swing at you." He was one of the strongest guys around and he had probably heard it all during his twenty-plus years in the majors. He just smiled and ignored me. So I yelled at the pitcher, calling him every name I could come up with. Well, he walked me on four pitches, and I cussed him all the way to first base. As he turned away and picked up the rosin bag, I was sure I shook him up. I can still see the amused expression on Coop's face.

I wasn't always mad. One day when we were playing in Indianapolis, they had the bases loaded and one out when the hitter, a guy by the name of Garcia, hit a semi-line drive to my right. I got a good jump on the ball and backhanded it on the short hop. I threw it behind my back to Samford at short, who threw to first for the double play. There were some bleachers down the right field line where black fans sat, and when I came off the field after that play, they were cheering hard. I waved and tipped my cap to them, and they cheered even harder. After that, every game we played in Indianapolis, I made a point of walking down to those bleachers and talking to the fans there.

I watched Twig play with my "hometown" Charleston Senators. That was my first wide-eyed baseball experience, watching players "just a breath away from the majors." The feeling returns every time I take a grandchild out to the ballpark. . . . Twig still brings back the memories. Thanks for a career well worth the price of admission.
—Tom Bailey, Dallas, Texas, e-mail, July 4, 2004.

Probably the only downside to playing for Charleston was the travel. We flew on Purdue Airlines out of Indiana. It was a C47 charter plane, a pretty small two-engine prop with a couple of pilots and one female flight attendant, all of whom always looked as if they got to the airport just in time for takeoff. One day, we took up a collec-

Teammate Ozzie Virgil waves before boarding the team plane, a two-engine prop based at a mountaintop airport with a runway "just long enough to get us airborne." *Photo by Wayne Terwilliger*

tion to buy coffee for everybody, not because we wanted it but because we thought the crew needed it. The airport was on top of a mountain and the runway was just long enough to get us airborne. Landing on it was like having to hit a silver dollar. Early in the season, I told our manager, "If this f—ing plane doesn't crash, we'll win the pennant." It didn't, and we did.

We didn't have a bunch of stars that year, but we did have experience—we could catch the ball, and our pitching held up well. And that was enough to win the American Association championship. It wasn't a hitters' league that year; a guy from Denver won the batting title with a .328 average. But we did all the right things— move a runner over, take the extra base, be patient at bat. I had another really good fielding year—I led the league in putouts for a second baseman (361) and fielding percentage (.988). Offensively, I also led in stolen bases (24) and runs scored (103), so the league writers didn't let my .269 batting average stop them from electing me the league's Most Valuable Player. Our fans added a couple more honors; they voted me Charleston's MVP and the most popular. Beckley, a town 60 miles south of Charleston, sent me a plaque naming me their "favorite Charleston Senator." All of this, and the fact that my son, Steve, was born in June, made 1958 a pretty special season for me.

When I got home after the season, I said to Mary Jane, "Instead of playing winter ball, I think I'll stay home and get a job." I had barely made the decision when I got a call from Horace Stoneham, the owner of the New York Giants. He said the Giants had a lot of young players from their farm system playing on a team in Escogido, and he'd like me to join them. "I've decided to stay home this year," I said. "How much would it take to change your mind?" he asked. Here was my chance to ask for some big money . . . and I choked. Whatever I had been making the year before—I think it was $1,500 a month—I asked for $500 above that. "Fine," Mr. Stoneham said, and I immediately had the thought that I should have asked for more. I guess I never was very good at bargaining. Anyway, it was off to Escogido again.

About a week into the season, I came down with a virus. I felt weak as a baby, and my bat felt like it weighed a ton. A Dominican doctor checked me out and took X-rays of my chest. "Do you smoke?" he asked me. I had tried to quit a couple of times before, but yes, I smoked. He showed me my X-rays and in very broken English he told me that smoking was "not good." He had seen something on the film that he didn't like and that was enough for me. I was a pack-a-day smoker and I quit cold turkey—probably the best "play" I ever made. My illness wasn't related to the smoking, though, and there wasn't much he could do for me. I continued playing and I wasn't feeling much better, so a week later when I got a letter from the Kansas City Athletics saying they had drafted me, it was a "no-brainer"—Mary Jane and I packed up and went back to Michigan. I was getting another shot at the majors, and I wanted to be ready for spring training.

12

Better Hide the Watches

Kansas City—liked the song,
Don't see how I can go too wrong.
Fifth big-league team in my career . . .
Be nice to stay more than a year.
. . . And barely did.

Coming into the Athletics' spring training camp in West Palm Beach in '59, I was excited and confident. I'd just had a great season with Charleston, and I was feeling good again after that virus. I hit a home run in the first or second inter-squad game, a good sign that the rest of the spring would go well. As we headed north, I was on the club as an extra infielder.

Hector Lopez started the season as the regular second baseman. He could hit, but he was no middle infielder, and it didn't take long for the organization to realize it. I'm not blaming this on Hector, but we had one game in April when we blew a six-run lead against the White Sox by allowing eleven runs on only one hit in the seventh inning. Nellie Fox, the White Sox second baseman, had two RBIs in that inning, both on walks. Ten years later when Nellie and I became friends, we laughed about it, but I sure didn't think it was funny in 1959. I got into a number of early games, but I wasn't hitting very well. Then in May they traded Lopez to the Yankees and brought in Jerry Lumpe, who started playing regularly at second. At some point, manager Harry Craft moved Lumpe to short in place of Joe DeMaestri and put me into the lineup. In late July I got hot with the

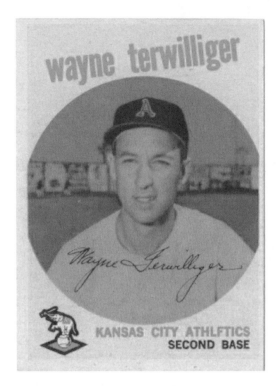

1959 Topps, #496.
Nancy Peterson personal collection

bat. It happened just as some of our big hitters also got hot, and we got some great pitching. Before we knew it, we had an eleven-game winning streak. To celebrate our streak, a Kansas City jeweler presented the whole team with nice watches.

Since the Athletics inaugurated their drive from the American League cellar 10 days ago, Roger Maris, Bob Cerv, Bill Tuttle and Dick Williams have been making most of the noise with their bats. But don't overlook Wayne Terwilliger, [whose] defensive work and timely hitting have been an integral factor in the A's surge.
—Kansas City Star, *July 24, 1959*

I played the last few games of the streak with a badly swollen middle finger on my throwing hand. It was getting worse, and I didn't want to screw up when we were playing so well, so I told the trainer about it. Wrong move. Without any discussion, Craft took me out of the lineup. I wish he had talked to me about it, because if he had

Old-Timers' games held before regular Athletics-Yankees games were a treat for Twig, who loved meeting some of the game's legendary players. These photos were taken at a 1959 Old-Timers' game at Yankee Stadium. Upper left: New York outfielder Joe DiMaggio, Philadelphia and Boston pitcher Lefty Grove, and Brooklyn outfielder Zack Wheat are three Hall-of-Famers who represent nearly fifty seasons in baseball. Upper right: Dave "Beauty" Bancroft began his sixteen-year career at shortstop in the National League in 1915, and is still considered one of the all-time best fielders. Lower left: Tom Zachary pitched for Washington in 1927 when he gave up Babe Ruth's sixtieth home run. Lower right: Chuck Connors, TV's *Rifleman*, played one game for the Dodgers and a half-season for the Cubs and became Twig's friend during Cubs' spring training in Catalina.

All photos by Wayne Terwilliger

said, "Try to play, see how it goes," I would have. For some reason in August we began to skid and ran up a thirteen-game losing streak. As we kept losing, the word in the clubhouse got to be, "We'd better hide the watches; they're gonna want them back."

I had a young teammate named Roger Maris who was so damned quiet and efficient you hardly noticed him. He had been a rookie

Twig, center, with future Yankee Bob Cerv and former Yankee Hank Bauer, both Kansas City teammates, at 1960 spring training in West Palm Beach.
Wayne Terwilliger personal collection

with the Cleveland Indians the year before, and how they let him go to the Athletics I don't know—maybe he was so quiet they didn't appreciate him. I could see that he had all the tools—he was a steady fielder and quick base-runner—and he played the game the right way.

During the winter the Athletics traded Maris to the Yankees (you know the rest of *that* story) along with a couple of other guys. In return, we got Don Larsen, Hank Bauer, Norm Siebern, and Marv Throneberry. I got a contract for $11,000, the largest player contract of my career. The way things had gone for me, I quickly signed it and breathed a sigh of relief. We also had a new manager, Bob Elliott, a former third baseman with Pittsburgh and the old Boston Braves. He

Another Old-Timers' game—this time in Kansas City—featured Ty Cobb, center, shaking hands with one of Twig's teammates. *Photo by Wayne Terwilliger*

was a big, strong guy who was "old school" all the way. I don't remember him saying much, at least not in my direction. I started and finished my season on the bench. The first game I got into was the second game of a doubleheader on a cold, blustery day in Cleveland. In an early inning I screwed up a tough hop and wrenched my back, and then I struck out in my only at-bat. In the dugout, I told the trainer about my back. I can still hear Bob Elliott muttering about "candy-ass ball players" as I hobbled off to the end of the bench. We lost the game, too. A few weeks later, I was sold to the Yankees, who optioned me to their Triple A team at Richmond, Virginia.

My memories of Kansas City weren't all bad. I ended up hitting .267 in '59, my highest seasonal average in the majors. One of my two home runs that year came in Tiger Stadium, which was special in itself, and off Jim Bunning, another Hall-of-Famer and a tough right-handed pitcher. Al Kaline hit a homer for the Tigers that day, and I remember my mom, who listened to the game at home, complaining that announcer Ernie Harwell had described Kaline's homer as a "blast" and mine as a long fly that dropped into the first row in left field. She was upset, and her loyalty made me smile, but Ernie got it right.

The Yankees had just purchased the Richmond Virginians, known as the "Vees," and they brought in former Yankee and Tiger Steve Souchock as manager. He did a good job; we finished in fourth place and made the International League playoffs, where we eliminated the first-place Buffalo Bisons but eventually lost to the Havana Sugar Kings. We had a few future major leaguers including infielder Deron Johnson and pitcher Bill Short, who won seventeen games for us. I played regularly for a month or so, but then my back started acting up and my playing time was limited. Late in the season, when I had been playing off and on, the Richmond general manager asked me whether I had ever considered managing. He said the Yankees needed somebody to run their club in Greensboro, North Carolina, the next season. I thought, here I am, thirty-five years old with an aching back, playing part-time in Triple A . . . it's time to move on!

Looking back on my playing career, I have a lot of things to be happy about. I wasn't one of those "phenoms" for whom everything is easy; I had to work hard and it took me a while to learn. I didn't have much minor league experience, so I learned "on the job." When I first started, I sometimes was better with the spectacular plays than the routine ones. But with a couple of years' experience and some confidence, I ended up as one of the best-fielding second basemen, especially in turning the double play, because I had quick hands and quick feet—and I still do!

I hit twenty-two home runs, some of them off Hall-of-Fame pitchers. So why am I not satisfied?

I should have been a much better hitter than my .240 average. I was hit in the head in my first pro season and a couple of times later, and each time it took me a little longer to stop thinking about it when I went to the plate. When I did get the bat going, I'd see in the paper that I was hitting .300 or so and I'd think, "I'm no .300 hitter." At that point I would expect bad things to happen, and eventually they did! When I was struggling, I'd spend time deciding what batting stance to use next. I'd use that one until I took an "O-fer"

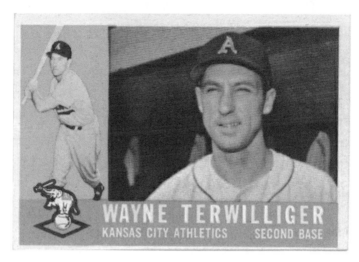

1960 Topps, #26. Twig's last card as a player. The photo of Twig batting was printed in reverse, making him look like a lefty.
Nancy Peterson personal collection

and then try another. The last time I checked at the Louisville Bat factory, I had used seventeen different models trying to find the "right" one. I had coaches tell me I needed to hit to right field, and in my last couple of seasons I started to figure it out, but it was a little late. And if I could have hit a curve ball, none of the rest would have mattered! So hitting was my weak spot, and in all these years as a coach and a manager, I still think about what I might have done to be better at it.

Sometimes I think I quit playing too soon, but as it turned out, retiring as a player didn't mean I was out of the game.

Editors' note: In 2,091 at-bats in 666 games over nine seasons in the major leagues, Wayne Terwilliger hit for a .240 average with 501 hits including 93 doubles, 10 triples and 22 homers. He batted in 162 runs, scored 271 runs and struck out 296 times. He reached base on a walk 248 times (one of them intentional), and he stole 31 bases. If Wayne Terwilliger the player had played for Wayne Terwilliger the manager, that last number would have been much higher!

13

The Whole Shebang

Where have you gone, Marshall Bridges?
You should know
You gotta show
To get the dough.

Right from the start, I loved managing. I loved assembling "my" team, even when it required a struggle to get players I wanted. I loved figuring out which pitchers should be starters and which should be relievers and how to use them in a game, even though I had to learn the hard way a couple of times. Heck, just making out the lineups was a turn-on! I told my players, "Run, don't walk," and followed my own advice so that some of my hustle and enthusiasm would rub off on them. I learned early that if you want to tell a player something he should do better, it helps to start by telling him something he does well. I intended from the get-go to be aggressive in every phase of the game, and I learned that some opponents aren't too happy about that. I thought there was no better high than the late innings of close games when the adrenaline really kicks in— except for the high of *winning* the close ones right at the end. And no lower low than losing them.

I had played for the Gashouse Gang's Frankie Frisch, the laid-back Bucky Harris, Leo "the Lip" Durocher, Eddie "whatever-it-takes" Stanky, quiet man Harry Craft—and for Charlie Dressen, who actually believed he was the catalyst of those talented Dodgers. I learned from all of them—things to do and things *not* to do—and by 1961 I had some ideas I couldn't wait to try out.

The Yankees gave me that chance when they made me skipper of their team at Greensboro, North Carolina. The Greensboro Yanks played five other teams in the Class B Carolina League—the Burlington Indians, Durham Bulls, Raleigh Capitals, Wilson Tobacconists, and Winston-Salem Red Sox. Jack McKeon—the same McKeon who led the Florida Marlins to a World Series title forty-two years later—was in his second year as the Wilson manager. Enos "Country" Slaughter was the head man at Raleigh. He was forty-five and had recently retired from the majors but still managed to get himself into the lineup now and then.

Farm director Johnny Johnson assigned me about twenty players at the start of spring training at Augusta, Georgia, and then made a lot of changes as he reassigned players to different levels. I knew that was how things worked and I had no problem until he was about to send a pitcher named Ed Merritt to a lower league. I fought to keep him; I insisted that he could win at our level and that I needed him. Johnson finally said okay, and Merritt became my number-one starter. I had expected a lot of advice about how to develop various players, but Johnson left that up to me. We didn't have a pitching coach or specialty coaches to help with hitting or base running; back then, as manager you were the whole shebang. As opening day approached, I found myself getting butterflies in my stomach. It was a little hard to eat my tuna sandwich before our first game.

Greensboro's Yankees, who led last year's composite standings by a whopping 10fi games and who swept the play-off championships after riding to the first-half crown, are one-sided favorites to accomplish the trick again, according to the annual Daily News *poll of writers who cover the league's activities.*
—Moses Crutchfield, Greensboro Daily News, *April 15, 1961*

We got off to a slow start, losing five of our first six games, but with a couple of lineup changes we settled down and played just over .500 ball for the season. Johnny Johnson sent me a pitcher and a hitter who helped, and a couple of infielders came off the bench to make a big difference.

When my regular second baseman pulled a back muscle, I put a guy named Ron Retton into the game. Retton used the opportunity to show what he could do both in the field and at bat, and the next night I put him into the lineup to stay. He developed into our best hitter percentage-wise, and he started getting more than his share of extra-base hits and home runs. After a week or two I moved him to shortstop; he immediately made a nice double play and pretty soon we led the league in that department. At 5-foot-7 Ron was a real sparkplug—flexible, quick, aggressive on the base paths, and a battler. He figured in a lot of our wins. He later had a daughter, Mary Lou, who won an Olympic gymnastics gold medal in 1984; her power and agility reminded me a lot of her dad.

A young guy named Don Keller had changed his mind about retiring from baseball and joined our squad just before opening day. He got some timely hits and made some big plays coming off the bench, so he became our starting third baseman. Pitcher Dooley Womack was the only member of the club to reach the majors; he had some early success and then bounced around between the big leagues and the minors. In 1969, when he was traded for Jim Bouton, Bouton gave him a little joking name recognition in *Ball Four*.

> *Dropped a ball I shoulda caught*
> *With the bat went four for naught*
> *Picked off first in inning eight*
> *But heck we won . . . let's celebrate*

We had streaks when the whole team was hitting well, and other times when we were manufacturing runs on singles, walks, a stolen base, or the occasional suicide squeeze. We had four players chosen for the All-Star team and we had the highest team batting average for the first half of the season. Ron Retton was the league's player of the month for June, and first baseman Chuck Reidell led the league in home runs. Pitcher Norm Forsythe won eleven straight games after losing his first three starts. Ed Merritt, the pitcher I had fought to keep, pitched eight innings and hit a single, a double, and a grand slam to win his tenth game of the season. Before that he had been 0-for-32 at the plate.

Unfortunately, we also had our share of injuries, a couple of six-game losing streaks, and some bad breaks here and there. One pitcher missed a start because he burned his hand checking the water in his car's radiator. Chuck Reidell was hit in the back by a thrown ball during a play, went down in a heap, and was carted away by ambulance. Don Keller went on the disabled list because of a bad back. Gene Domzalski, whose hitting gave us a boost once he arrived in late May, left so he could have knee surgery before going back to college.

I noticed that some of the players seemed to lose their concentration when things went wrong. That was especially true of the pitchers, but I usually couldn't pull them because I didn't have much of a bullpen. At one point I overused our most reliable reliever and he lost his effectiveness for a while—a lesson that stayed with me. I found that I didn't like losing as a manager any more than I had as a player.

Johnny Johnson came down from New York in July to see a couple of games, and we gave him quite a show. At home against Wilson, we managed to lose 8-7 with the help of three errors. The next night, last-place Raleigh came in and beat us 21-12. We walked in two runs and looked terrible. The next day we turned around and beat Raleigh 13-1 and played like champs. Our brand-new pitcher, just in from the University of Kentucky, struck out fourteen hitters and we made a great double play. Unfortunately, Johnson wasn't there to see any of it.

I was getting the feeling that the front office wasn't too happy with us. The 1960 team had drawn big crowds, played well, and won the league championship. I would have loved to do the same, but I knew for a fact that the 1960 team was stacked with talent that we didn't have. And, the weather was terrible. On opening day the temperature was in the 40s and a few hundred fans huddled under blankets. It didn't really get warm until about the middle of July. For a doubleheader on May 27, they sold 358 tickets. They tried all kinds of promotions—free Coca-Cola, autographed balls, a diamond giveaway, a new car giveaway—but nothing made much difference except better weather.

By late July and for most of August, we played pretty good ball. With an eight-game winning streak, we were in first place for a short time and in the hunt right up to the end. Then a pair of rainouts meant we had to play four doubleheaders in the last six days of the season. Our pitching had improved, but that kind of schedule put too much pressure on both the starters and the bullpen. Before the week was over, Jack McKeon's Wilson Tobs had clinched first place and we finished third. We ended up with a 70-68 record and I thought I'd done a pretty good job. Unfortunately, the Yankees didn't agree.

In those days, a manager had to write up a game report, cut out the box score from the next day's paper, and mail it in. I usually did that, but once in a while after a tough loss I would have a couple of beers and let the report go for a day or two. Nobody said a word about it.

At the end of the season, Johnny Johnson called. "We're not bringing you back," he said. I asked why. "You didn't turn in your game reports on time." I've always thought it had more to do with those two awful games he saw in July than with late paperwork, but whatever the reason, getting fired taught me that I'd better pay attention to details and not take *anything* for granted. (A few years later, managers started phoning in their reports. Once that happened, I was never late again.)

Don Keller, our third baseman, used to talk about our games with his dad Charlie—a big hitter for the Yankees in the '40s whose autograph I collected as a kid—and he told Charlie that he liked me as a manager. Charlie told his brother Hal, who was the Washington Senators' farm director, and Hal called to offer me a job. It was the first of many breaks that Hal Keller would give me.

Terwilliger got a bit of everything—good pitching, good hitting and a lot more of that blazing speed—from his Senators Thursday night as they made it a clean sweep of a four-game series with Montgomery, 15-3. The victory enabled the Senators to remain 3fi games ahead in the league standings.
—The Pensacola News, *May 11, 1962*

In 1962 Hal Keller did for me what Johnny Johnson and the Yankees had not done the year before: He gave me a team that could win. In fact he gave me my ideal team: good left-handed pitching and lots of speed on the bases. I avoided most of my first-year mistakes and we ended up with a 79-38 record, winning the pennant by twenty-two games.

I had a core of ten returning players. Six were pitchers, including the previous year's ace, Fred Waters. Fred was a high school coach in Pensacola and had pitched a couple of seasons in the majors. A lefty who still knew how to get 'em out with a little of this and a little of that, he went 11-2 for us. I also had three young left-handers with good arms—Bob Baird, Don Loun, and Barry Moore, each of whom eventually got in some big-league time. Carlos Medrano, a right-handed reliever, had a good little slider, which was a big advantage in Class D because some of those young players had never seen one, let alone learned to hit it. To avoid burning out the pitchers, I started keeping a chart showing the date each pitcher worked and how many innings he threw, along with how many times he loosened up before or during a game.

The business community was very supportive; they paraded us down the street in convertibles on opening day, and the mayor threw out the first ball that night. The papers ran big stories and the writers seemed optimistic about our chances, even if the new manager was unproven.

Our opponents in the Alabama-Florida League were Fort Walton Beach, Florida, as well as Montgomery, Selma, Ozark, and Dothan, all in Alabama. We won our first game 9-2 on a combination of Waters's strong pitching, some good hitting, and three stolen bases. I knew we were on track. A week into the season we took over first place, and we stayed there the rest of the year. We had two steady hitters—outfielder Lou Abrahams and first baseman Joe Klein—but no real power. We made up for it with speed. I taught my players everything I knew about base running and we poured it on all year. We ran in close games and it helped us many times. We ran when we were behind, and we ran when we were ahead. If it was early in the game, we ran. When we were ten runs ahead, we ran. It drove the opposing managers crazy. When the Fort Walton Beach manager got on me one day, I just said, "You manage your way and I'll manage mine," and he shut up. I built the team around speed, and I was going to use it—the same way a power-hitting team with a big lead still sends batters to the plate. If I ever questioned that idea, I had a rude reminder one night when we blew a 10-3 lead and lost 14-11. We put together some nine- and ten-game winning streaks, and I kept waiting for losing streaks to catch up with us, but it didn't happen. We were aggressive, we were winning, and it was fun. There was no budget for fireworks, so we did the next best thing. I had a wild pair of boxer shorts with huge red polka dots, which the players had kidded me about during the season. The night before the final game of the season, general manager Howard Schulman said, "Bring those shorts of yours to the ball park tomorrow and we'll run them up the flag pole." So that's how we celebrated.

We beat Dothan in the play-offs and then lost to Selma. After the way we dominated the league, we still considered ourselves champions.

Admiral Mason Park wasn't far from Pensacola Bay, so we had lots of mosquitoes on humid nights and a not-too-nice smell from a sewage treatment plant across the street. Still, we would rather have played there every night than go on the road. I hadn't ridden buses on a regular basis since I played for Des Moines in 1948. In Triple A and the majors we traveled by train or plane, and in Greensboro we went by station wagon. In Pensacola we had The Black Bus. It was a run-down old school bus painted an ugly dull black. Whenever it rained, the players had to stuff newspapers into a good-sized hole under one of the seats to keep from getting wet. Sometimes the windshield wipers didn't work and I had to reach out and move them by hand. The bus broke down on the road, I don't know how many times. The day after the season ended, that bus went directly to the junkyard.

Between our black bus and our black driver, we drew a lot of attention on the road. Selma and Montgomery were not good places to be black in the early 1960s, and Paul Raibon, who was both our trainer and our driver, had a tough time. When we stopped to eat, he went around to the back door to get food from the cooks. When we checked into a hotel, he went to another part of town. Even at the ballpark, he took abuse. One day in Selma a player was hurt on the field and Paul wouldn't venture onto the field so we had to bring the player to the dugout. Paul was in his early fifties, and he handled it the way he had to in order to survive, but young black players were refusing to play in the league. Right after that season, the league folded.

(Forty years later, Pensacola would get another professional team. The Pensacola Pelicans started play in 2002 and two years later joined the Central League, where I was managing the Fort Worth

Cats. The Cats' first road trip to Pensacola was my first time back in all those years, and as we rolled into town at 3 a.m. the memories came flooding back. I could still see those polka-dot boxers flying.)

Driving into Wisconsin Rapids, Wisconsin, for my new coaching assignment in 1963, I noticed a bunch of bloated, dead carp lying along a riverbank. I wondered whether it was an omen. In terms of our performance, the answer would be yes. At the end of the first half of the season, Wisconsin Rapids—the Senators' new Class A Midwest League team—stood tenth out of ten teams. We were much better in the second half thanks to a future major-league catcher from Ohio University named Jim French—he was a leader, he played hard, and he really took charge back of the plate.

Our general manager was a rosy-cheeked guy named Elmer Collar who always smiled, win or lose. I was a little leery of any guy who was always cheerful, but Elmer won me over one day when he showed his other side. On any club, you're going to have discipline problems and guys acting stupid. One day Elmer came to the club-house to discuss some relatively minor off-field incident with one of my infielders, and the kid cussed at him. Elmer reached for him, the kid took off, and Elmer took off after him. He chased the kid around the clubhouse and almost caught him. We released the kid soon after. For one thing, he had a bad attitude. For another, he was no speedier on the base paths than in the clubhouse where he could barely outrun Elmer.

The Minnesota Twins took over the Wisconsin Rapids franchise after that season, so in 1964 and 1965 I managed at Geneva, New York, a Class A team in the old New York-Pennsylvania League. Geneva was a pretty area, and there was something special about the way people supported the team. The owner and general manager was a big Irish former motorcycle cop named Joe McDonough. His wife, Molly, and their daughters ran the concessions; they made *great* sandwiches and the biggest, juiciest hot dogs I ever ate. They treated the players like family, and so did the townspeople. My son, Steve, was six at the time, and he loved to be out there shagging balls or playing catch with the players. During batting practice one day, he was standing in center field when somebody hit a line drive toward him. Steve took a couple of steps in to try to catch it on the hop, and it bounced up and hit him just below his left eye. He came running in, crying of course, but when it developed into a big shiner, he was as proud as could be. (Today as a paramedic in a hospital emergency room, he treats other people's black eyes, along with other injuries and illnesses.)

In spite of the fact that the military draft was having some effect on availability of players, I had a talented team in Geneva. We played better than .500 ball and finished high in the standings, just missing the championship in '64. At one point we had a lot of injuries and I was so short of pitchers that I actually pitched in one game—something I hadn't done since high school. I came into the game in the seventh with two men on base and one out, and I got a ball hit back to me. I turned and made a throw to second, a little wide, but shortstop Dave Hirtz caught it and threw to first for a double play. I got them out in the eighth and ninth, and I got the league's leading home run hitter to swing at a 3-2 fastball in on his hands to end the game. That was exciting! So the line on my professional pitching career is two and two-thirds innings, one hit, one walk, two strikeouts. If there had been such a thing as a "save" back then, I'd have had one.

The Geneva Senators of the mid-'60s were a great team to watch, and I came to deeply revere the game of baseball because of it. Two players, Jimmy Munoz and Tony Libertella, roomed at a nearby neighbor's house and they had me shagging fly balls at the ballpark during BP. I still recall how perfectly the players' spikes were spit-shined each day.
—Brian Rogers, Belmont, Massachusetts, e-mail, January 15, 2003

In 1966 I went back to the Carolina League, this time at Burlington, North Carolina, where I had as likable a team as I've ever managed. Two of them reminded me a bit of myself. Second baseman Fred Jacobs didn't hit much but could turn a double play as fast as anyone. Outfielder Ed Mouton had trouble hitting the curve ball and didn't mind admitting it. Shortstop Eddie "Stick" Griffith had great speed; he couldn't stand to wait on base more than a pitch or two, so I gave him the green light nearly all the time and he made the game exciting. First baseman Jim Martin, a little older than the others, was steady and helped keep everybody on an even keel. Outfielder Rich Billings had what I thought of as a catcher's mentality, and he was tough and durable. I suggested to the Senators that they give him a chance behind the plate, and by 1971 he was their starting catcher. Dick Such, a pitcher from Elon College with a pretty good slider, had pitched in the Eastern League for a season and went 0-16 with a two-point-something ERA—not easy to do! Later, he and I would coach together with the Rangers and the Twins. Bill Haywood, an assistant coach at North Carolina University, pitched for us when he could. He would wait for us along the highway in Chapel Hill. We'd stop the bus and open the front doors, and a bunch of equipment bags piled on the steps would spill out. Bill would climb in and then reach back down and pull the bags back in after him. It was an especially fun year of baseball, and with a 76-62 record we finished second in the league.

In 1967 Hal Keller called me and said, "We have an opening at the Triple A level and we'd like you to take it." As if moving up to Triple A wasn't enough, the team was in Honolulu. I pictured a dream season of talented players and perfect weather. That dream lasted through the spring and a couple of weeks into the season.

Spring training in Florida went pretty well, although I needed a little more pitching. On the last day Hal told me a left-hander named Marshall Bridges would either join us for the flight to Hawaii or meet us over there. Bridges had been with four teams as a reliever and had some success, and I figured he would be a good addition to our bullpen. We boarded the plane for the long trip across the Pacific Ocean without our new hurler, but I wasn't particularly concerned. It was a long trip from Florida and we all got a little stir-crazy, but the stewardesses were serving drinks and after the hard work of spring training, we relaxed and enjoyed ourselves. The players got silly grins on their faces as they received the customary leis from the bronzed Hawaiian gals, but who wouldn't? I was feeling pretty good myself.

We had a few workouts in Honolulu—minus Mr. Bridges, who had yet to show. Just before opening day, a "Welcome Team" party drew a good-sized crowd to a big auditorium. There was a band on the stage along with some club officials, and I was introduced to lead off the program. Speaking wasn't exactly my thing, so I had a mai-tai for courage. I had rehearsed my opening line: "You've heard that expression, 'You can't win 'em all.' Well, who says you can't?" I said I always thought it was a negative thing to say, and a cop-out when you lose. Why not plan to win every game? The crowd was into it and cheering, so I called a couple of veteran players up on stage. Gene Freese and Hector Lopez were both fresh from the majors, and they were a perfect combination. Freese was operating with a couple of flowery Hawaiian drinks under his belt, and he was funny. Hector, on the other hand, said the kind of things Tim Robbins' character said in *Bull Durham:* "We're happy to be here," and "We just want to play well and win for you great fans." Meanwhile, I talked my way into playing the drums with the band. I had no training, and I proved that I hadn't inherited any of that particular talent from my father, but the crowd ate it up anyway.

We opened the season without Marshall Bridges, and we won five games in a row. Now we had the media and fans saying, "Who says you can't win them all?" Then we lost game six. It was a game we should have won, and I was disappointed because I wanted to leave for our road trip with a sweep of our home series—and with a left-handed pitcher named Bridges, who never did show up. I guess you *can't* win 'em all.

The Hawaii Islanders were in the Pacific Coast League. The closest teams were in California and Oregon, and the farthest was Indianapolis, Indiana. How Indianapolis got into the PCL I don't know. Why they put a Triple A team in Honolulu I don't know, either. Going back and forth through all those time zones will really mess up your system and affect your play. Worse, it gave players an *excuse* for not playing well. At home we played just fine, but on the road we were awful and we ended up the season well below .500.

I reached my low point during a late-season road trip. We had a chance to snap a seven-game losing streak, taking a one-run lead into the ninth inning. Freese was having a tough day at third base, so I replaced him with Lopez. We got two outs and then let a couple of runners reach base. The next batter hit a soft line drive right toward Hector. It was just a couple of feet over his head; a little jump would make it an easy catch to end the game. Hector "jumped," but his feet never left the ground. The next batter hit a two-run double and we had ourselves an eight-game losing streak. I was mad, and the sight of the post-game spread in the locker room made me madder. With a couple of swipes, I scattered the food around the room and we headed for Tulsa.

The next day I called Hal Keller. "I need a break," I told him. "I don't want to manage tonight; I want to get a hot dog and a beer and be a spectator and remember what's fun about this game." Hal said, "Go ahead; I hope it works." We lost, but the break helped me get through the rest of the season.

> *Pot or pills need not be taken*
> *Beer and broads can be forsaken.*
> *What keeps my day from turning bleak?*
> *A simple one-game winning streak.*

The player least affected by our travel was pitcher Dick Bosman, who ran a lot and had his own set of conditioning exercises, all of which helped him adjust to the jet lag. Dick's fastball probably topped out at about 85 mph, so he worked hard at fine-tuning his two best pitches, a sinker and a "slurve." Whoever named that pitch got it just right—it was a combination of a slider that broke too much and a curve that didn't break enough. Bosman was managing to win despite everything, and it wasn't long before Washington called.

Whatever else happened, we did spend half the season in Hawaii, and that was hard to beat. I found a nice apartment on the Aliwae Canal, the club gave me a car to use, and they flew my family in. At ages nine and fifteen, the kids were old enough to really enjoy their Hawaii experiences. About the time I decided it wouldn't be so bad to manage there again, the Senators decided they didn't want their Triple A club to be halfway around the world.

The Buffalo Bisons had just been dropped by the Cincinnati Reds, and in 1968 the Senators became Buffalo's fourth major-league affiliation in seven years, a fact that should have sent up a red flag. The Bisons were struggling, drawing fewer fans, and losing more money every year. War Memorial Stadium was a beat-up old place that everybody called "The Rockpile." It was built as a football stadium and expanded for the Buffalo Bills. It was all wrong for baseball. The field had taken a lot of abuse and was full of places for the ball to take a bad hop or for a player to trip or twist an ankle. The Bills' locker room, which we used, was in no better shape than the field. The neighborhood had experienced some racial violence and night games were ruled out, so we played Sunday and holiday afternoon games at War Memorial and night games at a makeshift ballpark in Niagara Falls. This was my new Triple A job.

There were never a lot of fans at our games in Buffalo, even in daylight. The few who did come were rowdy and obnoxious. One afternoon we played a game that went extra innings. There was a bunch of guys sitting behind our dugout drinking and yelling, and the loudest one yelled, "Hey, give me your cap!" Each inning as I came into the dugout from the third-base coaching box, he got surlier. "Goddam it, I want that cap," he'd say with no trace of humor. This continued all through the game. I avoided looking directly at him, but I glanced over and saw that he looked like a character right out of *The Godfather*. At the end of the game he and his buddies spilled out of the stands and onto the field. I was getting worried about what this particular jerk might do. Security was no help, so we all grabbed the caps off our heads, clenched them in our hands, and ran as fast as we could toward the locker room.

After the game I found out that some fans had gotten mugged in the restrooms. At that point, we moved *all* of our games to Niagara Falls. The park there didn't seat many fans, but not many were going to show up anyway. The locker room was cleaner, and the fans didn't present behavior problems. Unfortunately, we didn't play much better there.

It wasn't that we had no talent. We had a handful of "gamers" including Hector Lopez, who could still hit even though he had lead feet, several young future Senators, and a couple of players who had been up briefly but were back for more experience. Outfielder Brant Alyea got off to a hot start, hitting a whole lot of home runs that seemed to energize the team. When the writers asked his secret, he would point to a couple of big jars of honey sitting in his locker. (If he thought eating honey helped him hit, I wasn't going to argue.) Part way through our season, Brant was called back up and hit another half-dozen home runs for the Senators. First baseman Mike

Epstein had been *Sporting News* Minor League Player of the Year in 1966, but he was having some trouble on defensive plays because of his eyesight.

I also had a couple of future Senators pitchers who had some talent but didn't always like to take direction. Depending on the situation, I sometimes let it go. Steve Jones was a left-hander with an assortment of pitches. One night he was having a tough inning and gave up three straight hits, all off fastballs. I went out to the mound and told him to use his curve ball more. He didn't say anything, and I went back to the dugout. He struck out the next two hitters with six straight fastballs. Inning over. I gave him a look for ignoring me, but I had to respect the fact that he had confidence in what he was doing and he got the job done. (In the off-season, Steve was working with a small company that had an odd-tasting new product called Gatorade. I hope he stuck with it!)

In some situations, though, it's not about confidence, it's about strategy, and the manager needs to be the boss. Jim Hannan was our starting pitcher in the first game of a series with Columbus. Our big left-handed-hitting first baseman Bob Chance had worn out Columbus's pitching in a previous series, and the first time he came to bat in this game, they knocked him down with a pitch up and in. Next time up, they hit him on the right arm. The way their manager, Johnny Pesky, was yapping at us from his dugout, I knew this could go on all night unless I put a stop to it. I told Hannan to hit their lead-off batter in the next inning—first pitch, on the elbow. I was happy with the timing, because the batter was going to be their best hitter, Manny Jimenez. We made our last out, Hannan took his warm-up pitches, and in stepped Jimenez. First pitch—high and outside! I nearly tripped over my own feet rushing to the mound. "What the f— was that?" Hannan didn't say a word. The catcher shrugged as if to say, "I don't know what to tell you." I repeated, "Hit this s.o.b. on his elbow, with this pitch, goddam it." Hannan nodded, but I didn't see the look in his eyes that I had hoped for. His heart wasn't going to be in it. I got back to the dugout as he delivered the next pitch, and sure enough, there was the unmistakable sound of ball meeting bat—crack, line-drive base hit to center field. I directed Hannan to the clubhouse, using all the profanity I knew.

Terwilliger stepped back and filled the locker room with right-hand uppercuts. One glanced off [Buster] Narum's chest, another nicked his lip. Buster . . . got a head lock on his manager—and, apparently, on his baseball career.
—Jimmy Mann, Saint Petersburg Times, *1968*

Only once in my life did I ever take a swing at a player, and I'm not proud of it. Pitcher Buster Narum had enjoyed some success with the Senators—he had average stuff but a good change-up—but he hadn't been consistent. He wasn't happy about being sent down to Triple A. One night he got knocked around pretty good, so I took him out of the game. He stormed straight into the locker room, and a while later I heard the guys talking about Buster raising hell in there. I thought, let him get it out of his system and he'll be gone by the time I get in there. When I did go in after the game, I found my dress clothes on the floor in front of my locker. The trainer said he didn't know how they got there. The players either hadn't seen anything or weren't telling. I had to figure it was Buster's work. He was mad coming out of the game, and the players had said he threw a tantrum. Deliberate or not, this had to be his work. I was trying to think it through logically, but I also was getting more pissed off by the minute. I said to myself, "I'm not going to let him get away with this."

Once everyone else was gone, I went to Buster's locker and took everything out. I piled it up in the middle of the floor—all his equipment, everything. Then I got dressed and left. I had a beer and thought about all the different ways he might react, so I could be ready. I figured either he'll come in and see it and laugh, or he'll be pissed. If he gets mad, I figured I would hold my ground. I'd say maybe spilling my clothes on the ground was an accident, but if so he should have picked them up. If it wasn't an accident, he should have stayed around to talk to me. I went to the ballpark early the next day, and as the players drifted in, I told them not to touch the stuff piled on the floor. When Buster came in, I was at my locker getting dressed and trying to ignore him. I heard him say, "What the hell is this?" and then ask Hector Lopez who did it. Hector told him I said to leave it, and that's all Buster needed to hear. He came over to where I was sitting and he got behind me. "What the hell is going on?" I didn't turn around and I pretended not to know what he was talking about. "You know what I'm talking about," he said. "Why is my stuff all out of the locker and on the floor?" The best I could come up with was, "Buster, let's just say 'an eye for an eye' and leave it at that." "What the hell does that mean?" he wanted to know. I told him my clothes didn't throw themselves on the floor last night. "Well, goddam it," he said, "I didn't do it."

Now he was right over my shoulder, brushing against me. I said, "Get away from me, Buster, we'll talk about it later." He said, "No, I want to talk about it now." He was leaning over me from behind my chair. I said again, "Buster, get away from me." I stood up and he was right there, not directly in front of me but a little to the side and leaning into me. I repeated, "Get away from me, get out of here." Every time I moved, he moved with me. Finally he moved directly in front of me and put his face right up to mine. I stepped back and took a wild swing that grazed his face. I had avoided looking right at him the whole time, so I didn't even realize he had his glasses on until my fist sent them flying. At that point, he came at me like a bull. He's a pretty big guy, and when I bent over to duck, he got his arms wrapped around my head and neck. He was squeezing me and dragging me around. I tried to yell for him to let me go, but nothing came out. Jim Miles, a young pitcher, probably saved me from getting hurt. He grabbed hold of Narum and pulled on him while somebody else was pulling on me. We finally got separated, and I coughed and wheezed until I caught my breath.

We got squared off again and I said, "F— this, we don't wrestle. If you want to fight, fine, but we're not going to wrestle." I was hoping somebody would stop us before we started up again. He didn't offer to fight, and some of the players got him to back away. He'd probably have cleaned my clock big-time if they hadn't.

I got on the phone to Hal Keller in Washington. "Hal, I just took a swing at one of the pitchers." I explained the whole thing. He said, "Want me to send somebody up there?" I asked what for. "To kick him off the club," he said. "If you don't want to be the one to tell him, I'll send a couple of guys to handle it." "Shit, no," I said. "I'll tell him myself." When I gave Buster the news, he just turned around and walked away. Later that season, there was an interview with Buster in the *Saint Petersburg Times,* where he was living, and he told this story. He told it pretty much the same way, except in his version he was an innocent bystander. I suppose I'll never know for sure. The story said he was still trying to get back into baseball, but he never did.

We ended up with a 66-81 record, seventh in the league—the same record the Bisons had the year before, when they were a Cincinnati Reds' affiliate and Don Zimmer took over as manager in the middle of the season. In spite of our poor season and all the other problems, I was scheduled to manage the team again in 1969, until Ted Williams picked me to be his third-base coach with the Senators. Senators' president Bob Short named Hector Lopez as my successor in Buffalo, making him the first black man to manage a professional baseball team in the United States. I was glad for Hector, but all of Buffalo's problems continued during 1969. The team went back to playing some games at War Memorial Stadium, but there were more rowdies, and one day guys with knives broke into the locker room just before the game. Even with big promotions, the fans stayed away. By the end of the season, the Senators had broken off their affiliation with the team. I got out just in time.

14

Ted Said . . .

Known as "Teddy Ballgame,"
"Number 9" and just "The Kid,"
None since 1941
Has done what Williams did . . .
. . . and maybe never will.

In 1939, the summer I turned fourteen, Ted Williams made his major-league debut. I followed his rookie season in the newspaper, and since I listened to all of the Tigers games on the radio, I paid attention to Ted when the Tigers played the Red Sox. The Tigers were my team and I loved them, but Ted Williams was something special and I was a fan from the start. After his great rookie season, I wrote him for an autograph and he sent back a signed postcard with a color picture of him swinging a bat.

Little did I know that fourteen years later I would be playing against him, and that eventually I would work for him as a coach and come to consider him a friend. The highlight of my fifty-plus years in baseball is the 1969 season, Ted's first year as manager of the Washington Senators and my first year as his third-base coach. We surprised everyone—we finished ten games over .500—and Ted was named Manager of the Year. For four years I experienced his passion for the game, his competitiveness, his incredibly detailed way of analyzing the hitting game, his larger-than-life personality, his way of taking over a room just by walking into it, and his sense of humor—more than once I saw him laugh so hard the tears just streamed down his face. We stayed in touch, and even though illnesses slowed him down, he still showed the same spirit until not long before he died.

Ted was an outfielder, but in 1940, his second season with the Red Sox, I was listening when he pitched two innings against Detroit. I was selling ties in a clothing store in downtown Charlotte, and we had the radio tuned to the game. He pitched in high school and once in the minors, but this was the only time he ever pitched in the majors; he gave up three hits and a run and got a strikeout. Years later, he was still proud of having a curve ball with a real tight spin on it that a lot of pitchers would have envied. He would demonstrate how to snap it off, throwing his whole body into it saying, "You gotta *crack* down on it." He had thought of himself as a pitcher, and he probably could have been one if he hadn't been so valuable as a hitter.

The 1941 All-Star Game was played in Detroit, and a friend of our family took me to the game. The American League came up in the bottom of the ninth trailing 5-3. With one out, the bases were loaded for Joe DiMaggio. He hit a ground ball that looked for sure like it was going to be a double play, but the fielders only managed one out. The lead runner scored and DiMaggio was safe at first. So with two out and two on and the score 5-4, Ted Williams came to bat. He got hold of a pitch and put it on top of the right field roof. In 1969 I sat with Ted in the visitors' dugout at Tiger Stadium and asked him about that home run. "Claude Passeau was the pitcher," he said. "He was having a great year with Chicago. He had a fastball that he spun just a little bit. It was kind of like a slider, but nobody that I know of was actually throwing a slider then. I had taken a couple of swings and I said to myself, 'I've got to be quicker with this fellow because he's got the ball coming in on me'—instead of coming back over the plate like it normally would from a right-handed pitcher. About that time he threw the pitch again, I got a little quicker and I got it up in the air." Ted always believed that a batter needed strong, quick hands and wrists. The quicker your bat came through the hitting zone, the longer you could wait in order to see the ball before trying to hit it. As a manager he was constantly telling hitters to "quicken up"—to get their hands and hips into it, especially when they were a little late with their swing. So it was interesting to hear that he told himself that as far back as 1941—which, of course, was also the season that he ended up with an average of .406.

"It was the biggest damn thrill of my career up until then, and it is still one of the biggest," Ted told me in '69. "Imagine a twenty-year-old kid with all the great players in the league, in his second All-Star Game, the first one as a starter, hitting the winning home run in the ninth inning." There is film from that game showing him half-galloping to first base, with an expression of pure joy and excitement. I don't think he ever showed that kind of emotion for a home run again. By the time of that All-Star game, he had already vowed that he would never again tip his cap while running the bases, because he was angry with fans who booed him. So for his whole career he generally ran with his head down and a sour expression on his face.

> *On the last day of the 1941 season [Ted Williams] was hitting .39955, which in baseball statistical terms rounds off to .400. Joe Cronin, the Boston manager, offered to let him sit—the .400 would be his. . . . He played both games of a doubleheader, went 6 for 8, and finished with a .406 average.*
> —David Halberstam, "The Perfectionist at the Plate," New York Times, *July 9, 2002*

Ted was a real *student* of hitting, and his goal was to be not just a great hitter but the all-time best. As a boy, he spent hours swinging at imaginary pitches, the same way that I fielded imaginary hits. Playing in the minor leagues, he got to know the veteran pitchers and soaked up information about how pitchers think, how they work the count. In the majors, he systematically picked the brains of Rogers Hornsby and Al Simmons and all the best old hitters. It didn't take him long to figure out that since Hornsby stepped into the ball and Simmons stepped away from it, there must be more than one way to hit.

Ted and I both got hitting advice from Rogers Hornsby, but Ted must have gotten better advice than I did! Okay, nobody could have turned me into a .400 hitter, but Ted probably got better advice from Hornsby than anyone else ever did. After his playing career, Hornsby served as a batting instructor for various teams. In 1950 he was at our Cubs spring training camp on Catalina Island. He would demonstrate and try to explain the mechanics of different aspects of hitting.

Whatever he said was too abstract for most of us, and we didn't think he was a very good teacher. But in 1938 Hornsby had worked for the Minneapolis Millers, where Ted spent his initial season after being signed by the Red Sox. The two of them—the rookie kid just out of high school and the veteran who was one of the last to bat over .400 in the majors before Ted came along—spent a lot of time having hitting contests and talking about hitting. Ted always said Hornsby gave him the greatest hitting advice he ever got, and Hornsby's cardinal rule became Ted's: "Get a good ball to hit." It means be patient and wait for a ball that you can see, that doesn't fool you, that's in the right spot for you. To do that you have to know what the right spot is—what you hit well and what you don't hit well. Wait for *your* pitch, at least until you have two strikes against you and you can't be quite so selective. Ted followed that advice, and preached it, his whole career.

"Teddy Ballgame" led the American League four times in home runs and runs batted in, was an All-Star nineteen times, and won the league batting title six times including 1957, when he hit .388 at age thirty-nine. Despite missing most of five seasons to serve in the Marines, he ranks among the game's leaders with 521 home runs and 1,839 runs batted in. Only Rickey Henderson and Babe Ruth have drawn more walks than he did, and no one has posted a higher career on-base average (.483).

I played against Ted when I was with the Senators in 1953 and '54, and again when I played for Kansas City in 1959. Whenever we played against the Red Sox, our players would line up in the dugout to watch Ted take batting practice. Eventually a couple of guys would drift over and ask him about some aspect of hitting. Ted loved talking about hitting almost as much as he loved hitting itself, so he would always take time to answer, no matter who was asking, and he would talk and talk as long as anybody was still standing there.

In 1953 Senators owner Clark Griffith had arranged for Ted to give me some batting advice. In our twenty-five minutes together before a game, Ted suggested waiting a little longer before swinging, said I should experiment to find what was comfortable, and quizzed me about what kind of pitch I looked for. When I started coaching with Ted in 1969, I mentioned that day. Immediately he asked, "Did I help you?" I told him I'd gotten three hits that night, and he said, "Good," and headed to the bat rack. I'm sure he would have liked to hear that he had made more of a difference. He probably could have, if I'd been able to work with him over a period of time.

When Ted became a manager, guys from the other teams still came over to talk with him. He'd stand there and give them all kinds of advice. Nellie Fox, our first-base coach, was really competitive, and it made him mad that Ted gave advice to opponents. He'd say, "Damn it, we're playing against those guys and there's Ted telling them how to beat us." He'd march over and say, "Why are you helping those guys? Cut it out!" Ted would just laugh it off with his big booming laugh. Ted usually didn't question a hitter's technique; most of the time he would talk about how to *think* about hitting—how to concentrate, how to remember every pitch, how to anticipate what the pitcher will do. Ted was a very good teacher—as long as the guy he was talking to understood what he was saying. If the guy didn't get it, Ted wasn't too good at finding some other way to explain it. He would just shrug his shoulders and let it go.

While we were working together, Ted was putting his ideas on paper. I have a seven-page memorandum that he dictated about how to be a good hitter; it seems to be the basis for his book *The Science of Hitting*. It was the same stuff he always preached, and what he'd tell you if he were here today. Number one: Get a good ball to hit. He said if a pitcher sees you going after bad pitches, that's all he'll throw you. Ted always knew where his strike zone was, and exactly where in the strike zone he was most effective, and he taught himself to wait for those pitches. He was so patient that some people criticized him for passing up too many decent pitches. But he was convinced that you do better to pass up pitches that aren't exactly where you want them, or pitches that you get fooled on, until you're down to your last strike. Then you have to go after what the pitcher wants to throw you, if it's in the strike zone.

Ted figured out that in part of the strike zone—belt-high, middle of the plate—he could hit .400, and in other parts of the zone he hit lower percentages until you got down to the low outside corner, where he only hit .230. He developed a chart showing a cross-section of his strike zone divided into small sections, each the size of a baseball, and in each section was a number representing his batting average for pitches thrown to exactly that spot. The chart was a great way to show a batter that you should get to know *exactly* where you hit the ball best and where you're not quite so good. In other words, "Get a good pitch to hit."

In 1999, at the thirty-year reunion of our 1969 team, I brought up that rule with Ted, and he said, "Yep, that's right." I was setting him up. I said, "What about Kirby Puckett? He'll hit *this* ball—I held my hand high and outside—over the fence in right field. Then he'll hit *that* ball—I moved my hand low and inside—over the fence in left. It doesn't matter where the ball is; he can hit anything." I thought I had him. I should have known better. Ted looked at me and said real slow in his John Wayne style, "Well, then, for him that's a good ball to hit." I laughed, and then he added, "Not too many guys are like that," and we both agreed that was true.

Ted had another great piece of advice. I can't tell you how many times I've said to a young hitter, "Let me tell you what Ted Williams did when he was having trouble with a particular pitcher"—and yes, there were some who gave him trouble—"especially if he had two strikes on him. One, he came up off the end of the bat, choked up on it a little, and two, he concentrated on hitting the ball right up the middle. This gave him a little more bat control and it allowed him to wait on the pitch a little longer. This is *Ted Williams* talking—the greatest hitter who ever lived. Don't you think it's worth trying?"

Shortly before the 1969 season, Ted Williams was coaxed out of a nine-year retirement to manage the Washington Senators. He guided the club for three seasons at RFK Stadium and one in Arlington, Texas, when the Senators became the Texas Rangers.

Even now, I sometimes have trouble believing that Ted Williams chose me to be his third-base coach. That first season in Washington was the most exciting in my career. Ted gave me a lot of responsibilities, we were winning, and I was coaching for the greatest hitter who ever lived. We had some down years after our first season, but working for Ted was always great.

The way it came about was a little unreal. I had been managing the Buffalo Bisons, the Washington Senators' Triple A club, and as bad as that job was, I was set to return for the 1969 season. Over the winter, Minnesota businessman Bob Short purchased the Senators, fired the manager and coaches, and talked Ted Williams into taking the job. After saying "no" three times, Ted surprised everybody when he agreed to give up his full-time fishing to manage, but I think he saw it as a challenge, a chance to try out his ideas. A few of my players from the '68 Bisons were going to the Senators' spring training camp in Pompano Beach, and the club asked me to spend a couple of weeks there before the season opened in Buffalo to help them make the transition.

Ted used to say, "You've got to have enthusiasm to play this game." Well, I was busting my butt the way I always had, and maybe a little more. Ted appreciated that. One day a couple of weeks into spring training, he sidled up to me and said, "Did you coach third base when you were managing in the minors?" I said, "Yes, sir." He said, "Is there any reason you can't coach up here?" "No, sir." "Okay, you're my third-base coach." Just like that. It wasn't only a promotion, it was a minor miracle. Just before the season started, Ted came to me again and said, "Listen, I know the part of the game between the pitchers and the hitters, but I don't know much about base-running, stealing, hit-and-run, all that stuff. You take care of that part and I'll handle the pitching and hitting." I said, "Wait a minute, I'm going to call the bunts and hit-and-runs?" He said, "Yes, you take care of all that." I said, "What about hitting on 3-and-0?" He shrugged. "Look in the dugout. If I take a swing, that means we're hitting." I can't think of another manager who ever gave a third-base coach that kind of responsibility.

Ted's coaching line-up was strong on former infielders, partly because he needed our help and partly because as an outfielder, he didn't want any other outfielders trying to give him advice. First-base coach Nellie Fox was an outstanding second baseman; he played with the White Sox most of his nineteen-year career. He held all kinds of records—ten years leading the league in put-outs, five years in double plays, 1959 American League MVP. He was a three-time Gold Glove winner and would have had more, but the award was only invented halfway through his career.

The bullpen catcher was George Cyril Methodius Susce (pronounced "Susie"), a major-league catcher in the '30s and '40s. The

Gold Glove and Hall of Fame second baseman Nellie Fox became Twig's closest friend in baseball while they coached for Ted Williams.
Wayne Terwilliger personal collection

fingers on George's throwing hand pointed off in different directions from all the foul tips and balls in the dirt, and his face looked as if a few pitches had missed his mask. George worshipped Ted. He was a Red Sox coach while Ted played there, and he helped Ted get back into playing shape after Korea. In spring training, George was in charge of calisthenics, and although he was over sixty, he could twist his body into all kinds of positions. He wanted everybody to do eye exercises, too. He'd sit in the front of the bus moving his eyes this way and that and ignoring all the wisecracks about how strange he looked. Nobody would sit close to him in airports because he did the same thing there.

Sid Hudson, the pitching coach, pitched with Washington and Boston in the '40s and early '50s. Sid and Ted handled the pitchers together and they did really well, especially in 1969. Because Ted was always so thorough about every aspect of hitting, he knew a lot about pitching, and he shared that with Sid. It was said that as a player Ted didn't like pitchers or pitching coaches much. But he and Sid had a ball, especially that first season.

Joe Camacho was Ted's bench coach—maybe the first bench coach ever. He was in his early 30s, and he had been running Ted's baseball school just outside of Boston for several years. Joe had reached Double A in the Cleveland organization and decided he wasn't going to make it to the majors. He went into education, but he jumped at the chance to work for Ted. Nellie was often annoyed that Joe forgot the rest of us had considerably more experience. But Joe knew the game pretty well, and Ted liked being able to talk things over with him in the dugout.

One day during spring training, Nellie and Joe and I were going over run-down plays with the infielders. We didn't do a lot of that; with Ted it was mostly hitting, fielding, and pitching. Nellie and Joe set up the situation—you've got a guy trapped in a run-down play and you fake the toss of the ball a time or two. Then they started arguing about whether, at that point, you give some kind of signal to your teammate to say, "Okay, here it comes." They were getting louder and more heated by the minute. Nellie—nineteen years in the majors, three-time Gold Glover, great base-runner—was pissed about Camacho—this young guy, this *minor-leaguer*—telling him how it should be done. I was just enjoying the whole thing. Players were standing around watching—everybody but the outfielders, who were off working with Ted. Pretty soon Ted noticed all the commotion. He came over and he was mad. "What the hell's going on here?" I started to explain: "We're going over a run-down play, and Nellie says it should be done this way, and Joe says—" Before I could say another word, Ted threw up his hands and bellowed, "F— it, let's hit." And he turned around and walked away.

People were wondering whether Ted could still hit. I was throwing batting practice one day early in spring training, and Ted was standing by the cage, watching. He had a bat in his hands, and he was itching to use it. Everybody was saying, "Come on, Ted, take a few swings." So he called time and stepped into the cage. All of a sudden *I'm throwing BP to Ted Williams*. The reporters perked up, waiting to see Ted take his first swing in nine years. I was nervous as hell. I had a three-quarters delivery, not quite sidearm—Ted told me later that he liked the way I threw because the ball tailed a little bit. He began to narrate the action for the benefit of reporters. "Here is Ted Williams stepping into the cage; let's see what he can do." Then, "If I can't hit one of these f—ing balls out of the park in ten or fifteen swings, I'll buy all you guys dinner." I threw a couple of bad pitches, and then I got in the groove and he started roping them—he was hitting line drives but he wasn't getting them into the air, and it was bothering him. Finally, he hit one over the right field fence. The minute the ball went out, he walked out of the cage, flipped the bat and kept right on walking. It was a wonderful moment.

People sometimes called Ted Williams the John Wayne of baseball. (Somebody else, probably a baseball-lover, said John Wayne was the Ted Williams of the movies.) Ted was a big, good-looking guy with a big, booming voice, just full of self-confidence. Wherever we went, the room would start buzzing when Ted walked in. Even if you didn't know who he was, you would know he was somebody special. Everybody around him could feel his confidence, and if you liked him, it gave you confidence, too. Once in a while, when the team flew in and out of Washington, we'd get into a little bad weather. When that happened, it was nice to look back and see Ted sitting there in the middle of that United Airlines charter plane. I always figured, "Nothing could happen to this baby with him aboard." For one thing, with his experience as a combat pilot, he could probably take over and fly out of any situation.

Ted just naturally took over wherever he went, and he liked to control all the little details. He was always asking questions about whatever he saw, quizzing a waitress about how the food was prepared or checking out a photographer's camera or talking to a sales person about something he was going to buy. Once he figured out the best way to cook a steak, or the best kind of camera, or the best after-shave, he was sure that was best for everybody. When we went out to eat, he'd order for the group. One time in Cleveland he took the staff out to eat at a nice restaurant down near the railroad tracks. "Salads for everybody. And the best steak you've got in the house." Then he told them *exactly* how to cook it, and everybody got their steak cooked the same way.

I was sitting next to Ted that night in Cleveland. Before the food came he had a bottle of Budweiser and I had a bottle of Schlitz. He pointed at my beer and said, "What in the hell are you drinking *that* for?" I said, "That's my beer, I like it." He said, "Jesus Christ, are you kidding? Pour your beer in your glass and watch what happens." He poured his Bud into his glass and a big old fat collar of foam came up, and I poured my Schlitz and my collar wasn't as big. "There you go," he said. "You can tell a beer by the collar." I've been drinking Bud ever since. I've switched to Bud Lite now, but it still has a nice collar. Another time we went into a store so he could pick up some aftershave. He asked me, "Have you ever tried this British Sterling? It's got a good, fresh smell." I said no, I hadn't tried it. He immediately told the saleswoman, "Make that two bottles." I've been using British Sterling ever since, and it *does* have a nice, fresh smell.

During the 1972 season, there was a short strike early in the season, and during the strike Nellie and Joe and I invited Ted to a cookout at our apartment building. We had steak and all the trimmings. Ted walked into the kitchen and saw Camacho cutting lettuce for the salad. "Hey," he said, "you don't cut lettuce, you *tear* it." He picked some up and showed us how it's done. People who cook will say, "Well, of course, you never use a knife on lettuce." But we didn't know; we all looked at him like he was crazy. Then Nellie went to get the charcoal ready, and Ted said, "Put a lot of starter fluid on it. No, no, don't just sprinkle it, that's not enough, you gotta *saturate* your coals so the fire burns evenly." I was supposed to cook the steaks that night, but no way was I going to try grilling steaks in front of Ted. So Nellie brought out the steaks and we let Ted run the show.

Some people really didn't appreciate being told what to do. Years later when I was with the Twins I was talking with Ralph Houk, the former great Yankees manager. Ted Williams's name came up, and Houk bristled. "That son-of-a-bitch took me bone fishing in Florida one time. They're tough to catch. We found a school of them, and Williams told me to cast out in front of the school. I did, but the wind blew my line back into the fish. He went crazy, jumped all over my ass. I'd never go fishing with that son-of-a-bitch again." There were plenty of others who felt the same. But I enjoyed Ted's company, and I never minded his suggestions or his manner. That was just Ted—enthusiastic and confident—and it was fun to be around him, on and off the field.

He even gave me a lesson in manners. I ran into him one morning in the hotel lobby, and he said, "Good morning, how ya doin'?" I said, "Fine, thanks," and kept on walking. I'd taken about six steps when I heard, good and loud, "*I'm fine too, Wayne.*" From that day on, nobody ever asked how I was without me asking in return, "And how are you?"

The Senators finished last in the American League in 1968, and we had pretty much the same team in '69. Ted set out to build their confidence and to improve their skills, especially in the hitting department, and it worked pretty well, at least in the first year.

Williams apparently has decided it would be foolish to remind the club how bad it is. Instead, he is telling his men how good they can be. In the pregame practice session . . . he had nothing but kind words. . . . "This guy could do it, sports fans," [he] said as Ken McMullen stepped in.
—Steve Cady, New York Times, April 3, 1969

The guys were very much aware that this was the great Ted Williams, and they were on edge at first, watching to see what he would do or say. After all, this was one of the all-time baseball heroes, and on top of that, a guy known to have a temper. But nine years of full-time fishing had made him a lot more even-tempered than when he played, and besides, he saw it as his responsibility to set a positive tone. He knew he already had the players' respect; that was never an issue for him. So he wanted to encourage them, give them a little self-confidence, and then help them live up to it. He was loud and kind of boisterous, and he used a lot of cuss words; that was just his normal way of speaking. It took a little while to get used to that, and to realize that when he was mad at you, you'd know it, but once he said what was on his mind, it was over, he let it go. He was unhappy if we didn't have good at bats—if we swung at a bad pitch and stranded a guy on third, for example. And if somebody didn't hustle, you'd see him take a sharp breath and bite his lip to keep from saying too much. But Nellie Fox was always on top of that—if somebody didn't run out a fly ball or didn't get over fast enough to make a play in the field, Nellie would tell them, so Ted didn't have to. If a pitcher threw something Ted didn't agree with, once in a while he would shake his head and then walk down to Sid Hudson and say something like, "Geez, Sid, he had him all set up for a curve ball, so why would he throw that fast ball?" Whatever Sid told him would calm him down.

Ted didn't get along quite as well with the pitchers as with the other players. When he was younger, he often said pitchers were stupid by nature. Unlike the old-time veterans he got to know in the minors, his contemporaries didn't seem to *think* about the game. As a manager, he liked to needle them. He'd say things like, "Pitchers are the dumbest sons-of-bitches in the world," just loud enough so whatever pitchers were around could hear him. Almost always, somebody took it personally—which he took as further evidence of their stupidity. Other times he'd give somebody a little jab about something they had done, and just walk away and leave them standing there cussing. Ted would be chuckling and he'd say, "He didn't like that, did he?" Over the years, I didn't hear too many pitchers give him compliments. And yet he worked very closely with our pitchers, especially in that first season, and they did great.

Ted's debut as a manager was the big story all across the country as the season got under way, and we had reporters everywhere, through spring training and at home leading up to opening day. He was working very long hours, and he spent at least half his time giving interviews. He wasn't bitter like he was as a player, and he knew working with the press was part of the job, but if he enjoyed it you'd never have known by watching him. Like he did with the pitchers, Ted was willing to get some of the reporters upset for his own amusement and just leave it that way. He'd answer a question with some little dig that *he* knew was tongue-in-cheek, but he never explained himself, never gave that little wink to say he was putting them on. So they wrote it the way he said it and before long he'd get pissed off about what they had written. After that, when he said something vaguely insulting, he wasn't kidding any more.

The Senators' 1969 home opener brought out a rookie President who sat with a new owner and a new commissioner of baseball—in a newly renamed stadium—to watch the rookie manager and his team lose to the Yankees 8-4 in spite of fourteen Washington hits. Williams's first managerial win would come the next day.

There was always a lot of excitement on opening day for the Senators, and part of it was that the President always came to throw out the first ball. When I played there in 1953, Dwight Eisenhower was attending his first home opener as President; in 1969, Richard Nixon was doing the same. Ted liked Nixon politically and liked the fact that Nixon was a real baseball fan. Before the game Nixon told reporters he hoped we could get him to come out more often. Bowie Kuhn was at the game as the brand-new baseball commissioner, and the ballpark itself had just been named Robert F. Kennedy Memorial Stadium. We had fourteen hits including a two-run home run—but we stranded twelve guys on base, and the Yankees made much better use of their nine hits. The papers reported that when the public-address announcer used the Senators' new promotional phrase "It's a whole new ballgame," the crowd roared with laughter.

One of the photos that went out over the national wire services on opening day showed Ted arguing with the umpires over a ruling on a dropped pop fly. The picture fit people's expectation of what he'd be like as a manager, but in fact he rarely argued. He knew it wasn't going to change things very often, and Ted Williams didn't usually go around looking for an argument he couldn't win. Ted's first regular-season victory as a manager came the next day when we beat the Yankees 6-4. It was another milestone in his career, so everybody made a very big deal about it. There were lots of reporters in the locker room after the game, and there was a big, noisy celebration. After the game, somebody asked Yankees manager Ralph Houk whether he thought Ted Williams was improving the Senators' hitting skills—we'd had twenty-three hits in the first two games. Houk said it was too soon to tell. The next day we got sixteen more hits and beat the Yankees again, 9-6. The *New York Times* said, "Senators Show Williams Touch."

> *[Pitcher Joe Coleman said,] "He's got everybody pulling for everybody else. . . . And he's helped the hitting, just by telling us to make contact. Last year, everybody swung for the fences because they saw Hondo [Frank Howard] knocking the ball out of sight. Now they're just trying to meet the ball, like Ted says."*
> —*George Vecsey,* New York Times, *April 20, 1969*

In the third game of the season I thought my major-league coaching career might be over. At home against the Yankees, Jim Hannan was pitching with a seven-run lead in the sixth inning. The Yankees had loaded the bases, there was one out, and Yankee catcher Frank Fernandez came to bat. Hannan had been fooling him all night with a little slider; Fernandez hadn't managed to come anywhere near it. I was standing in the corner of the dugout when Ted walked over to me and said, "Whaddya think, should I take him out?" I didn't think about the fact that the pitcher might be tired, or that the batter might have learned something from his first three at-bats. I just said, "Geez, Ted, Fernandez hasn't come anywhere *near* that slider." Ted said, "Okay," and left Hannan in. Hannan threw the slider and Fernandez hit it for a grand slam home run. I thought, "Nice going, Wayne." I spent the rest of the game avoiding eye contact with Ted. We won the game, thank God, and Ted and I never discussed our conversation. Later, I wished I had said, "I *told* you to take him out." He would have appreciated the humor. Anyway, he told the *New York Times* it was his first significant mistake as a manager.

"He was getting weak, we recognized it, he was pitching high,"
says Williams. "[With the bases loaded] we decided to leave him
in. Fernandez is up. Fernandez hasn't gotten a foul all day. Not
a foul. Then, VOOM!" Williams laughs, liking the sound of the
word "VOOM."
—*Robert Lipsyte,* New York Times, *April 17, 1969*

In the second series of the season, we played the Orioles at Baltimore. We knew it would be tough because they were a great team
and had beaten us up pretty well in exhibition play. We won the first
game, but then lost three by a combined score of 20-0, leaving us
with a season record of 3 wins and 4 losses. Bob Short was upset
about the way things were going, and Ted was upset that Short was
upset. We had a staff meeting at the hotel in Baltimore, and the two
of them got into it big-time, yelling and cussing each other out. It's
the one time I saw Ted really angry, and *he was furious.* He came up
with curse words I had never heard before, and I was a Marine. They
had invited all the coaches to this meeting, and we sat there listening,
not saying a word. The argument went on and on, and they both
made some threats, like "I oughtta fire you" and "I'll quit first."
They both knew they had gone too far, but neither was willing to
back down and they couldn't figure out a way to stop. Finally Bob
Short turned toward us and said, "Well, what have you guys got to
say about all this?" I raised my hand and said as calmly as I could,
"We just lost three straight to the Baltimore Orioles. But the Orioles
are the *very best team in baseball* right now. You've gotta remember
that. They're going to win a lot of games this year, and some will be
against us." Each of them could find something to agree with in what
I said, so they each mumbled some final comment. Ted went out and
slammed the door hard enough to make us jump, and that was the
end of it. I was a little hesitant about speaking up at first. But I was
glad I did, because it gave them a way out, and they both got to have
the last word. I was right about the Orioles, too, because they won
the pennant and played "the amazing Mets" in the World Series.

Eventually, things started going well for us, too. Guys began playing great—most of them better than they ever had before. In July I
used my tape recorder to capture sounds of a celebration at the end

of a series at Fenway Park. On the tape I narrated like a sports commentator. "Coming to you from our locker room in Boston. We've just taken three out of five from the Red Sox and we're happy about it, as you can tell from the noise in the background. We preceded this by taking three out of four from the Cleveland Indians, so we've had a pretty fair road trip!" You hear a lot of chatter and laughter, and then you hear Ted walking somebody around and introducing them to his coaches. Everybody is happy. It was like that a lot of the time.

Ted kept his word about giving me free rein with the signs from third base. I could put on the hit and run, the steal, the bunt; I could try things, take chances. With the kind of year we were having in '69, things usually worked out. Even when they didn't, he only second-guessed me once. One night we had runners on first and third with one out, and I had the runner on third going on anything on the ground. The ball was hit to the third baseman, and he elected to throw home. Our base runner was an easy out, but we were still alive with runners on first and second. Ted questioned the wisdom of sending the runner, but if the fielder had gone for the double play and completed it, the inning would have been over. I knew I had made the right decision, but after the game Ted called Joe McCarthy, his old manager at Boston, to discuss it. McCarthy told him I had made the right call—that it was worth the risk. From then on, Ted figured I knew what I was doing, and I continued to call plays and take risks.

Sometimes it takes a while for players to understand that you *want* them to take risks, that they shouldn't always settle for the sure thing. One day we had our big hitter, Frank Howard, on second base with two outs, and when the batter got a base hit, I tried to wave Frank in. I figured it wasn't a sure thing but it was worth going for. Frank was lumbering along, trying to accelerate, and I was waving and yelling, "Ya gotta *go*, Frank, ya gotta go!" As he got to third base, he pulled right up and stopped. I walked over and looked up at him—he's 6-foot-7 or so—and I said, "Frank, why did you stop? Didn't you see me waving?" He looked down at me real slow and said, "I didn't think I could make it, coach." All I could do was shrug.

Some of the pitchers were pretty good hitters, so I'd let them hit. Young Joe Coleman could make good contact (he was the first graduate of the Ted Williams Baseball School to make the major leagues). We'd have a man on first, and the other team would be looking for a bunt, and I'd let Joe swing away. Two or three times that year, Joe got a base hit while they were creeping in on him for the bunt.

We finished the 1969 season fourth in the American League East, one game out of third. If we'd won *one more game* we'd have been in the bonus money. But we won twenty-one more games than the team had won the previous year, and we were ten games over .500. Since 1901 there had only been six other seasons when the Senators finished at .500 or better. The most recent one had been 1953, my first year with Washington.

Ted also took great satisfaction in the fact that the players' individual statistics were much, much better than the year before he took over. We started with a team of good position players, most of whom had not been great hitters. Just about every member of the team started hitting better than they ever had, and their statistics showed it. For many 1969 was the best season of their lives. Frank Howard started out with four home runs in the first three games. By the end of the season, he had equaled his best-season average of .296; he had also increased the number of runs he scored, cut down on strikeouts from 141 to 96, and increased his walks from 54 to 102. (His attitude was as great as his performance. One of my great locker-room memories is a naked Frank Howard, without the partial plate that provided his front teeth, leading his version of the team fight song after a win.)

The most dramatic changes were the guys who weren't born power-hitters. Shortstop Eddie Brinkman was one of the best fielders in baseball at the time, but in '67 and '68, he'd hit .188 and .187. In 1969 he hit .266, his career high. Mike Epstein at first base had hit .234 in '68, with 13 home runs and 33 RBIs. In 1969 he hit .278 with 30 home runs and 85 RBIs. Center fielder Del Unser's great defensive work had made him the *Sporting News* Rookie of the Year in 1968 despite hitting only .230; in '69 he came up to .286. Infielder Zoilo Versalles joined us late; he hit .267 in the thirty-one games he played with us and his season average went from .196 in

'68 to .236 for '69. Others also had numbers to be proud of. Although he struggled later in the season, outfielder Brant Alyea, who told a reporter he had been hitting "like an old woman," hit a home run in his first at-bat of the season after getting some personal attention from Ted just before the game. Our pitchers were doing well, too. Joe Coleman had been great in training camp and then struggled early in the season, but when he regained control of his forkball, he pitched three consecutive shutouts and was back on track. Dick Bosman became the 1969 American League leader with an ERA of 2.19.

> *"I took a seventh place team and won my division,"* [*Minnesota Twins Manager Billy*] *Martin moaned, "and they voted Ted Williams manager of the year. Then I find out that Williams doesn't even give the signs from the dugout. His third base coach, Wayne Terwilliger, gives them. I told Williams he should give the trophy to Terwilliger."*
> —*Pete Waldmeir,* Detroit News, *September 20, 1971*

Ted worked hard, he was smart, and he deserved every bit of recognition he got, including the Manager of the Year award. He was feeling very generous toward us, and the last game of the season, each of us found a fishing rod and reel in our locker as a gift. Ted had become as passionate about fishing as he was about baseball, so it was a nice personal touch. Ted knew my son liked to hunt, and he gave him a shotgun. Steven, who was eleven at the time, was thrilled.

My dad died before the season started, so he never knew that I coached for Ted. But my mother and her sister came to some of our games in Detroit and sat right behind the dugout. At the first game they came to, Ted came up to say hello to them. My mother had known all about Ted Williams for thirty years; when I got his auto-graph, she was excited right along with me. So it was a big deal for her that I coached for him and she loved being part of it. After the season I went home to Charlotte, Michigan, tended bar, and talked about Ted Williams. I was invited to speak at some Rotary and Lions Club lunches that fall; everybody wanted to know what it was like to work for him, and I was more than happy to tell them.

Ted Williams's coaches were the last coaching staff of the Washington Senators and the first of the Texas Rangers. From left: George Susce, Wayne Terwilliger, Nellie Fox, Ted Williams, Joe Camacho, and Sid Hudson. *Wayne Terwilliger personal collection*

Ted had such a good time in '69 and everything went so well that he thought managing was a snap. By comparison, the next two seasons were down years. We started out 1970 with a lot of optimism, and the program for that season showed a smiling Richard Nixon on the cover, with the words "Our No. 1 Fan." Things didn't come together on the field as well as we thought they would, but we didn't lose hope. After the 1970 season some trades were made and that made 1971 even worse.

The Detroit Tigers had been looking to get rid of pitcher Denny McLain. McLain had thirty-one wins in 1968 and he won the Cy Young Award two years in a row. Unfortunately, he also got involved with some gamblers and was suspended for part of 1970. When he returned to the mound, he had lost his fastball. There were other problems and more suspensions—Detroit decided he had to go. Bob Short must have seen it as a terrific opportunity, because he gave up four players including half of our infield and our best pitcher. Apparently he thought, "This guy is a big name and a big star; he'll draw crowds and he'll win thirty games for us." But Denny

McLain was washed up. His arm had given out, his reputation was ruined and there were rumors of financial troubles. He was also not a good teammate. He treated me fine, but he was overbearing with other players and deeply angry. He had been known as fun-loving and arrogant. Now the fun was pretty much gone, and the arrogance had turned to bitterness. The three players who came along with McLain were Elliott Maddox, a young outfielder; Norm McRae, a pitcher who spent the season in the minors; and Don Wert, a third baseman who I had liked when he played for Detroit but was washed up at thirty-two and was released in June. They couldn't make up for the talent we had lost, including Eddie Brinkman and Aurelio Rodriguez, a young third baseman we had gotten in a trade with the Angels in 1970.

The strangest part of the deal was trading away Joe Coleman, who won sixty games for the Tigers over the next three years. Twins owner Calvin Griffith had once approached Short about a trade for Coleman, and Short had said, "I might as well give up my right arm." Ted and Joe didn't always see eye to eye on Joe's pitching progress, but Ted knew Joe's best days were still to come and McLain's were over. Ted was unhappy with the trade, to say the least. So were fans and baseball writers. To this day, people talk about that as one of the worst trades in baseball, and as the start of the downward spiral that ended with the Senators leaving Washington.

In another odd acquisition, Curt Flood came to our club in '71. Curt was still a young man, but he, too, was finished as a ballplayer. As recently as 1969, he had been a big star with the Cardinals—three times an All-Star, seven Gold Gloves, a pair of World Series championships. But in 1970, after the Cardinals traded him to Philadelphia, he refused to report, filed his antitrust suit against the reserve clause, and then sat out the season as the suit went through the courts. During that time, he got out of shape and lost his playing skills. I was surprised at the time, although looking back I'm sure all the turmoil over his lawsuit affected him greatly.

Curt's lawsuit was based on the principle that a team shouldn't be able to "own" a player forever, something he compared to old-time slavery. When people pointed out that he was making $90,000 a year, he answered that even so, he had no freedom to negotiate in an open market or to choose where to play. Jackie Robinson and a number of other players came out in support of his cause, but most of the media and most of the public branded him as an ingrate trying to destroy baseball. Bob Short was so eager to get him that he agreed to give Philadelphia a player just for the right to *talk* to Curt. Curt still wanted to play, he needed money, and his lawyer assured him that playing would not jeopardize his case. When Curt signed a contract with the Senators for $110,000, many of the people who had supported him decided he had "sold out," although his suit was still in the courts. So he felt like everybody in the world was mad at him, and he kept to himself a lot.

On top of that, he just couldn't get back to his old self; he couldn't hit the ball, couldn't field, couldn't do much of anything. I'm sure he was very disappointed, but he didn't talk about that, either. I just knew him as a nice, quiet guy. His book had just come out, and he autographed a copy for me, but we didn't talk about it. Eventually, a lot of people came to agree that the reserve clause should go, and they praised him for taking up the fight. When players became free agents and started negotiating huge salaries, somebody asked him whether he felt guilty about it and he said no, because all he did was make it possible for players to have the same negotiating rights that owners did. I guess he was right about that; nobody forced the owners to pay those huge salaries.

Bob Short had acquired Curt Flood from the Phillies, whose team he had refused to join after the Cardinals traded him. Flood's lawsuit against baseball's reserve clause went all the way to the U.S. Supreme Court, which ruled against him. In 1975 an arbitrator effectively overturned the reserve clause by granting free agency to a couple of pitchers, and baseball was changed forever.

Ted was frustrated with how the team was shaping up, and everybody—with the possible exception of Bob Short—knew we were in trouble going into the '71 season. We got a lot of preseason publicity over Flood and McLain, but it wasn't the kind of publicity that helps a club. Flood played in thirteen games, struggled badly, and in mid-April quit baseball and went to Europe. McLain not only failed to

draw crowds but lost twenty-two games to lead the league in losses—
the only title anybody on the team earned that year.

Not surprisingly, given our performance, attendance at our games
fell off. In 1969 we drew more than 11,300 fans per game; by '71 it
was about 8,200. Bob Short had been threatening for a long time to
move the team, and he stepped up his campaign during the '71 season. On September 20 the other major league owners voted to let
him take the franchise to Texas. Baseball lovers in Washington were
very upset. We may not have had huge crowds, but there were very
loyal fans who had loved the Senators through the years. The original Senators were there from 1901 through 1960. (The Senators
were officially the Washington Nationals from 1905 to 1955, but I
don't think the fans ever called them that.) When Calvin Griffith
moved that franchise to Minnesota to become the Twins in 1961,
Washington immediately got an expansion club, which they also
named the Senators. But there was no replacement club on the hori-
zon for 1972, and people were both sad and angry. Most of the
anger was focused on Bob Short, and that set up one of the strangest
games I've ever seen.

The final game of the 1971 season—and the last major league ballgame at RFK Stadium—was against the Yankees on September 30.
More than 14,000 paying fans showed up and another 4,000 or so
pushed their way in—some to say farewell to their team, others just
to get on Bob Short. The authorities must have expected trouble
because there were about fifty extra police officers providing security. People had signs and banners protesting the move and insulting
Short, and they made their feelings known throughout the game.
The only positive moment of the evening came in the sixth inning
when big Frank Howard, who was the most beloved player and
also the one who most hated to leave Washington, hit a home run
off Mike Kekich into the left-field stands. The crowd gave him a
tremendous standing ovation that went on and on. After Hondo had
circled the bases and gone into the dugout, Ted and some of the
players made him come back out to acknowledge the crowd, at least
twice. Once he blew the crowd a kiss, and once he tossed his helmet
to the fans. There were tears in his eyes when he went back into the
dugout.

Howard's homer started a rally that tied the game at 5-5, and then in the eighth we went ahead 7-5. In the top of the ninth, we got two men out, and it seemed like we were minutes away from going out with a win. But all of a sudden—I don't know what started it—fans began jumping over the walls and streaming onto the field. They pulled up the bases and home plate, they dug up pieces of sod, they climbed up onto the bullpen roof to reach the scoreboard and pull off light bulbs and letters. Anything they could pry loose, they grabbed as a souvenir. We got our players off the field, and both teams headed for their clubhouses. There was no way the authorities were going to restore order, and no way the field was going to be playable, so the umpires called the game and gave the win to New York with a score of 9-0. One of the New York owners was in attendance, and he asked the umpires to give the win to the Senators, which was very unusual. The umpires bumped the decision up to Joe Cronin, who by then was the league president, and he chose to let the forfeit stand. And that's how we left. Washington would be without a team from that night until 2005.

As much as the fans hated to lose the team, and we understood that, we all perked up over the chance to get a new start in a new place. Ted had two years left on his contract, and he wanted to enjoy them more than he had enjoyed '71. Unfortunately, the move did nothing at all for the team's performance, which was even worse than the year before. Just like everything went right in '69, it all went wrong in '72. Our team batting average was .217. Our record of 54 wins and 100 losses put us last in the American League West, 38fi games out of first place. (We should have played another eight games but the season opened with baseball's first general strike, and those games weren't made up.) It was clear that Bob Short was not going to put any significant new money into the team, and it was clear, as Ted pointed out, that fans in Texas were no more eager to see a bad team than fans in Washington had been. Although attendance was a big reason for the move, the average attendance only went up a tiny bit, from 8,241 in Washington in '71 to 8,610 in Arlington in '72. So at the end of the season, Ted announced that although he had another year left on his contract, he was stepping down. In 1973 the Rangers went through three managers including

Whitey Herzog and Billy Martin, and they lost five more games than we had in '72.

Ted . . . would argue with anyone about politics, sports, deter-gents, anything. He would question. He would tell stories. . . . There was a liveliness about him that was different from the ordinary. He was larger than larger-than-life, if that makes any sense."
—Leigh Montville, Sports Illustrated, *July 15, 2002, writing about Ted at age sixty*

When we were on road trips, Ted and I often spent time together. He liked to walk and so did I, so he'd ask me to go along. The fact that we were both Marines gave us something else in common besides baseball. We were both in the Pacific during World War II, and Ted also served in Korea. We talked about getting shot at, and how after a while you just took it for granted, unless something dramatic happened like having your plane get hit or being chased by a tank when you're on foot. Ted often said that his two greatest accomplishments in life were his service in the Marine Corps and being elected to the baseball Hall of Fame. I've always said I'm as proud of being a Marine as anything I ever did in baseball.

I liked to walk around with Ted and watch people react. They'd be so surprised to see him walking down the street, or in their store or their restaurant. We stayed in downtown hotels, so we'd walk all around the downtown and through the department stores. It was on one of those walks that he introduced me to British Sterling. A lot of times we would wind up our walks with chocolate milkshakes at a drugstore ice cream fountain. He told me that back in 1941, when he got his six hits on the last day of the season to lock up his .406 batting average, he celebrated with a chocolate milkshake.

Ted was aware of people recognizing him and watching him, and one of the ways he responded was to play a little trick. When we were in an elevator with other people and he noticed somebody looking at him, he'd say to me, "Isn't it a shame about that boy who lost his leg to an alligator? You wouldn't think that could happen here." He never did this in Florida, only in places where they didn't have alligators. It was my job to nod and keep a straight face. A lot of

times people would react and they'd ask, "Where did it happen?"
He'd make up a vague answer like, "Over on the west side of town,"
and he'd time it so that we'd leave the elevator and walk away before
he'd have to answer any more questions. The people in the elevator
would be left saying, "Oh, that's terrible," and "Gee, I didn't hear
about that." Sometimes he did it as we walked through a hotel lobby,
talking loud enough so that people who were watching him could
hear, and then just strolling out of their earshot. He thought this was
hilarious. He did it over and over, and always the same way. Any of
us who were with him knew exactly what was coming if we heard
the words, "Isn't it a shame . . . "

When we moved to Texas in '72, neither of our families came
with us for the season, so we sometimes went out together to do a little shopping. Because Ted had a contract with Sears to endorse and
promote a line of Ted Williams fishing gear, he had a discount that
was good at any of their stores. We walked into a Sears store in Dallas, and everybody working there perked up. He bought sheets and
towels and blankets for his apartment, and I remember him making
sure that they gave him his 15 percent discount. He asked the
saleslady several times, "Did you remember to give me my discount?"

One day in Cleveland when we were walking around downtown,
we came upon one of those little X-rated movie places. We went in,
each going behind a separate curtain, put quarters in the slots and
watched nudie movies. We'd watch for a while and then he'd say,
"Hey, this one's not too bad," so I'd leave mine and go over to his
and watch that one for a while. We didn't stay there very long.
Instead, we went to a drug store and had chocolate milkshakes.

Once in a while he'd ask, "What are you doing tonight?" And
whatever it was, I wasn't doing it any more! There was a pizza place
outside of Arlington that showed old movies—Charlie Chaplin and
other really old classics, which he loved. We'd order pizza and beer
and watch those old-time movies. Another evening, Ted said, "A
friend of mine is playing the piano tonight; do you want to take a
ride?" We drove to a jazz club in Dallas, and the place was packed;
Errol Garner was playing. We sat at the bar, right next to the piano,
and Ted would turn and talk with Garner while he played. Ted was a
real fan of his music, and they had been friends for years. Sometimes

Ted would say that the sound of the bat hitting the ball was as beautiful as listening to Errol Garner, meaning the most beautiful music he could think of.

Ted never did much drinking, at least while we were together. He'd have a beer or two with dinner, and one year in spring training he introduced me to "Navy Grog," a kind of rum drink, but even that night we didn't overdo it. I also never saw Ted chasing women. When he was younger, I'm sure women chased him. But when we worked together he was newly married, his son John Henry was just a baby, and he seemed happy with his life.

Ted's sense of humor was usually very dry; he found great entertainment in the alligator story, or in saying something a little insulting with a perfectly straight face. But a few times, I saw him laugh until tears ran down his cheeks.

It always surprised Ted when players who had been around a while didn't think about hitting the way he did, when they didn't learn to pay attention to what a pitcher was throwing and how the ball moved. He told a story about watching a game on television and seeing Boog Powell, Baltimore's big left-handed-hitting first-baseman, being fooled again and again by a slow looping curve ball. Powell had a big stride and big swing; he'd swing himself almost into the ground. Ted said that as he watched the game, he thought for sure Powell would start looking for that curve ball but he never seemed to, and it had made Ted laugh to see Powell keep making that big swing of his and keep missing the ball. I don't know who the pitcher was in the game that Ted saw on TV, but in '70 and '71, we had a young left-handed pitcher named Denny Riddleberger who also had a big slow curve ball. When we played Baltimore, Ted would bring Riddleberger in to pitch to Powell. Denny would serve up that big slow curve and Powell would stand there and cock and cock and cock the bat, and then swish, he'd swing and miss it entirely. Every time Denny pitched to Boog, Ted would be hiding in the corner of the dugout where the fans and the reporters couldn't see him, laughing, with tears running down his face. Riddleberger would throw another one and Ted would throw up his arms and his legs and laugh and laugh. Once in a while Powell would foul one off. I don't know how many times Powell faced Riddleberger but I doubt he ever did hit a fair ball off of him.

Ted wasn't what you'd call a pay-attention-to-the-road driver under any circumstances. He'd step on it for a while, and then kind of slow back down, and he'd turn around to talk to people in the back seat. During spring training in Florida, we'd all take the bus to our games on long trips, but for shorter trips Ted would drive his big Ford station wagon and some of the coaches would ride with him. On one particular trip, we stopped along the way at a strawberry stand, and we all had orange juice and strawberries. We got back into the car; Joe Comacho was sitting in the front with Ted, and Nellie Fox and I were in the back. Pretty soon Ted passed some gas. It was audible and it also was smellable. He knew he did it, and he started smiling a little. Then Nellie said. "Geeeeez," and Ted started kind of chuckling. Then I smelled it, and I said, "God damn." At that point, Nellie said, "That was no strawberry fart." Ted just completely broke up laughing. I thought we were going to run off the road, he was laughing so hard. He kept it up for the longest time. He'd just about stop laughing and then he'd start all over again.

After we left the Rangers, Ted sent me a very nice letter.

Dear Twig:

I just found out last month that you were back in baseball and am really delighted because you are what I consider a top baseball man—in knowledge, enthusiasm and loyalty. It's too bad things had to end up in Texas the way they did, but I had really had it up to my neck and thought it better for everyone if a change of scene was made. The other day, after three weeks of Spring training, I was out fishing and said to myself, "The base-ball season has begun and for the first time in five years, I'm not a part of it" . . . and then I said to myself "I don't miss it a bit!" (especially when you lose the way we were losing). In any event, I wish you all the luck in the world. I know you will do a good job. I suppose you are in the Astros system—they have a good man.

Best regards, Ted

I saw Ted a couple of times after that, and we talked every so often by phone. At a 1999 reunion of the '69 Senators, in Baltimore, he was in a wheelchair. He wasn't signing balls anymore because his handwriting was bad. I had never wanted to bother him with that

Ted Williams signed this ball for Twig at a 1999 reunion of the 1969 Senators. It is one of the last balls—perhaps the last—that Ted signed.
Photo by Lin Terwilliger

sort of thing when we worked together, and I felt bad asking him now, but I did anyway. It's a shaky "Ted Williams," and it may be the last ball he ever signed.

Our last real telephone conversation was about a year before he died. I was with the Saint Paul Saints, and we were playing in Fargo, North Dakota. I called from my hotel room. When he came on the line, he sort of growled, "Wayne Terwilliger—*who's that?*" As often as he did that sort of thing, it always took me a split second to realize he was kidding. But he laughed and asked, "Wayne, how are you? You're still in the game, I know." And then without waiting for me to reply, he asked, "Who is that Yankee pitcher who is having so damn much trouble lately—the right-hander who has been struggling?" I got my first words in: "David Cone?" "That's the guy. You know what's wrong with him don't you?" "No," I said, "what's wrong?" "Chrissakes, he's dropping his arm to throw that slider and it's *flat*." At age eighty-two, even with all his health problems, Ted sounded like he always did, sitting in the dugout with his voice booming to make a point. You'd never know he had slowed down. "Tell him he's got to get that arm up and crack down on that thing." I said, "He drops down a lot, Ted." "I know, but that's no good . . . ," and his voice trailed off. I didn't mention that I wasn't in a position to offer advice to David Cone, even from Ted Williams. We talked a few more minutes. Ted said he was doing better, and I told him everybody was pulling for him.

I called him one more time just a couple of months before he died in 2002. A nurse answered and said, "Oh, I'm glad you called. He's sleeping and he needs to get up." When he came on the line, he was pretty groggy. I started talking about the time he pitched a couple of innings against the Tigers back in 1940. "I was listening on the radio," I said. "Do you remember that?" "Yeah," he said. "I was just wondering whether you used that good curve ball of yours." "Yeah," he said again, but he wasn't really into the conversation. After a couple of minutes the nurse came back on the line and said, "I'm sorry; I can't wake him up enough to talk."

In 1999 when the Saint Paul Saints organized a celebration of my fifty years in baseball, Ted recorded a tape that they played on the public address system. "I wanna tell ya," Ted starts out in his big enthusiastic voice, "I picked him as one of our coaches in Washington . . . and *I wanna tell ya,* he was one of the best decisions I ever made in my life. I picked three infielders because I didn't know the infielders and I didn't know the plays that have to be made, but I thought I knew something about hitting and something about the outfield. So I said I gotta go to my weakness to strengthen the club as much as I can. And hell, I ended up with a *helluva* group of coaches. And *I wanna tell ya,* Wayne Terwilliger is one of the greatest guys I ever met, *terrific* guy. As a coach, he taught me a lot about the game and couldn't have been a better guy to have on the ball club. Baseball's richer that they had him. I'm *so happy* that I have a chance to talk to people that are helping honor him tonight, because everything I know or remember about Wayne could not be of a higher caliber, so they're lucky that he's there tonight." Then his tone changes to a more personal one and he says, "My very best wishes to you, Wayne, because I really sincerely feel about you as one of the greatest guys I ever met. I wish I was there with you tonight."

I wish he were, too. Thanks, Ted. Thanks for everything. All my life I've loved going to the ballpark, but there was something especially exciting about finding Ted Williams there every day. Each and every day, I heard him say something new. It was always worth hearing, and over the years I've found that it was often worth quoting. I can't tell you how many times I've heard myself say, "Well, Ted Williams said . . . "

15

Up and Down
with the Rangers

Surprise—could work—might sometimes lose,
But if I had my way to choose
With a move some people might call lame,
I'll grab the chance to win the game.

The summer of 1972 was the start of a lot of change for me, in the game and in life.

By the end of the season, Ted Williams had had enough of losing. Moving the Senators from Washington to Texas hadn't improved anything, so with a year left on his contract, he called it quits. Like many good things that come to an end, this could have been another big break for me. I was interviewed for the managing job, and I was a reasonable choice—experience as a Triple A manager and major-league coach, and in the Senators' system eleven years. The interview went well, and we were wrapping up when I said to Mr. Short, "Ted has been a great manager, I hate to see him go. I'd rather coach for Ted than manage." I thought they had blamed Ted for things beyond his control, and I wanted it to be clear that I admired him. Short hired Whitey Herzog and Whitey hired his own coaching staff. For the first time in eleven years, I didn't have a job with the Senators.

I also didn't have a marriage. Early in 1972 Mary Jane and I had decided to split after twenty-five years. All those years of my being absent, or finally coming home and then being a jerk, had caused problems for everybody, and she was finally tired of it. When I left for Texas for the '72 season, she stayed in Michigan, and we said we'd work out the details of a divorce in the fall.

I wasn't looking for a new relationship just yet, but that summer I met the woman who would change my life. I lived in an apartment in the same building with Nellie Fox and some other coaches. Our mailman came by one day and said, "A couple of nice ladies who work down the street are wondering whether any of you baseball guys are single." I said, mostly joking, "Hell yes, some of us are available." I didn't imagine anything would come of it. But the next time we saw the mailman, he had a couple of names and phone numbers. One was a woman named Lin. I called her and said, "Let's have lunch today." I liked her right away. She was lively and attractive—great smile, really personable and easy to talk to. But she was wearing black stockings so I couldn't really see her legs. It was summer in Texas, so being a life-long leg man, I started wondering, are her legs alright? It must have been obvious because pretty soon she said, "In case you're wondering, black stockings are in style." I soon found out her legs were fine, and she looked great in a miniskirt. She was a strong woman; she was making it on her own with two young sons after two bad marriages. She did writing, photography, and artwork for a newspaper in Arlington, and she was an artist besides. It didn't bother either of us that I was forty-seven and she was only twenty-nine, and I didn't care that she wasn't a baseball fan.

The Rangers played at night so we met a few times for lunch; once we had a picnic by a lake. Just when I was starting to think this might turn into something, Lin said she couldn't see me any more. She had met a guy earlier in the summer and had to decide what to do about him. They had a whirlwind romance and within a week he had bought her an engagement ring. She hadn't said yes, but he was wealthy and he took her to fancy places and treated her better than anyone else ever had, so she hadn't said no. She was going to spend some time with him out of town to see how she felt. Before long she realized there wasn't enough between them and she didn't want to marry for money, so she came home. But meanwhile, I had started dating a nurse, so for a few weeks Lin and I didn't see each other at all. Then one day the Chamber of Commerce threw a big picnic for the team, and Lin's newspaper asked her to go. I was there with the nurse, but when I saw Lin and her sons across the way I went over to

Lin was not a baseball fan before she met Wayne in 1972, as he was ending his first stint as a coach for the new Texas Rangers. They returned to her native Texas when he rejoined the Rangers from 1981 to 1985.

Wayne Terwilliger personal collection

talk. The nurse must have found her own way home, because I left the picnic with Lin and the boys and we saw each other every day through the rest of the summer.

I had bought my dad's bar before he died in 1969, and my mother was living in the front apartment on the second floor. When I went back to Michigan in mid-October, I moved into the apartment at the back, with a refrigerator and a bed and not much else. Lin and I wrote one another, and as Lin says, our letters got "hot and heavy." I even sent rhymers that were romantic and a little racy. Mary Jane and I had not yet sorted out our divorce, but Lin and I needed to figure out whether we had a future. In early November she flew to Charlotte for a few days and we talked it out. After years of struggle, Lin was enjoying life; she loved her job, her boys Mike and Kevin were having a great time in their schools, and she had lots of family around her. She hadn't gone looking for any big changes, including marriage. But we wanted to be together. I asked her, would you be willing to move here? Within a couple of weeks she quit her job, sold most of her furniture, and pulled the boys out of school. She packed the boys and a cat into a Kharman Ghia convertible, piled all their stuff in a little U-Haul trailer hitched on behind, and drove from Fort Worth to Charlotte. I was tending bar one day when they showed up at the door, and I thought, "Oh, geez, I hope this works."

I rented a tiny apartment for Lin and the boys, although we could hardly afford it. She worked part-time for a local newspaper and helped me tend bar. We weren't sure what kind of welcome she would get. My mother and sister treated her well; my kids had a harder time. They never had enough of my attention growing up, and now they saw me smiling and laughing with Lin and her boys. My son Steve was fourteen and playing three sports in high school, just as I had. We went to all his games, but it wasn't the same for him as it had been for me growing up, and we both missed out because of that. Marcie, at twenty, hit it off with Lin because they were both artists, but for a time both Steve and Marcie blamed Lin for breaking up our family. Eventually, they came to understand that it was my doings that broke up my first marriage, and not anything Lin had done.

With all this going on, I still needed a job for the baseball season. Fortunately the Houston Astros called me to manage their Double A club at Columbus, Georgia, in the Southern League. On the way to spring training, I stopped in Columbus and took part in a press conference at the Chamber of Commerce headquarters. People seemed surprised by the Van Dyke beard and long hair I had grown over the winter. I assured them I wasn't some kind of hippie freak and I promised to shave and cut my hair. I said I didn't know much about the team's prospects yet, but I *promised* it would be fun to watch.

I was back in the bus leagues, but happy to be managing again. I had learned from Ted Williams how much you could help a player by boosting his confidence, so when I talked to a player about a mistake he'd made, I tried to let him know I was confident he wouldn't make it again. The players appreciated my approach. Apparently the previous year's manager had been kind of a jerk, and the returning players said I made them want to show up and play.

> *Texas Ranger outfielder Elliott Maddox was so right when he described Wayne Terwilliger as a pepperpot. . . . The former Ranger coach sprints to the coaching box before every inning and has his pitchers running off the mound and relievers running in from the bullpen. It's an innovation baseball ought to copy from top to bottom.*
> —*Richard Hyatt, Columbus (Georgia)* Sunday Ledger-Enquirer, *May 6, 1973*

We won our first eight exhibition games, and the sports writers started using the word "pennant." I wasn't so sure. We had good pitching and I thought our hitting would come together, but we were inexperienced. The two guys playing shortstop had no experience at that position and our third baseman served National Guard duty every few weekends.

Our first win of the season came in a six-hour, twenty-three-inning game against the Savannah Braves. Not many fans stayed for the post-game fireworks, which started just before 1 a.m. I missed not only the fireworks but most of the game because I was thrown out in the seventh for arguing with the umpires.

A day or two later, we won our home opener and gave the fans an idea of our speed with five stolen bases. We got three or four key hits from center fielder Al Leaver, a good fielder and base runner who had never batted much more than his weight. I had been working with him, using some of Ted Williams' advice to struggling batters. I was really pleased when I heard Leaver tell a reporter, "I'm choking up on the bat, just trying to meet the ball and go up the middle." Amen.

We were in first place much of the year, but it was a tight race and we ended the season third in the standings. I was disappointed in our 69-70 record. Still, I had promised that Columbus fans would enjoy watching us play, and I kept my word. Management did their part, too, with crowd-pleasing promotional stuff including square dancers, a guy who parachuted into the stadium, a band of cowboy characters who performed skits between innings, and a young lady named Billie Jean who wore "hot pants" and dusted the plate. Even Max Patkin, "The Clown Prince of Baseball," made an appearance. The season was more fun than I'd had in a couple of years.

About halfway through the season the Astros signed pitcher Joe Sambito out of Adelphi University. Joe spent eleven seasons in the majors, and a reporter once asked about his most embarrassing moment. He said it was his first day in pro ball, when he joined the team on the road. Twig, irritated with the team that day, pointedly reminded them of 1 a.m. curfew. Team members told Sambito not to worry because the manager never checked. He did check, and he fined half a dozen players including Sambito $25 each, due on payday. Said Sambito, "I don't think I earned $25 that day and I was already in the hole."

Lin had joined me for a couple of weeks during spring training in Florida (she took the boys out of school, got all their assignments from the teachers, taught them every day and mailed their work back to the school), and after school was out we lived together in Columbus. When we went back to Michigan, we all moved into my place above the bar. We said it was for economic reasons, and I don't remember people giving us too much grief. Mary Jane had filed for the divorce, but for some reason we hadn't made a lot of progress. After a few months Lin told me to get it done or she was going back to Texas. She would have, too. So in December of '73 the divorce was final, and in March of '74 Lin and I got married.

We got back from Georgia in September. We had only recently gotten a liquor license for the tavern and I wanted to see how busi-

Twig enjoyed taking over his dad's bar in Charlotte, Michigan, and managing it in the off-season. When he made it his full-time job, he only lasted a season before he got back into baseball.
Wayne Terwilliger personal collection

ness was doing, so without anybody noticing me, I went in and sat at the end of the bar. The place was crowded, and I thought, "Holy smoke, we're doing pretty good." For about twenty minutes, I watched the young lady tending bar. She was pouring double shots for everybody and charging for singles and giving them a big smile. I said to myself, "Whoa, I don't think this is going to work out." I decided to take off the 1974 season—the only year I've been out of baseball since I signed with the Cubs in 1948—and Lin and I straightened things out. We let the manager go, Marcie worked part-time for us, and we all worked our butts off. My dad had run it as a men-only establishment; when I took it over from him, I put in a women's john and a new tile floor and gave it a baseball theme. With Lin's good design ideas, we duded the place up and meanwhile we tended bar, made chili and hamburgers, washed dishes, and scrubbed floors. The next day we did it all again. We drew good crowds and cleared about $20,000 that year, but it was long hours and hard work and I missed baseball.

I was working at the bar one day when Hal Keller called. By the time I got off the phone, I had a job for the '75 season. Lin and some of our regulars were there, trying to be quiet because they knew I was talking about a job. When I hung up I said, "I'm going to manage Single A ball at Lynchburg, Virginia." Everyone cheered. Lin said they were just glad to see me move on because I was getting grumpy away from baseball. So Hal Keller rescued me twice. When the Yankees fired me in '61, Hal started me on an eleven-year career with the Senators-Rangers organization. In 1975 he brought me back for what turned out to be another eleven years. (We'd had enough of the bar and sold it in 1976.)

The Lynchburg Rangers, in the Carolina League, were a combined club—the Atlanta Braves and the Rangers each furnished half of the players. There was rivalry between the two organizations. Unlike my earliest managing years, when I got little input from the higher-ups, I was hearing from two different sources whose ideas often clashed. No matter what I did, somebody was going to question my moves.

The organizational rivalry extended to the players, and it caused all kinds of conflicts and discipline problems, including a couple of shoving matches in the dugout. I had learned long ago how to deal with pitchers who called their own pitches and runners who went when you told them to stay and who stopped when you told them to go. I had learned that when you do bed check and a guy tells you his roommate is in the shower, you go in and look, and if you find the shower running into an empty tub, you fine the absentee *and* the roommate. I had learned to recognize the smell of marijuana when the Columbus trainer pointed out that players were smoking it on the bus. Usually, those were isolated cases.

But I had more than the usual problems at Lynchburg. One player from the Rangers organization was out of control half the time, off the field and on. Bobby Thompson—not to be confused with Bobby Thomson of the '51 Giants—was a speedy outfielder with some talent, but he was a real pain in the ass and he didn't last long with the organization. Some of the others weren't much better. I chewed them out when I had to, and I benched them when that wasn't enough. One day the Braves' farm director called to say he'd heard I was favoring Texas players. I told him he was wrong, but what he said really pissed me off so I sat down and wrote him a letter, and sent a copy to Hal Keller. I said I treated each player as he deserved, which in some cases meant I had to be more of a baby-sitter than a manager. If that's the kind of guys they were going to send me, that's how I would manage them. When he got my letter, he called to ask for details. At the end of our conversation, he said it sounded like I was doing the right thing. So I got him off my back, but the players' attitudes didn't improve.

Overall, 1975 was a tough season. In the middle of it my mother died. We went home for the funeral and it took a lot for me just to come back and finish the year. We ended up in fourth place both halves of the season—not awful, but not a year I wanted to repeat in any way. I guess the Rangers felt the same, because at the end of the season they ended their association with Lynchburg.

Lin and I loved our next assignment—four years in Asheville, North Carolina, with the Rangers' new Single A club. It's beautiful country—we lived in a round house up in the hills, enjoying the scenery—and the people were friendly. We played good baseball, there was no craziness to deal with like I had in Lynchburg, and for the first time I had a pitching coach. Jeff Scott stayed with me all four years and made a *big* difference in helping our pitchers improve.

The Asheville Tourists had just joined the Western Carolinas League. Our competition the first year consisted of only three teams, all in South Carolina—the Greenwood Braves, the Spartanburg Phillies, and the Charleston Patriots (a Pirates affiliate). (During the time I was there, Charleston was in and out of the league, and new members included Shelby, Gastonia, and Greensboro, all in North Carolina.) Just before the season, they built a new clubhouse at McCormick Field, improved the concession areas and painted the stands red, white, and blue for the Bicentennial.

The Asheville Tourists . . . run almost at will and in almost every situation. . . . "That's our style," explains Terwilliger. "It's exciting for the fans and it wins games. . . . I'm like the football coach who's got the ball on the two-yard line. . . . What do I do, tell 'em not to score?"
—Larry Pope, Asheville Citizen-Times, 1977

I emphasized speed from the very beginning, and it helped us play winning ball even when our pitching or hitting wasn't consistent.

We won nine in a row during spring training in Florida in '76, and with the warm sun and the fresh orange juice, I thought I was in heaven. Reality set in—eight-hour bus rides, rained-out games, injuries—but we led the league most of the first half and clinched the title in late June thanks to a stolen base and a perfect two-out bunt single. We started the second half with eight straight wins, during which it seemed every situation turned out great, so we were really upbeat when we returned home for a huge Fourth of July Bicentennial celebration. We got blanked 10-0. At least the fireworks gave the fans something to celebrate that night.

During that season I was writing a short column—three or four paragraphs—for the local shopper newspaper back in Charlotte. It ran as an ad for the bar, and each week I would say a little something about whatever the Tigers were doing and talk about life with the Asheville Tourists (the ad signed off with "watch the games at Twig's Saloon"). Late in July, I described a really miserable weekend on the road at Charleston, S.C. Friday night we were leading 2-0 in the sixth and it thundered and threatened for two innings, but it never rained, so Charleston rallied to score three in the eighth to beat us. Sunday, they led in the sixth and the skies did open up, so the game was called and we lost again. In between, on Saturday, we scored a run in the top of the tenth to go ahead, only to have them pull it out with two runs in the bottom of the tenth. Somewhere during these games, our left fielder hit a ball over the fence and the umpire ruled it had bounced over, our shortstop got spiked, our catcher was hit by a pitch on the elbow, our right fielder twisted his knee—and the mosquitoes were terrible. In the rainstorm that cancelled Sunday's game, we piled onto our bus to go home and it wouldn't start, so we had to get out and push. I described all this in my column and then said, "Despite all this, the sun came up this morning. Keep smiling." That doesn't sound like the Wayne Terwilliger who was so disagreeable early in his career. I'm sure Lin had a lot to do with it.

We finished the '76 season with an overall record of 76-62; the next year we went 81-58. A big factor in our success was Pat Putnam, a first baseman-outfielder who had become the one bright spot at Lynchburg when we signed him in June out of the University of Southern Alabama. I liked his skills and his attitude right away. At Asheville in '76, he hit .361 and set league records in hits, RBIs, and total bases. The league named him MVP and *Sporting News* named him Minor League Player of the Year. In 1979 he went up to the Rangers, and *Sporting News* named him American League Rookie of the Year. Pat stayed in the majors for eight seasons, mostly with the Rangers, and I was glad to work with him again when I coached there in the early 1980s. In my four years at Asheville I had a handful of other position players who later spent time in the majors. Thanks partly to Jeff Scott's coaching, nine pitchers went on to major-league careers that ranged anywhere from seven innings (Jim Farr and Mark Mercer) to thirteen years (Paul Mirabella and Gene Nelson).

In '78 we had a pair of middle infielders named Vic Mabee and Izzie Gutierrez. Someone would ask, "Izzie?" and someone else would answer, "Mabee." That went on all season in the clubhouse, on the PA, even on the radio. Vic was a funny guy, always thinking up ways to have a little fun. One day he and some of the other players were joking around in the outfield, pretending to be professional wrestlers. There was a metal fence that made a big noise when you hit it, so they were throwing one another against the fence and making loud grunting noises, "Ooof," and they'd all crack up laughing. From this, somebody got the idea of staging a wrestling show before a Sunday afternoon game. Several of the players got decked out with costumes and masks and props—even a dog on a leash—and each "wrestler" made a grand entrance. They really hammed it up, and it was a great show. Vic Mabee had a big hand in planning this event, and of course he was one of the wrestlers. During the match, Vic got punched in the face, and down he went. Pretty soon there was blood all over the mask. Some of the other guys carried him off the field, still in character, while the crowd cheered and laughed. Like the fans, I thought it was all part of the show until I noticed that the blood was real and Vic had a huge split lip. He was so pleased about the success of the show that he never complained about the lip. Vic Mabee, wherever you are, that show was the highlight of the season!

I was "Quasi" and Vic Mabee was "Moto" as a tag team and we were supposed to win that wrestling match until Len Whitehouse ("Blackshack") tagged Vic with an unscheduled left uppercut early in the first round. I can still hear Twig screaming at me as I carried Moto into the locker room.
—Scott Peterson #18, member of the 1977 and '78 Asheville Tourists, e-mail, March 16, 2005

In 1980, I moved up to Double A Tulsa in the Texas League. It was the last year of Tulsa's old ballpark, which was on its way down and almost out. The surface of the field was bad and they didn't do much to fix it because a new ballpark was on the way. The outfield fence had been patched and re-patched, but they had given up long ago and a section in left field had fallen off. In spite of the facilities, the crowds were good and we played well. The first half we were 40 and 27, the best record in franchise history—but still five games out of first. Some of my Asheville players had already moved through Tulsa on their way to the majors, and in 1980 I had eight or nine of them again. As usual, we ran whenever we could; one of my infielders, Nick Capra, led the team with fifty-five stolen bases. Another infielder, Wayne Tolleson, had played football in college; he was quick and had good hands and he became a good switch-hitting infielder for the Rangers and Yankees. I worked with him on the pivot because when he went to his left he took an extra step before throwing the ball.

After the season, I got a call from Joe Klein, who had played first base for me in the early 1960s. He now had Hal Keller's job as the Texas Rangers' farm director. Joe told me that Don Zimmer was going to be the Rangers' new manager and if I wanted, I could be a coach. I called Zimmer and asked him, "What's my assignment?" He said, "I've got you penciled in for the bullpen." If this was going to work, I had to talk him into something more suited to what I could offer. He said Darrell Johnson, his boss at Boston in the mid 1970s, was going to coach at third. I asked, "Is that written in stone?" He said, "No, we'll sort things out during spring training." "I could help you much more at third base than in the bullpen," I told him. "I'm an infielder, I know the game, I've coached third when I managed, and I coached third for Ted Williams. I hope you'll let me show you what I can do." We started spring training with Johnson at third; then one day Zim put me there for a game and left me there. After a few days he said, "You've got the job at third." I missed being the guy in charge, and I didn't have the same leeway at third base that I had under Ted Williams, but there were plenty of positives. The money was better than in the minors, flying beats riding buses, we stayed in better hotels, and after eight years away, Lin was happy to be living back in Texas.

Twig gives a word of advice and a pat on the rear to outfielder and designated hitter Johnny Grubb, as George Brett guards the base.
Used by permission of the Texas Rangers Baseball Club

Don Zimmer was the best manager I ever worked for. He knew the game and how to play it. He was a real positive guy even when things weren't going well, which was often. He always gave the sense that he had things under control and everything was going to work out. Playing in Boston in April, we were going to face young side-armer Dennis Eckersley, who Zimmer had managed there in '78. Eckersley was a heck of a pitcher, but Zimmer walked into our locker room and said, "Bet the farm on today's game, guys. We're going to win this baby, no question. Bet the farm." We knocked Eckersley out of the game in the first inning and beat the Red Sox 16-8. Just like Zim said we would. Once in a while since then I've had that same feeling about a game, and when it happens I'll tell the team, "As Don Zimmer used to say, 'Bet the farm on this one.'"

There were similarities in Zim's and my careers, as far as where we played or managed. We played for the old Saint Paul Saints a year apart, the Dodgers three years apart and the Cubs about ten years apart. He managed the Buffalo Bisons in 1967; I managed there in '68. He managed at Tulsa in 1979; I was there in '80. I always liked Zim as a player, because he was a tough old son-of-a-bitch, and I say that with respect. The fastball in the head that almost killed him early in his career kept him from being quite as good a power hitter as he could have been, but surviving it made him one determined and scrappy guy. And he's the only guy still alive who has been in the game as long as I have.

It didn't take long to see that Zim wasn't getting the support he needed from the Rangers. Both he and general manager Eddie Robinson got a lot of interference from the owner, Eddie Chiles, who was an oilman and not a baseball man. Chiles wanted us coaches to help the players develop performance goals, just like salespeople in his car dealerships. How many hits in the next month, how many runs scored, how many homers, etc. You can imagine how popular this was in the clubhouse. Managers know it's not going to help a player's performance to have him thinking, "I've got to get three hits today" or "I'm a little behind in my quota of runs." We agreed that this little experiment was going to do more harm than good, and pretty soon Zim said to forget it.

Midway through the season, we were leading the league in team batting average and runs scored, and we were winning games. One night we played Milwaukee with a chance to move into first place. We lost. The players went on strike the next day. Winning that game would have put us in the play-offs because the team in first place when the strike began played the team in first place at the end of the season. By the time the strike was over, our bats had cooled off and we ended up far out of the running.

The bosses made a lot of trades over the winter, trying to get more hitting into the lineup. Zim wasn't thrilled with most of the trades, and he was right. We sacrificed some promising pitching and decent fielding, and we didn't get the offense they were looking for. We got off to a terrible start in '82, including a twelve-game losing streak. I didn't help things; I sent a couple of guys and got them thrown out at home. Eventually they fired Robinson as GM, and a week or two later they fired Zim. It was messy, both behind the scenes and in

Twig has spent forty-five years hitting fungoes for infield practice; he does it here for the Texas Rangers. *Used by permission of the Texas Rangers Baseball Club*

public. Zim deserved better. And once he left, most of the fun went out of the job for me.

Right after he fired Zim, Mr. Chiles came into the locker room looking for Darrell Johnson. Chiles didn't know any of us, so he looked around for the names on the lockers. Johnson happened to be standing in front of my locker, so Chiles went up to him and asked, "Wayne, where can I find Darrell Johnson?" When D.J. identified himself, Mr. Chiles said, "You're the manager for the rest of the season."

New manager Doug "The Rooster" Rader introduced many unfamiliar routines to spring training in 1983. Among them, he would smack the same tree every day . . . with his car. Team GM Joe Klein delicately described his prized hire as having a "hint of unsteadiness."
—Roger Edwards, posted on www.stormeyes.org/tornado/rangers/ htm, based on information from Texas Rangers: The Authorized History *by Eric Nadel*

In 1983 Doug Rader became the Rangers' twelfth manager in the twelve years since Ted Williams left. He was a Gold Glove third baseman for the Astros and a hell of a ball player, but too volatile to be a good manager. He often blew up when he didn't like what somebody said or did. Once during a clubhouse meeting he threw a can of Coke that just missed a couple of guys. Another time he brought pitching coach Dick Such into his office and started shouting about some little thing. He got more and more incensed, and all of a sudden he jumped right over his desk so he could shout directly into his face. Dick said it scared the hell out of him. In spring training in '84, Dave Stewart was pitching an exhibition game, and he walked a guy. A player from the other team said something and Dave kind of laughed and turned around and went back to the mound. Rader went nuts and called Stewart all kinds of names in front of everybody. You might understand it if a player was goofing around, but that wasn't the case with Dave, or most of the other guys Doug yelled at.

He did it to me, too. He told me in spring training that he wanted our guys to run more often, so I should put on the hit-and-run when I wanted to. One day outfielder Gary Ward was at bat with a 2-0 count, and I thought, well, that's not a great count, but he should get a good ball to hit. Ward popped it up. When I got to the dugout, I really heard about it. "Why the hell are you putting on a hit-and-run with that horseshit count?" Et cetera. I didn't say anything right then, but I went to Doug's office after the game and said, "What the hell was that all about? You told me you wanted us to hit-and-run." He said, "You don't hit-and-run on two balls." I told him as far as I'm concerned, in baseball you shouldn't rule out possibilities. He said, "You want possibilities? Gary Ward might have hit a home run." "Look," I said, "it's the preseason. If you want to hit-and-run, this is the time to work on it. You don't have to get on me, and you certainly don't have to do it like that." But he still had to have the last word, "You should have known better." He just wasn't my type of manager, or my type of guy. He was there for two seasons, and then in '85 we got off to a 9 and 23 start and he was fired.

Bobby Valentine came in as the manager in the middle of May 1985. After a ten-year playing career with five teams, he'd been a minor-league instructor and then the Mets' third-base coach. He brought a couple of his own guys as coaches, and I figured he'd bring others eventually, but he kept me at third and I supposed he was checking me out. I screwed up during one of the first games we worked together. Valentine told us that first-base coach Art Howe would be giving the signs that day. At some point, out of habit, I looked in at Valentine. It dawned on me too late that I was looking at the wrong guy. Immediately I looked over at Howe, and he was looking up in the air, like Jesus Christ, why look at me now? I didn't make any excuses, and I knew my days were numbered.

Valentine never said much to me, so one day late in the season I decided to ask him about my job. He was standing with one foot on the top step of the dugout like he always did, watching something on the field, and I was standing behind him. I said, "Bobby, I'd like to know whether or not I'm going to be here next year, so I can make some plans." After a very long pause I said, "Just yes or no, that's all." Without looking at me he said, "Well, a bird in the hand is worth two in the bush." I walked down to the other end of the dugout and turned back to see whether he would look in my direction. He never did. I had just turned sixty, an age when a lot of guys are retiring, but I never gave that a thought. I just figured it was time to start job-hunting again.

16

At Home in the Dome

*Coached for Texas Rangers
And Minnesota Twins.
Not much success in Texas, but
With Twins a lot of wins . . .
. . . and a couple of rings, too.*

When I was a kid, I heard the World Series on our living-room radio, and I felt like I was right there. When I was a Dodger in '51, the Series was a sure thing—until I watched it disappear over the left-field wall along with Bobby Thomson's home run. When I signed on as a coach for the Minnesota Twins, the World Series was the far-thest thing from my mind, but we got there twice, and it was a lot like being a kid again.

It was looking like I would manage in the minors in '86, until I got a call from Twins manager Ray Miller. "Dick Such told me you do a good job with infielders," he said. "My infielders are young. They have talent but they need some help adjusting to this level." I told him, "I'm your man." Then Ray said he had promised to talk to a guy in the Dodgers organization about the job. I said, "Don't do that—it's the perfect job for me. I can really help you out." He said, "Don't worry, I'll get back to you soon." True to his word, he talked with the guy from the Dodgers and then called me back and said, "You've got the job." So Lin and I moved to Minnesota and I became infield and first-base coach for the Twins.

I loved Minnesota when I played there in the '50s, and I liked the fact that the Twins were a young team—the players would still be open to advice and I could make a difference. I liked all the coaches, and we worked well together. I had known pitching coach Dick Such and bullpen coach Rick Stelmaszek a long time. Former Twins star Tony Oliva was batting coach. Tom Kelly, who I hadn't known before, was coaching third base after managing in the Twins minor league system.

Over the previous five years or so, the Twins had put together a team of young players with little experience but lots of talent. Many had come up through the Twins' minor league system, including first baseman Kent Hrbek, third baseman Gary Gaetti, shortstop Greg Gagne, catcher Tim Laudner, second baseman Steve Lombardozzi, pitcher Frank Viola, and an outstanding young outfielder named Kirby Puckett. A few, like outfielder Tom Brunansky, were acquired from other teams. And in 1985 pitcher Bert Blyleven, a curve-baller who had started his career with the Twins in the early 1970s, came back.

Working with the infielders was just as much fun as I had hoped. Lombardozzi was in his first season as a regular second baseman, and I worked with him on fundamentals. He had a tendency to rush his throws. He had slow feet but fast hands, so I told him he was quick enough and didn't need to hurry the throws. Gagne was still pretty fresh, too, and they had told me he wasn't getting a good jump on the ball because he squatted way down before every pitch. I assumed that was going to be a problem for Gags until I watched him play. He was getting to the ball and making all the plays just fine. Whatever advice I did give him, I never said a word about him squatting too low. Gaetti at third and Hrbek at first had a little more experience; they both had very good hands and played like veterans.

Blyleven and Viola each had a pretty decent year, but overall the pitching came up short. There was some grumbling about that, because pitching was supposed to be Ray Miller's strong suit. Kirby Puckett had a great year at the plate in '86 but the other big hitters—especially Hrbek and Brunansky—struggled. Overall, things just didn't gel, and in mid-September Miller was fired. Tom Kelly—"TK"—managed for the final few weeks, and we finished sixth in the American League West.

There was talk about hiring a new manager from outside the club, but a lot of us on the staff were pulling for TK to get the job. He had played in the minors for thirteen seasons, and the Twins had brought him up as a first baseman for a couple of months in 1975. He didn't hit well enough, I guess, but he did hit one home run. He knew the game, and the Twins gave him a managing job in the minors. He had worked with most of the young players who came up through the minors, and he had a good relationship with them. He was a good teacher of fundamentals, and he liked an aggressive style of baseball. Even though he was only thirty-six, I thought he would do a good job. I also thought there was a better chance of my staying if TK was manager. He got the job, and I got to stay.

It's still hard to understand how everything could come together so well for the 1987 Twins after the year we'd just had. It didn't happen right away; we started out as a bad team just trying to be better. We never did win many on the road, but we kept finding ways to win at home in the Metrodome. It's a strange place to play. It's built for football, so when it's set up for baseball, most of the fans are far from the field—some facing away from the infield—and giant "baggies" line the outfield walls. The artificial turf we had at that time was tough to play on and pop flies disappeared against the white Teflon dome. By '87, though, the Twins had pretty much figured out how to adjust for all these features, and we won two out of every three home games. Brunansky, Gaetti, Hrbek, and Puckett combined to hit 125 home runs in the Dome in 1987.

Tom Kelly had a sure hand as manager and he got better all year. The guys were getting more experience as a team. Our pitching came together. And a couple of new players—pitcher Jeff Reardon and outfielder Dan Gladden—made big contributions. We already had a team of young players who hustled their butts off, but Gladden added some fire, in the clubhouse and on the field. The players liked to horse around and keep things loose in the clubhouse. Gladden joined in the fun, but he was gritty, intense, and competitive. On the field he always looked like he was mad at the other team. Somebody gave him the nickname "Wrench," and somehow that fit him.

Jeff Reardon, a relief pitcher from the Mets, became our closer. He had a hard time of it at first, but he kept getting better. He didn't have great stuff, but he was a gutsy guy, he worked fast, and he really went after the hitters. When he pitched, his arm dropped down from the side a little and the ball would pretty much stay at that level. When he'd get it in just the right spot, it would ride in a little bit on the hitter. The hitter would swing and miss, making it look like Reardon was throwing really hard. Other times he'd come in with a dinky little curve ball that fooled them. Jeff appreciated the way Kelly handled him. It's not easy being a closer, and sometimes if he had a bad outing, he'd get down on himself. But Kelly would put him back in as soon as he could and Jeff would bounce back.

There was a pivotal moment early in the year in Boston, after a game that Reardon wasn't able to save. TK called a team meeting on the bus. He said among other things that some days the pitchers do well but the hitters don't hit, and some days the hitters do well but the pitchers don't. It was a good talk; he left everybody feeling that we were all in it together. It helped Reardon to get that kind of support from his manager. But more than that, the whole team picked up after that talk. You could see it in the clubhouse. There was still a lot of humor—with Puckett and Hrbek leading the way—but the guys were focused on the game, and their energy would just build. At times I worried that they were getting *too* keyed up, that they might get on the field and lay an egg, but they carried their enthusiasm right into the game. Sometimes I think team chemistry is overrated, but in 1987 we really had it, and it worked for us.

"I've never seen a team get so charged up before a game and then carry it onto the field and play the way they do," Terwilliger said. "It scares me sometimes. I want to tell them to calm down. But they seem to be able to channel it in the right direction."
—*Jim Reeves,* Fort Worth Star-Telegram, *October 17, 1987*

Puckett and Hrbek were well on their way to being fan favorites, and they clearly earned it with their play and their team leadership. But everybody stepped up, and often it was the role-players who made the difference in a game. In late September we were in a tight pennant race with Kansas City, and we were playing them at home. Before the game the guys were talking it up even more than usual in the dugout. Hrbek said, "The guys are really fired up for this one." I hoped that was a good sign. Bert Blyleven started the game, and in the first inning the first two batters got on base, at first and third. The guy on third was Willie Wilson, who was quite a speedster. I was thinking, oh, no, we're in trouble already. The next batter hit a ground ball to Gaetti at third, who fielded the ball and threw it to utility infielder Al Newman at second without ever looking at Wilson. Wilson figured they were going for a double play at first, so he broke for home. But Newman saw Wilson take off, and he threw the ball to catcher Tim Laudner, who tagged Wilson out at the plate. That changed the whole feel of the game. Blyleven took a big deep breath; now he had two out, no runs scored, and a runner at first. He got out of the inning and sailed through the rest of the game. We scored five runs in the bottom of the first and won the game 8-1. I was proud of my infielders. Al Newman's great decision to throw to the plate—because of something he saw out of the corner of his eye—changed the game and maybe the season. A week later, we clinched the division in Texas, finishing two games ahead of Kansas City in the American League West. The party that evening was led by pitcher Steve Carlton, who brought a case of Dom Perignon and charged it to the club.

Our success at home brought out more and more fans, and by the time we started post-season play we had big, enthusiastic crowds at the Dome. We found out that when the place was full, it could be so loud that it actually hurts your ears. I wore ear plugs and even those didn't help much. It was surprising at first; the place was five years old and nobody had ever created that much of a roar. We never got used to it, but we learned to make it work for us. Besides, having all those fans cheering for *you* pumps you up and keeps you going.

We played Detroit—my childhood World Series heroes—for the pennant. This time I wasn't cheering for the Tigers! They had a better overall record, but we had the best home record and we had home-field advantage. We won our first two games at the Dome with screaming fans, good pitching, and timely hitting by Puckett, Brunansky and others. We were 2-0, but we went into Detroit with people saying, "It's over, the Twins can't win on the road." We lost Game 3 on a late-inning home run, so the nay-sayers could say, "I told you so." But I had a good feeling that our team was better than that. I had walking pneumonia and had to watch Game 4 pacing around in a Detroit hotel room. I could see, even on television, how

For a 1992 feature in *Twins Magazine* Twig, then sixty-six, re-created the leap photo taken of him as a Senator (see page 102) nearly forty years earlier . . . *Photo by John Mowers*

much presence and enthusiasm our guys brought onto the field. We came back to win Games 4 and 5, and we were on our way to the World Series!

We were in high spirits flying back to Minnesota. About an hour into the flight, the pilot announced, "People are gathering at home to greet you." I pictured a few hundred fans lined up near the stadium, but he said, "There are 10,000 or 15,000 people in the Dome, waving Homer Hankies." Our wives were aboard and we were happy that they were going to be along for a fan celebration. A little later, the pilot said, "The crowd is growing; there are 20,000 to 25,000 now." When we got on the buses and headed from the airport into downtown Minneapolis, we saw some people along the freeway and up on the overpasses, and by the time we got to the Metrodome, more than 50,000 people were inside waiting for us. We could hear the buzz as we all lined up beyond the gates in right

. . . and laughed at his landing. *Photo by John Mowers*

field, and when they opened the gates and we started walking in, the buzz turned into a roar that just kept growing. By the time we got to the infield, quite a few of the players and wives were choked up. We milled around soaking it all in, and nobody wanted to leave. I don't know who organized that night at the Dome, but it was amazing, and I'm sure those players remember that night as much as the World Series itself.

Our opponent in the Series was the Saint Louis Cardinals, who won the National League pennant in seven games against the Giants. Whitey Herzog, their manager, had them playing "Whitey Ball," emphasizing speed on the bases and everything that goes with it. Once again, we had home-field advantage. In the first two games at the Dome, Frank Viola and Bert Blyleven were just about unhittable and we got plenty of offense including a grand slam by Dan Gladden. We won those games 10-1 and 8-3.

Then we went to Busch Stadium and lost three games. In Game 3 they got to reliever Juan Berenguer and beat us 3-1. In Game 4 their one power hitter, Jack Clark, was out with an injury but they brought in a guy named Tom Lawless, hitting .080, who hit a three-run homer and they beat us 7-2. The next night they stole five bases and beat us 4-2. We came home knowing we had to win two in a row.

We were trailing in Game 6 until designated hitter Don Baylor, who came to us in a trade on September 1, tied it up with a two-run homer. In the bottom of the sixth, Kent Hrbek put us ahead with a huge grand slam; the final score was 11-5. Frank Viola pitched a great Game 7, and we were ahead 4-2 at the end of the eighth when TK sent in Jeff Reardon, who closed it out one, two, three. The last batter hit a little bouncer to Gaetti at third, who threw it perfectly, head high, to Hrbek, and with that the whole team ran onto the infield to celebrate. I stayed in the dugout and congratulated Tom Kelly. I remember hearing that general manager Andy McPhail dropped his head into his hands when Kelly took out Frank Viola, our ace pitcher, after eight great innings. But Kelly had trusted Reardon all season, and Jeff gave us exactly what we needed, three quick outs. The Minnesota Twins—a team of mostly young low-salary guys and a young rookie manager—had just won their first World Series.

Can a baseball team they called ragtag and ragamuffin dine with the royalty? It can, because today it is royalty, the best in major league baseball and the winner of the 1987 World Series, a team everybody in Nevada said had one chance in 150 to win the championship.
—*Jim Klobuchar*, Minneapolis Star-Tribune, *October 26, 1987*

The celebration, the noise, the cameras, the fans . . . I just watched and listened and let it all soak in. When we got into the locker room, everything was covered in plastic and the celebration continued with more noise, more cameras, more media people, and champagne spraying everywhere. Eventually I drifted off with the other coaches and we sat on the floor for a long time, drinking Canadian beer and trying to make ourselves believe it. "Fantastic," somebody would say. "Amazing." The word that came up most often was "unbelievable."

Two days after we won, there was a huge parade through the streets of downtown Minneapolis and downtown Saint Paul, and a rally at the State Capitol in Saint Paul. We were in open convertibles moving very slowly through the streets. The fans were packed in, practically up against the cars, and the police were pushing people back to clear the way for us. In downtown Minneapolis I looked up and saw people bunched together in office windows and overhead skyways. I picked out a guy in a window and made eye contact, and without thinking about it, I gave a little thumbs-up. He brightened up and waved back. So I picked out somebody else and the same thing happened. I looked at a group of people on the street and put up both hands with my thumbs up, and they all did the same. On the freeway between Minneapolis and Saint Paul, people were sitting and standing on the banks and crowded onto the overpasses. We were moving faster but the double thumbs-up still worked.

My two favorite moments of the Series were the grand slams by Gladden in Game 1 and Hrbek in Game 6. Gladden's, in the fourth inning, really got us going. If anyone had doubts about our hitting, that home run answered them. It got the fans on their feet, and the noise in the Dome registered about the same as a jet engine when a plane takes off. It was so exciting that when Dan came around first base, I accidentally gave him a high-five. The high-five was a fairly new thing in baseball, and I thought it was too showy. When somebody scores a run shake his hand, don't high-five him just because he did his job. The guys were always kidding me, holding their hands in the air, and I'd say, "No way. Shake my hand the way you're supposed to."

When Gladden hit that ball, I wasn't sure it would go out. I watched it all the way, and when it went over the fence, without thinking I raised my right hand in a fist to say, "Yes! Home run!" Even that is something I wouldn't usually do, but this was *big*. Just as I raised my hand, Dan was reaching first base. He reached up and slapped my fist, hard, and I thought, "Oh, no, that was pretty close to a high-five." He still likes to tell people he gave me my first high-five. If there was ever a time when a high-five was appropriate, this was it.

Kent Hrbek's homer in Game 6 sent chills down my spine. This was a game we had to win, and it was still tied in the sixth inning. He hadn't had a big hit in the series, and he hadn't been able to do anything against left-handers. He came to the plate against left-handed reliever Ken Dayley and boom—a huge shot to dead center. He knew immediately that it was out. He came around first with his arm extended, and he ran the rest of the way with both arms in the air. His hit broke the game open, and the fans sent the noise level higher than ever, cheering a great guy playing in the World Series in his hometown. It has been reported that as he ran, I was yelling and jumping around in the coach's box, but I only remember that it was a special thrill watching him go around the bases.

Twig has long been special to Charlotte residents and, as a coach with the Minnesota Twins, his dream was finally realized when the Twins won the World Series this fall. . . . The Charlotte Chamber of Commerce is sponsoring a dinner to honor Twig . . . tickets are available at $20 per person.
—*Lois Smith,* Charlotte Republican Tribune, *November 1987*

In 1988 we set an attendance record, drawing over three million fans. Most of the club stayed together, but the Twins made one trade that really fizzled. A few weeks into the season, they sent outfielder Tom Brunansky to the Cardinals in exchange for second baseman Tommy Herr. Lombardozzi, our second baseman, wasn't hitting well, and on paper Herr looked promising enough. He was a pretty good hitter for Saint Louis, and he and shortstop Ozzie Smith were a great double-play combination. But with us, Herr became one of those guys who try to make everything in the field look easy. Sometimes it isn't easy, and it takes a little extra to make the play, which he didn't do often enough. He wasn't a bad guy, but he didn't fit in with our team. He used to run around bare-assed in the locker room, and when he'd get a telephone call, he'd have one hand holding the phone and the other hand on his privates. When he wasn't around, one of the players would say, "Player quiz!" and put one hand up to his ear and the other on his crotch and get a big laugh. After the season, Herr was gone and the team continued to look for a second baseman.

In spite of the Herr fiasco, we played pretty well and just missed getting into the post-season. But '89 and '90 were down years, and nothing seemed to help. In 1990 we really hit bottom. We won 74 games, lost 88, and finished last in the division. Nothing seemed to go right—hitting, pitching, fielding, team chemistry, nothing—and we all knew that changes would be made during the off-season.

One big change was Gary Gaetti leaving to play for the Angels. Gaetti was a great third baseman, had a quick bat, and was a hard-nosed player. He was part of the group that came up through the minors together, and he was always right in the middle of the action. Gaetti and Hrbek were good friends, together all the time. We were all used to them sitting at the back of the bus shooting the breeze— with Gary sneaking a smoke now and then. Then late in the 1988 season, Gary tore some cartilage in his knee. While he was out he became religious, and his personality changed. No smoking, no swearing, no bantering with the others; instead he would go off by himself and read the Bible. Before long, he and Hrbek weren't as close, and there was tension between Gaetti and the rest of the team. For the next two seasons, he seemed to have things other than baseball on his mind and it showed in his performance. Even then, TK believed in him and the Twins tried to keep him, but the Angels offered him a lot of money. Gary once told me in the off-season, "Gee, Twig, I already have all the money I'll ever need," but he wanted to keep playing and welcomed a fresh start, so he took their offer.

For a while it felt like a big part of the team was missing, but we still had several players from the '87 team—Hrbek, Puckett, Gagne, Gladden, Larkin, Newman, and Bush—and some new players arrived to stir things up.

Kelly put together a great new combination at third. One was Yankees veteran Mike Pagliarulo, a left-handed hitter who the higher-ups hadn't really wanted to sign. TK believed Pags could help us win and fought hard to get him. The other was right-handed Scott Leius, a rookie backup shortstop in 1990 who learned to play third during spring training in '91. The two of them platooned all year, and they more than made up for the loss of Gaetti.

At second, we had a twenty-two-year-old rookie named Chuck Knoblauch, a first-round draft choice just up from Double A ball. The Twins thought he had a lot of promise, but he was a shortstop and we needed him at second base, where we'd had problems ever since Tommy Herr. In fall 1990 I went down to the instructional league to work with Chuck, to see whether he could learn the new position. I had made the same transition during college, and I knew from experience that the biggest thing he would have to learn was the double-play pivot. As a shortstop, you can see the runner coming; at second, you often have your back turned. You have to pivot quickly, get the ball off in a hurry, and hopefully protect yourself against the runner. It's hard to do, and some good shortstops who try to move to second never quite make the transition.

Chuck impressed me with his talent and his willingness, and at spring training in '91 my chief responsibility—along with helping Scott Leius learn third base—was to help Chuck become a major-league second baseman. He had talent, he worked hard, he drilled on the fundamentals, and he learned fast. He worked with the other infielders on special plays; for example, he and Gagne practiced a decoy maneuver to make a runner think they had the ball, a play they used a half-dozen times during the season. Chuck had a shaky first game, but with Gagne and Hrbek on either side of him, he gained confidence in a hurry. Our infield had the fewest errors in the league that year. As well as he was playing, Chuck was eager to learn the fine points of the position, and all season he continued to ask me how he could have improved on a particular play.

Shane Mack had joined Gladden and Puckett in the outfield, and we brought in Chili Davis as a designated hitter. Chili had played with San Francisco and California for nine seasons, mostly in the outfield. As a fielder, Chili was a good argument for the designated hitter—when he got into the field for a few plays in a World Series game in Atlanta, it was scary. But he was a hell of a hitter, a club-house leader, and a guy everybody loved. His arrival made as much of a difference as Gladden's made in '87.

The other new player who made a huge difference was Jack Morris, who after fourteen years with the Tigers signed as a free agent in order to play at home in Minnesota. Jack had a temper, but he usually kept pretty quiet, and Hrbek could make him laugh. Jack had been around long enough to know exactly what he needed to do and he gave us confidence in our pitching. He, along with young pitchers Kevin Tapani and Scott Erickson, gave us a lot of wins during the season. Meanwhile, Rick Aguilera had become a terrific closer. He saved games all year to help us win the pennant, and he was just as important in the post-season as Reardon had been in '87.

We knew from the start that we were a better team in '91 than we had been the year before. We were a little worried about our 2-9 start, but we straightened things out and when the season was over we had won twenty-one more games than in 1990—and we clinched the American League-West with seven games to go.

We played Toronto for the American League championship. Our fans cranked up the noise from the start, and in Game 1 it seemed to get to Tom Candiotti, the Blue Jays' starting pitcher, who gave up five runs in a couple of innings. Knoblauch lost a high pop-up against the white roof and the Jays got a rally going, but we pulled out a 5-4 victory, our seventh straight post-season win at home. The next night there wasn't much fan noise because the Jays took an early lead and held on to beat us. In Toronto, Game 3 was tied 2-all until a tenth-inning pinch-hit home run by Pagliarulo, and we took Game 4 on Jack Morris' strong pitching plus a Puckett homer and a couple of RBI base hits. In Game 5, the Jays again got an early lead but we came back with run-scoring hits from Knoblauch, Puckett, and Hrbek. We were going to the Series again.

The American League had been in business since 1901 and never had one team gone from last place one season to first place the next. Until the Twins did it this year. The National League,

though 25 years older, never had seen such a thing either. Until
the Braves did it this year.
—*Jim Caple,* Minneapolis Star-Tribune, *October 19, 1991*

We played the Atlanta Braves in a very tight, *very* exciting Series.
The teams were so evenly matched that three of the seven games
went into extra innings and five were won by a single run. Jack Morris pitched Game 1 at the Dome; we won it 5-2 with the help of a big
three-run round-tripper by Gagne and a huge upper-deck homer by
Hrbek. Knoblauch went 3-for-3 at the plate, and he killed a potential

Getting the 1991 World Series off to a lively start, the Twins' Dan Gladden
upended Atlanta catcher Greg Olson on a slide into home. Gladden was
out, but the Braves were on notice: We're gonna play hard.
Photo by Richard Marshall, Saint Paul Pioneer Press

Atlanta rally in the eighth inning with a great double play. There was also a memorable play when Dan Gladden slid into Atlanta catcher Greg Olson on a play at home. Instead of taking a hook slide, Gladden ran right smack into Olson and knocked him on his head. Olson held onto the ball and Gladden was out, but he made it clear we weren't going to make anything easy for the Braves.

Metrodome noise got us off to a good start in Game 2. Early in the game, Gladden popped up into short right. Outfielder David Justice and second baseman Mark Lemke couldn't hear each other call it, and they collided. Gladden made it to second on the error, and with two out Chili Davis hit a home run. The play Minnesotans still chuckle about happened in the top of the third when Ron Gant rounded first and then returned to the base as Hrbek was taking the relay. Hrbek somehow caught his hand under Gant's leg and lifted it up, throwing Gant off balance and off the bag. Instantly, Hrbek tagged him out. The umpires said Gant's own momentum carried him past the base, although the replay looks like he had a little help from Hrbek. Manager Bobby Cox was livid, and he stayed that way because Scott Leius homered in the eighth to win the game 3-2. Hrbek said later, with a straight face, that he didn't know how it happened.

In Atlanta for Game 3, we didn't have the designated hitter. TK had said that wouldn't be a problem, but he wasn't counting on extra innings. In the top of the twelfth, we had the bases loaded and nobody left on the bench, so TK had to send Rick Aguilera to the plate. Aggie flied out and the Braves scored in the bottom of the inning to win it 5-4. They won the next night, 3-2, with a ninth-inning RBI. In Game 5, they came out swinging and won a lopsided 14-5 victory.

Twins fans back home were tired of seeing Ted Turner and Jane Fonda on their TV screens and tired of watching the Braves fans' "tomahawk chop," and they showed up for Game 6 ready to raise the roof. We scored two runs in the first inning, but it stayed close and we got to the eleventh still tied 3-3. In the bottom of the eleventh, Atlanta brought in starter Charlie Liebrandt to pitch to Puckett. Kirby—who had already singled, tripled, driven in a couple of runs, and made a leaping run-saving catch against the fence—sent a ball over the left-field wall. Once again, the fans went crazy. Announcing the game on TV, Jack Buck said, "And we'll see you tomorrow night."

Game 7 was a classic pitchers' duel, with twenty-four-year-old John Smoltz up against thirty-six-year-old Jack Morris. Through seven innings, the pitchers dominated and the tension grew. It was clear that one run might be enough to win the game, and the Series. In the eighth, Morris gave up a single to Atlanta's Lonnie Smith. Terry Pendleton doubled to left, and Smith took off running. Everybody in the place could see he was going to score. But as Smith neared second, Knoblauch got down on one knee and *pretended* to field a ground ball and toss it to Gagne, who came running across second—just as they had practiced. They were so convincing that Smith, playing in his fourth World Series, slowed down. By the time he figured out that Knoblauch never had the ball, Gladden was fielding it in the outfield and Smith could only make it to third. A groundout and a double play later, Morris was out of the inning. The Twins loaded the bases in the bottom of the eighth but didn't score either. Smoltz was gone by the end of the eighth, but Morris refused to come out, and he continued to pitch scoreless baseball.

In the bottom of the tenth, Gladden doubled and then moved to third on a sacrifice. Atlanta walked a couple of guys intentionally, and TK sent in Gene Larkin as a pinch hitter. The outfield was drawn in, and Gene's long fly ball with one out brought Gladden home. All eyes went to Gladden. Morris had come running out of the dugout to escort him to home plate, and the two of them pushed their way through celebrating teammates so Gladden could stomp on home plate. Meanwhile, Larkin came trotting to first, where I was waiting to shake his hand. He ignored my hand and gave me a big bear hug instead. His pinch single at 11:01 p.m. on that Sunday night won the Twins' second World Series.

What would it have taken to get Morris out of the game? "Probably a shotgun," Twins manager Tom Kelly said. "I thought nine innings was enough. He said, 'T.K., I'm fine, I'm fine' . . . Dick Such said, 'he's fine, let him go.' I said, 'what the heck, it's just a game.'"
—*Claire Smith,* New York Times, *October 28, 1991*

There was the usual celebration—guys poured onto the field, hugged, took a victory lap around the field to thank the fans, sprayed and guzzled champagne in the locker room. The fans stayed in the stands, cheering and dancing and singing, until midnight. But it had been such a long and intense game, at the end of a long and intense Series, that we were all drained. It showed on the players' faces. I was exhausted too, and at some point I went into the trainer's room. There was Dan Gladden, lying on a table watching TV. "There's just too much excitement out there," he said. I stretched out on the next table and we both watched the rest of the celebration on television, quietly enjoying our beer.

At the end of the season, quite a few Twins won various honors and awards. TK was voted American League Manager of the Year, Puckett earned his fifth Gold Glove and was MVP of the ALCS, Jack Morris was MVP of the World Series, Chili Davis was the league's outstanding designated hitter, Randy Bush was the best pinch hitter, general manager Andy McPhail was Executive of the Year, and *USA Today* voted me the league's best first-base coach. (I give Kent Hrbek credit for that. Whenever an inning ended and Herbie was on base, I'd go to get his batting helmet to take it into the dugout. He'd always flip it in the air and I'd take off running to catch it. Sometimes I really had to turn on the afterburners, or make a tough low catch, but I always managed to get to it. I figure somebody in the media noticed that.)

Best of all, Chuck Knoblauch was voted Rookie of the Year. He hit .281 during the regular season, .350 in the ALCS and .308 in the Series. At the plate he was good with the hit-and-run all season, and he stole twenty-five bases, more than anyone else on the team. I wasn't responsible for his hitting, of course, but I like to think I helped him become a solid second baseman and a good base runner. Hrbek commented that Chuck never really played like a rookie. I thought Chuck was going to be another Roberto Alomar, who I consider one of the all-time great second basemen. He did go on to be a four-time All-Star and 1997 Gold Glove winner. I was proud of his success. He has always said he appreciated my help.

Chuck and I always worked together pretty well, but after he had been around a while, he started to change; he seemed angry a lot of the time and he could be rude and nasty. I'd just say, "Don't talk that

In December 1991, the world champion Minnesota Twins hosted a holiday party for the Minneapolis Boys and Girls Clubs at Cafesjian's Carousel in Saint Paul. A nonprofit group founded by Nancy Peterson and Peter Boehm rescued the antique carousel from being auctioned to collectors in 1988, operates the carousel as a community attraction, and donated the use of the carousel for the party. From left are Gene Larkin, Willie Banks, Peter Boehm, Lenny Webster, Rick Aguilera, Kirby Puckett, and Twig, who met his co-authors for the first time that evening and then again when he joined the Saint Paul Saints. *Photo courtesy of the Minnesota Twins*

way to me," and he would settle down, but it didn't work that way with everybody. After I left the Twins I heard stories about how he was acting—like what we used to call a "red-ass" guy—and I was disappointed. I don't know what was going through his head, although I do know that eventually he just wanted to get away from Minnesota.

Chuck made a good move financially by going to the Yankees. But there was a lot of pressure there, and something happened to his ability to throw. People started asking me what happened to his arm. If I could have answered that, I'd have been sitting in George Steinbrenner's office with a fat contract in my pocket. I did have an idea, though. As soon as he started having problems, I'd have dropped him down to a side-arm throw, which gives you more accuracy than the three-quarters throw he was using. And I'd have said throw the ball *hard*, don't try to baby it over there. I wanted to help him, and I almost called one time. But then I figured that between Don Zimmer and everybody else on the Yankees' staff, they probably didn't need any help from me. Maybe I should have called, because the Yankees never did solve Chuck's problem.

"Twig has meant everything to me," said second baseman Chuck Knoblauch. "From the first day I met him, I had 100 percent respect for him, from the time I met him in instructional league. . . . He not only has a great knowledge of the game, he's played the game, and he knows what we go through. He's very good at what he does."
—*Jim Souhan,* Minneapolis Star Tribune, *August 11, 1994*

Tom Kelly believed in letting the players enjoy themselves, and the locker room was a fun place to be. Many of the players were there the whole time I was, or nearly the whole time, and I got to be closer with them than with any other team I coached or managed. They started calling me the entertainment director because I introduced them to Fantasy Football and a card game called Casino, which we played mostly on the road.

They liked to kid around with me, too. One day Hrbek was playing catch with a football on the field, and I went out and intercepted the ball. He took off after me until I ran out of gas and he caught me and held me upside down. After that, any time I saw him playing catch I ran out and grabbed the ball, got chased, and found myself upside down. I joined in touch football once in a while during the off-season, but one day I ended up under a pile of guys with somebody's knee just grazing my head. It threw a scare into me—if it had hit me squarely, it could have broken my neck. That was my last football game.

Lin and I had a house on Lake Minnetonka, and sometimes I'd invite one of the guys to go fishing. Hrbek loved fishing and I knew he had a much fancier boat, but we went out in my little old rowboat and caught some northerns and had a good time. Kirby came out

Ice fishing was too cold for Chuck Knoblauch and not productive enough for Kirby Puckett, but for Twig and his son Steve, it's a great way to spend a winter day. Steve photographed his dad with a nine-pound northern.

Wayne Terwilliger personal collection

once, and after we got out on the lake, I asked whether he had a fishing license. He told me he didn't need one. I said, "Of course you do. Everybody does." He said, "Nobody will stop me." I knew people idolized him, but I wasn't about to take the chance. The bait shop was nearby, and I rowed him up to the dock and said, "Go get a license." He did. A while later we were sitting in a spot fishing for crappies and a guy going by in another boat said, "Hey, Al, how you doing." It was ironic. Here's a guy who believes he doesn't have to follow the rules because he's so famous—and some of the time he didn't have to—and then he gets mistaken for Al Newman! Kirby came out winter fishing, too, just to see what it was like. I had warned him to bundle up. When he got out of his car he was wearing enough clothes for two people. We went out on the ice and stayed quite a while. We caught two little fish and he said, "That's the end of my ice fishing." It wasn't so much the cold that got to him—he grew up in Chicago, after all—but he wasn't going to waste his time for so little success.

Kirby Puckett is one of my baseball heroes, right along with Jackie Robinson, Willie Mays, and Ted Williams. Kirby contributed a lot to the game of baseball. To start with, he was a great player who ran out every ball, hustled on every play, made the game exciting. He was also very smart about the game. He understood what pitchers were trying to do to him, and it helped him become a better hitter. Some fireballer would throw two neck-high fastballs; Puck would swing and miss them by a foot. But he knew they would go up the ladder. The pitcher would throw again, two or three inches higher than the first two, and Puck would hit it off the big blue baggie in right field. The pitcher would shake his head, and the catcher would wonder what happened. What happened was that Puck knew what was coming and was ready for it.

Kirby was also a major presence in our locker room. He could sense the mood in the clubhouse and he, along with Hrbek, would manage to get the whole team fired up. I can still hear him walking into the clubhouse and saying, "Jump on, boys, I'll carry you tonight." He was a real help to the younger guys, offering encouragement and advice. More than anybody else I knew, Kirby was always in a good mood. For nine years, my locker was directly next to his. I marveled at how he could stay upbeat, no matter what. His legs took a beating on the turf and he was hurting sometimes, but he'd jump into the whirlpool a while and then get out and say, "Okay, I'm ready to go." There was something about his personality that fans couldn't resist, and when it was time to renegotiate his contract, fan response seemed to be "pay him whatever it takes to keep him in Minnesota." He might have made more money in a bigger market, but in Minnesota everybody loved him, and he chose to stay until glaucoma suddenly ended his career in 1996.

When the news came out a couple of years ago about his troubled marriage—his infidelity and violence and all the rest—I couldn't believe it. All I knew about Kirby was that he was a cheerful guy who played the game of baseball right and that he was a good friend and a great teammate. I was so sad when I heard about his recent death from a stroke at age forty-five.

"By his example," [Andy] MacPhail says, "Twig shows the guys that baseball is something to make the most of, to enjoy, to give 100 percent to, game in and game out. His presence reminds them how lucky they are every day they put on that uniform."
—William Swanson, Twins Magazine, June 1992

The first few years that I worked with Tom Kelly we were fairly close, but we drifted away from that relationship. I respected his managing and the way he treated the players, but as the years went by he talked to me less and less, and when he did say something, it often sounded like a put-down. He had told all the coaches when he became manager that he wanted our honest feedback, and I always gave it. But I started thinking maybe I was speaking up more than the other coaches and maybe TK didn't really want that. Finally I went to him one day and said, "Okay, what's going on?" He gave me an I-don't-know-what-you're-talking-about response, but I could see that he did know, so I decided to press it. "It's like I can't do anything right. You always have something to say about what I'm doing wrong. Tell me what's bothering you." He tried to laugh it off, but at least I had gotten it into the open, and after that we got along better for a while.

There were some changes in the coaching staff—Tony Oliva became the team's Latin connection, Rick Renick became our hitting

He doesn't seem to be wearing a World Series ring, but Twig poses next to the 1991 trophy. Little-known fact: officially "The Commissioner's Trophy," it is major sports' only such award not named after an individual. A new one is created each year. *Wayne Terwilliger personal collection*

coach and then was replaced by Terry Crowley, and Ron Gardenhire came in as third-base coach. I supposed something could happen to me, but I felt pretty good about my situation.

After the great Series in '91, we should have won it all again in '92. We were having a good season, we had great attendance, and we were in first place for quite a while. But at the end of July there was a home game against Oakland in which a rookie outfielder named Eric Fox hit a ninth-inning home run off Aguilera to win it, and that seemed to be a turning point. We started to slide, we went 12 and 17 for August, and we ended up in second place behind Oakland. Then in '93 and '94 we knew pretty early both years that there wouldn't be a post-season for us.

Just after the '93 season, I had a talk with Andy MacPhail, the Twins' general manager. He told me they had a guy named Scott Ullger in their minor-league system who they wanted to keep in the organization, maybe to make him the Twins' manager some day. They didn't think he was quite ready for the majors, but if he got an offer from another team they would counter by bringing him up to the major-league club. That would mean I'd be gone. He could have offered to find me another spot somewhere in the organization, but he didn't. "That pisses me off," I told him. He fired back that my response pissed *him* off. I said, "Do you mean to tell me I have to spend the off-season not knowing whether I have a job?" He answered, "Do you want me to make that decision right now?" I wasn't ready to give up my paycheck just yet, so I said, "Whoa, take it easy now," and he calmed down. Andy MacPhail is a great baseball guy, no question about it, and he had treated me well in the past. But given the job I was doing, I thought it could have been handled better.

As it turned out, Ullger didn't get another offer that year, so I was back in '94. But it wasn't the same. I knew I was a lame-duck coach and so did the players. I knew the Twins would want to bring Ullger in before long. And Kelly definitely wasn't including me the way he had—instead of asking me to work with the infielders, which was my job, he'd get somebody else to do it. The '94 season didn't go well for us anyway, and it came to a premature end because of the players' strike.

At some point the Twins let it be known that I'd be "retiring," and on August 10, the last day before the strike, the players and coaches presented me with a very nice boat. They had told me there would be a pregame ceremony honoring radio announcer John Gordon, who had been out because of back surgery. But instead, they hauled this fishing boat onto the field and started talking about me. It took a while for it to register. Somebody had to shove me forward so I could accept the rod and reel and the tackle box they were holding out toward me. I was truly surprised. When they handed me the microphone, I mumbled something about filling the boat full of bluegills before it snows. It meant a lot to get this from the team, and I'm sure Herbie and Puck had a lot to do with it. They obviously knew what I needed! But I didn't want people to think I was planning to retire and spend my time fishing. I didn't know whether anybody would hire me, but there was no question I wanted to stay in the game. I was only sixty-nine, and I felt great.

I had been with the Twins for nine years, longer than any other team I ever played with or coached for, and I left with a bad taste in my mouth. But I also left with a lot of great memories.

> *Wayne "Twig" Terwilliger, so shoddily dismissed from the Twins after helping them win two world championships, was finally going to get his day on the field at the Metrodome. "I don't know why they're doing this for me," Twig said, "except that I've been riding buses for forty-eight years. Maybe if I do it another ten, they'll put me in the Hall of Fame."*
> *—Neal Karlen,* Slouching Toward Fargo, *Perennial/Harper-Collins, 1999*

For a while I didn't go back to the Metrodome. Then in 1996 they invited me for a special event before the game where they were going to give me a painting of me in my major-league uniforms. I wasn't going to go, but my new boss, Mike Veeck, said I'd be glad if I did, and he was right. Lin and I were walking toward the field when Puckett came out of the locker room. He wanted me to go in, but I didn't think that would be right, so he called Knoblauch and others out. It was great to see them again, and it was nice to take a bow on the field. I don't hold any grudges any more. I got a break by joining the Twins in the first place, and I had a great time. I'll never be able to thank the players enough for the thrills they gave me, and for the two World Series rings.

17

We Needed the Pants

A Saint in 1952,
Again in '95.
Eight years in "tailgate heaven";
Tough to say good-bye.

In 1992 when Kirby Puckett became a free agent, Minnesota Twins fans came up with bumper stickers that said, "Sign Kirby." Two years later when the Twins announced that I was "retiring," a couple of fans of the Saint Paul Saints made buttons reading, "Sign Twig in '95." They gave the buttons to Saints owners Marv Goldklang and Mike Veeck—who says he had already thought of the idea—and I found myself at lunch with Mike discussing a new job.

These were not the same Saint Paul Saints I'd played for in the American Association in 1952. The new Saints were part of the independent Northern League, established in 1993. They were an instant success. The team was promoted as "Rebel Baseball"—a contrast to the big egos, huge salaries, and high prices of the major leagues. The Saints played in the 6,300-seat Midway Stadium, where trains rumbled past the outfield fence several times each night. Fans loved the chance to watch baseball outside on a long Minnesota summer evening. The public address announcer would comment on a dramatic sunset or the Minneapolis skyline or a moon rising over the right field wall or a passing helicopter ("high chopper over the mound"). He didn't have to add that none of these could be seen

Button created and distributed by
Peter Boehm, late August 1994.
Photo by Nancy Peterson

from inside the Metrodome which, when the noise isn't cranked up
for a play-off game, is a pretty sterile place to watch baseball. The
Metrodome has luxury boxes; Midway Stadium has a hot tub and a
"ship" that used to be a parade float, both just above the left field
fence. The Saints' "owners' box" consists of four folding chairs on a
concrete pad just behind a chain-link gate—the same gate where fans
and staff involved in between-inning entertainment enter and leave
the field.

From the start the Saints drew national and international publicity
for their nonstop promotions, which helped bring in people who
weren't already baseball fans, kept people entertained and—especially in the early years—often poked fun at big-league baseball.
Every half-inning there were tire races or dizzy bat races or fans
wrestling in sumo suits or mimes re-creating key plays. There were
giveaways at nearly every game—seat cushions or rain ponchos or
coffee mugs or backpacks. There were theme nights like Halloween
or Saint Patrick's Day or Back to the '70s for which even the fans
dressed up. Many of the contests, themes, and giveaways changed
from season to season, but some were trademarks that may go on as
long as there is a team—things like a pig carrying balls out to the
umpire, a nun giving massages in the stands, and a barber cutting
hair just behind the dugout.

Mike Veeck was the man who made the Saints popular. He
dreamed up the promotions, attracted media coverage, invited the
fans to help run the place by giving him their opinions, and made

sure to promote the Saints as *Saint Paul's* team. Mike obviously learned a few things from his father, Bill, who owned a series of major and minor league teams and made a career of finding new ways to bring people to the ballpark and making the experience fun.

When we had lunch together, Mike told me that if the Saints were going to be successful in the long run, they had to build a reputation for playing good baseball. The team had won the league championship in '93, but the league was small and its quality wasn't well known. Several of the original '93 Saints had their contracts picked up by major league organizations and some had moved up pretty quickly to Triple A and the majors, but even then a number of local sports writers refused to believe that the Saints were worth watching, and they said so often. Most of them, of course, wouldn't come to a game to find out.

Mike said he thought my presence could help the team build credibility. People who followed baseball in Minnesota knew me—I had lived in the state and coached with the Twins for nine years, and the two World Series championships had made all of the Twins pretty visible. Besides, having a former major-league player and coach on the staff might help the team sign some of the better players.

Mike told me I could make the job whatever I wanted it to be. "You can coach at home and skip the bus rides if you want," he said. I just looked at him. "Why would I skip the bus rides?" I was sixty-nine but I still felt young. It was a while since I'd done ten-hour bus rides, but if they're part of the job, so be it. I told Mike I would coach home and away. I would throw batting practice, hit fungoes for infield drills, work with players on fielding and base running, and coach first base during the games. He said that would be fine. Then he asked if I would also do some speaking and public appearances around the community. I told him I enjoy doing that; I'm not a regular after-dinner speaker, but I'd make a few remarks and then invite the audience to ask questions. So in November 1994 the Saints held a news conference at Gabe's, a neighborhood bar that had become the "official" hangout for Saints players, staff, and fans, to announce that I was the new first-base coach. That's when I saw the "Sign Twig" buttons for the first time. It was my first chance to find out that Saints fans really went out of their way for the team—something that would make my eight years with the Saints very special.

Over the winter, community relations director Annie Huidekoper started arranging for me to make public appearances on behalf of the Saints. Two or three times a month, I'd go out and speak to a Rotary Club or a school. I'd say a few things about my career and about baseball and about the Saints, and then people would ask questions, usually about the World Series, Kirby Puckett, and Kent Hrbek. Older groups, like the Golden Kiwanis, asked about Ted Williams, Mickey Mantle, the '51 Dodgers, and about my time in the Marines. I enjoyed the speaking, but when major-league spring training time care around, I started to get restless. The Saints' camp didn't open until the middle of May, so to keep busy I went over to Minnetonka High School and helped out their coach, and as a Saints promotion, I spent a Sunday afternoon coaching for an amateur team also called the Saints, in the town of Saint Bonifacius.

"The independent league is an interesting concept," [Terwilliger] said. "There are a lot of players who fall through the cracks of major league organizations, which the Northern League has proven in just two years. If I can help these kids get back on the road to the big leagues, that would be great."
—Mike Augustin, Saint Paul Pioneer Press, *reprinted in the* Saints Souvenir Program, *1995*

Managing in an independent league like the Northern League is a little different from managing for a major league organization. Every team has a certain number of rookies and players with limited experience, and only a few veterans with five years or more in professional ball. You have a real mix—unsigned college players who were hoping to get picked up by an organization, players who were signed but released for some reason and want to prove the "experts" wrong, players who have been in the majors and hope to get back, and those players who just want to keep playing. A manager in an independent league always knows that part of his job is to help players do well and move on, but he is also expected to win.

After Mike Veeck hired me, he asked whether I knew a guy named Marty Scott. I said, "All I know is that he could hit and everybody likes him." The Saints were recruiting Marty as their new manager. I had known him in the Rangers' system, but not well. He played

In a 1995 "Sixty Minutes" interview, Morley Safer asked Twig how baseball had changed in the forty-six years since Twig first played. "Not much outside of the salaries," Twig replied. "You've still got to catch it and throw it." Then he added, "I enjoy the eighth and ninth innings of a close ballgame just like I always did. The old adrenaline starts flowing . . . I get excited. I love it." *Photo courtesy of the Saint Paul Saints*

while I managed, but always on a different team. Then he managed for a couple of years while I was coaching with the Rangers. They made him farm director around the time I moved to the Twins. Well, Marty did a great job for them; the Rangers' system became known as one of the best for developing talent, bringing up guys like Sammy Sosa and Ivan Rodriguez. After eleven years, there was some kind of front-office shakeup and Marty was out of a job. He wasn't sure he wanted to manage again, but he finally agreed to do the job for a year. It was a good choice, for him and for the Saints. Marty was an excellent manager. He knew the game, used his pitchers well, and had the players' respect. With hitting coach Barry Moss, pitching coach Ray Korn, and myself, he had an experienced staff.

The first Northern League Saints team, in '93, had included former Chicago Cubs first baseman Leon "Bull" Durham with his powerful bat, along with ex-Angels first baseman Jim Eppard. A walk-on
third baseman named Kevin Millar would soon be playing first base
for the Marlins—and a dozen years later winning a World Series ring
with the Red Sox. Pitchers Mike Mimbs and Eddie Oropesa, catcher
Frank Charles, and especially shortstop Rev Ordonez all spent some
time in the majors. I figured if we were going to have some talent like
that, it would be a fun year.

Our team in '95 was memorable, not for big names, but because of
the way the team came together. One of Marty's first and best moves
was signing Dan Peltier, an outfielder with the Rangers in '92 and
'93 who was living in the Twin Cities and had already started a successful business career. Dan was a smart and clever guy and a real
leader in the clubhouse. He had a great year with the bat and at first
base, and the next year he was with the Giants for a while as a bench
player. Former Cubs and Rangers outfielder Doug Dascenzo came to
camp with us, but a week into the season the Marlins bought his contract and he was gone. A few days later we signed former Royals'
outfielder Daryl Motley, an intense guy who got a lot of important
hits for us. Center fielder Doug O'Neill had been drafted by the
Expos right out of college in '91, and he was so talented I was sure
he would be in the big leagues soon. I liked several others just
because they played hard and were good guys. Shortstop Greg
D'Alexander had been with the team since '93 and rarely missed a
game. He didn't cover a lot of ground but he had good hands, a good
arm, and he knew how to play the game. Outfielder Terance
"Turbo" Frazier could fly and he was a likeable character besides.
Vince Castaldo didn't have much range at third base, but he was a
big hitter and became the league's Player of the Year. The fans sang
his name to the tune of "Volaré." Cas-tal-do, oh-oh, Vinnie
Castaldo, oh-oh-oh-oh. Joe Biernat, one of my favorites, started out
as a third baseman but moved to second when we needed him there.
The pivot was hard for him at first, but we worked at it and came up
with something that kept him upright while turning two. Carlos
Mota was a great defensive catcher from the Dominican Republic.
We had good pitching, including twenty-eight saves from closer
Bruce Walton, who later became a major league bullpen coach.

Saints first baseman Dan Peltier and teammates celebrate winning the first half of the 1995 season on a one-out Doug O'Neill ninth-inning double against Thunder Bay at Midway Stadium. *Photo courtesy of the Saint Paul Saints*

Our season was a little streaky, but we set a league record with fifty-three wins and we won both halves. When Marty wasn't named league Manager of the Year, the players gave him a plaque of their own. We played the Winnipeg Goldeyes in a best-of-five post-season championship series in early September. We split at home, but we had won at Winnipeg all season. We got excellent pitching, and we beat them two nights in a row. In a way, the celebration reminded me of those after the Twins' World Series wins—the players were excited, our fans were cheering, and we were going to get championship rings. I was glad for Marty, too. On the other hand, only a few dozen fans had made the trip, and we had a ten-hour drive back to Saint Paul. Another few fans would greet us at the stadium, the mayor would greet us at a victory parade, and the all-too-short season would be over until the following May.

Nobody has bounced around major and minor league baseball
quite as much as [Wayne] Terwilliger. Twig, as he is called, was
hired by the Saints after being ignominiously dropped last season
by those soulless fools over in Minneapolis.
—*Morley Safer, CBS Television,* 60 Minutes, *summer 1995*

Marty Scott had some conversations with major league organizations during the off-season, but I was glad when he came back in '96.
So was he, when he found out who would be playing for him. Darryl
Strawberry and Jack Morris, hoping to work their way back into the
majors, had both signed with the Saints. Nobody was sure what to
expect. They were much bigger names than anyone else who had
played in the league, and some people worried that just having them
in the locker room might be a distraction. One was known for his
temper and one for having drug problems, and it had been a lot of
years since either of them had to deal with long bus rides, second-
rate motels, and minor league ballparks. As it turned out, Darryl's
only infraction was sneaking a smoke in the back of the bus once in a
while, Jack toned down his temper, and Marty Scott handled both of
them really well.

Darryl was the best team member you could ask for. Even with all
the success he'd had, he was a humble and hard-working guy. He
showed up on time. He went to the outfield and shagged balls like
everybody else. He stayed mostly to himself at first, but after a few
days he started to relax and mix with his teammates. You could see
that he was having fun. He worked hard every day—nobody put
more effort into warm-ups, batting practice, and all the rest—and at
game time, he was ready to go. With those long legs, he still had
good range in right field and a strong arm. He hit a lot of home runs,
most of them long, high ones that seemed to be still rising when they
left the park.

After every game Darryl would sign autographs until there was
nobody else waiting. I remember watching him in Sioux City one
night. A bunch of kids had lined up after the game and they were following him like the Pied Piper. As he signed autographs, he was saying something to each kid. I think that's important, but a lot of guys
don't do it—heck, there was a time when I didn't do it. When I saw
him handling the kids the way he did, I said to myself, what a break
to get a guy like that on our club.

People sometimes ask Twig what it was like to coach Darryl Strawberry. "Nobody coached Darryl. I think it's fair to say that the coaches just watched him—like the fans did—and we told the players to watch and learn. Then we said, 'Nice job, Darryl.'" *Photo courtesy of the Saint Paul Saints*

> *"Playing in Saint Paul brought back that desire from when you are young and have all that energy and want to play the game,"* Strawberry said. *"I had forgotten those feelings. I had forgotten what it was like to really WANT to play baseball."*
> —*Mike Augustin,* Saint Paul Pioneer Press, *reprinted in Saint Paul Saints Yearbook 1997*

Jack Morris was as competitive as ever. He was just as serious about pitching in the Northern League as when I knew him with the

Twins. On days when he didn't pitch, Jack would talk with the younger pitchers. He told them to be aggressive, throw strikes, go after the hitter, pitch inside. And every time he pitched—even if he gave up a lot of hits, which he sometimes did—our pitchers paid attention. We had a twenty-year-old country boy named Scott Stewart with a great left arm, but not much discipline. Scott didn't like to take advice—which is why he was in the Northern League instead of with the Rangers, who had drafted him out of high school—but he listened to Jack. Maybe that helped him, because about five years later, Stewart was pitching with Montreal and doing pretty well.

On days that Jack pitched, he was a son-of-a-bitch—no worse than with the Twins in '91 and lots better than the reputation he built with the Tigers, but pretty unusual for a Saints team. You didn't talk to him before the game, and once he got on the mound he was all business. Jack helped us win the first-half championship, and he gave us everything he had.

Having Jack and Darryl on the team drew a lot of media from the first day of spring training. After a while, it slowed down to the usual Saints coverage—reporters and photographers from every sort of newspaper, magazine, and television station from New York to Los Angeles to Tokyo coming in to learn what the Saints were all about. Writer Neal Karlen was around all season, taking notes and doing interviews for a book about the Saints. And a big video crew was in our faces with cameras and microphones just about every minute of every day, making a documentary series for FX cable television.

We opened the season in Duluth with a loss, and the next night's game was fogged out—about 30 feet past second base, outfielders disappeared like in that cornfield in the movie *Field of Dreams*. When we did play the second game, Darryl hit a home run that disappeared into what fog was left; somebody measured it as 530 feet. We had two more home runs that night, from Kevin Garner and Marty Neff, and their homers looked like fence-scrapers compared to Strawberry's.

Garner had been drafted in 1987 out of the University of Texas, pretty high in the first round, as a pitcher. He gave up pitching and played outfield and first base, and he seemed to be a good prospect for the majors. By '96 he was mainly a DH. With his tremendous power Kevin could hit a ball out of any park. But he was a little bit late on a good fastball, and I'm sure the scouts noticed that. Still, he worked hard and he was a good team player on and off the field. His teammates liked him, and so did I. Marty Neff had been a good first baseman and solid hitter with the Sioux City Explorers for a couple of seasons, and he looked like a good addition to our team. Some folks had even formed an official Marty Neff Fan Club, and they'd come to the game wearing their fan club shirts and cheering for number 36.

Somehow the team was meshing, superstars and all. We were the defending league champions, but we soon found that the league was more competitive than it had been the year before. Our longest winning streak was four games—which was also our longest losing streak.

At the end of June, we were in first place with two weeks left in the first half of the season. Darryl was playing well, his drug tests were always clean, and his behavior was a model for anyone. He got his reward on July 3, when the Yankees told him they were picking up his contract. The Northern League and the Saints had done exactly what they were supposed to do—give somebody a chance to move up. Like everybody else, I hated to see him go. But I was happy for him, because I liked him, he had worked hard, and it was clear that he still had the talent. When he left Saint Paul, he played a couple of games with the Yankees Triple A team at Columbus and then went right up to New York. At the end of the season, no matter how anyone felt about the Yankees, we were all glad to see Darryl Strawberry back in the big leagues.

Darryl was with the Saints only a little over a month, but he made huge contributions. He hit .432 with 18 home runs and 39 RBIs. He showed a lot of class, helped our level of play, and gave fans all across the league something to remember. Playing with the Saints was a great experience for Darryl, too. He sometimes got heckled on the road, but he didn't have the kind of pressures that he had in New York. He liked the support he got from Marty Scott, on and off the field. He said Marty became like a father to him, and after he went to New York, he called Marty often. Darryl and his wife Charysse both said they had a wonderful experience in Minnesota and if the weather were warmer, they might have stayed. I

Popular with autograph seekers of all ages, Twig signs posters, balls, programs, and other memorabilia, looking each fan in the eye and engaging in conversation. The exception: If he's just washed his hands and is about to eat something, you'll have to wait until he is finished eating.
Photo courtesy of the Saint Paul Saints

was very sad to hear about Darryl's cancer and about his using drugs again.

Jack Morris was getting knocked around more than he had expected to in the Northern League. Unlike Darryl, Jack had not played in '95. In the beginning of the season, his arm tired early. He did get stronger week by week, but at age forty-one, it took longer than he expected and he was getting frustrated.

By July 17 we had lost the lead and were down by a game to the Madison Black Wolf. We were playing them in Saint Paul, in the final game of the first half. We had to beat them to tie for the lead and force a one-game play-off. It was a tight game, and we rallied to win it 3-2 in the ninth on a base hit by Greg D'Alexander. That set up a play-off game with elements of the Dodgers-Giants play-off in 1951 and Game 7 of the World Series in 1991. Plus, there were rumors that put everybody on edge.

Jack Morris pitched the play-off game—in the town where he grew up. He gave up five runs in the first four innings, but then he held Madison to a single run for six more innings. Marty Neff hit a grand slam in the first inning, Madison went ahead, and Kevin Garner tied it up 6-6 with a home run in the eighth. Morris pitched a tough ten innings—just like Game 7 in '91—but finally gave way to closer Paul Romanoli. In the bottom of the twelfth, Saints second baseman Carlton Fleming singled to win the game 7-6.

The win guaranteed that the Saints would go to the post-season again. The fans celebrated, but most of the guys were a little more subdued than usual.

Before the game, Jack Morris had gotten an offer from the Yankees. They intended to bring him up to New York, but first they wanted him to start three games at Columbus. Jack said no, he would only go straight up. He had promised to finish the first half for us, and he had done that. The Yankees weren't going to budge and neither was Jack. He had no other offers, so he decided his career was over. Without a word to anybody, he dressed, packed up whatever he had in the clubhouse, and left.

Meanwhile, Marty Scott had quietly been working on a trade. Our first baseman, Marty Neff, had an attitude that was wearing on everyone, especially the skipper. Neff could hit, but he was had too much hot dog in him and he never really hustled. Scott was willing to deal with Jack Morris being a loner and being grumpy on his pitching days, because he figured Jack had earned it. Marty Neff had not. A trade to get rid of Neff was supposed to happen on the off-day between halves of the season. But our tie with Madison meant we played for the first-half title that day. Marty Scott worked hard to keep the trade a secret, but somehow rumors got out. By game time the Saints still weren't confirming anything, but the whole Madison organization was talking about it—even though the trade didn't involve them. Neff hadn't been playing especially well for a while, but that night he contributed to the win, not only with his grand-slam but also with some good base running. At one point when he reached base, the Black Wolf first baseman asked him, "Why are you playing so hard when you're being traded?"

After the game, Marty Scott retreated to his office, and the rest of the coaches got out as fast as we could. The players dressed and went down the street to Gabe's, where first-half titles had been celebrated in the past with a gathering of coaches, office staff, a few fans, and a free beer or two. This time, the team filed in and sat quietly. The two fans who told me about it later sat at their usual corner table and watched. No staff, no "way to go" banners, no "attaboys," no free beers.

Eventually, Marty Scott drove over to Gabe's, but he wasn't going to celebrate. An FX video crew rode over with him, and on the way he talked about how much he disliked the way this deal was playing out. He believed that getting rid of Neff and his negative attitude would help the team but he had hated having to string him along a whole day, until after the play-off game. Besides, the Explorers would only take Neff if they also got Kevin Garner, and Marty knew Garner would feel that he was being unfairly linked with Neff. Marty went inside the bar, called Marty Neff from the back room where the players were gathered, and told him he'd been traded back to the Sioux City Explorers and was expected to join them the next day. Neff was unhappy, but probably not surprised. Garner took it hard. He told his teammates he was finished with baseball, although in the end he did report to the Explorers. A third player, rookie Dave Konigsmark, was also going, but it was a break for Dave because he would get to play regularly with his new team.

Trading Neff got rid of one headache, but it didn't solve the fact that we were a team without a leader. We brought in former Astros third baseman Chuck Jackson, who injured his ankle badly in one of his first games with us and couldn't recover, and then former Houston and Baltimore first baseman Glenn Davis. Davis played well and got a lot of big hits for us, but nobody was going to fill the gap left by Strawberry and Morris. Marty Scott was doing everything he could to keep the players focused on winning the second half. In late August we still had a chance, and something happened that made believers out of everybody.

On the last Sunday in August we were playing a 5 p.m. game against Thunder Bay. Marty wanted to get the pitching rotation aligned just right for the final series and the play-offs, so he decided to let one of the relievers start this game. He chose Joe Miller, an outfielder who early in the season had started learning to pitch. Joe's dad, a New Jersey police officer, had come to town just a few weeks before and had watched Joe struggle in relief, as he had in most of his pitching appearances. Marty was just hoping Joe would give us four decent innings.

A seasoned baseball man shares a secret with a young fan.
Photo courtesy of the Saint Paul Saints

Our hitters took a lot of pressure off Joe by getting nine runs in the first five innings. He responded with seven perfect innings. He gave up a walk to start the eighth, and another in the ninth, but he never lost his concentration. A second guy got on base in the ninth because of an error, and then with two outs a left-hander named Sean Hearn came up. Hearn was a good hitter, but he hadn't hit Miller all year, and besides, this was Joe Miller's day. Joe threw a hanging slider that Hearn hit right to the first baseman. A one-hop bullet. The first baseman grabbed it and stepped on the base, and Joe Miller's no-hitter was official. Glenn Davis was the first guy out of the dugout, and the whole team celebrated with Joe. A few minutes later, Joe called home and said, "Dad, I made my first start and I threw a no-hitter." His dad was sure he was joking.

We beat Madison in a best-of-five divisional series and swept Fargo in three games for our second straight league championship. We would all—including Darryl Strawberry and Jack Morris—get championship rings (Darryl got two that year; the other was from the Yankees for winning the World Series).

After winning the league championship two years in a row, I was beginning to think Marty Scott was the best manager in baseball, and to expect that we would just keep winning. But in the next few years, the other teams in the league got better and we spun our wheels a little. Still, things were always interesting.

The Madison Black Wolf are taking batting practice, so Wayne Terwilliger is making his customary rounds of the parking lot. . . . He looks as if he were running for mayor. He probably could. "If you'd walked that parking lot like this with the Twins," one 30-something fan says, "they'd still be selling out." —Kevin Sherrington, Dallas Morning News, *reprinted in 1998 Saints yearbook*

In 1997, college player-of-the-year and first-round draft choice J.D. Drew declined to sign with the Phillies because his agent believed he was worth more than they offered. Instead, he played out the season with the Saints so he would be eligible for the draft again in '98. After the first time I pitched batting practice to him, I told my friends, "I've seen the second coming of Mickey Mantle." His smile looked a little like the young Mick, his swing reminded me of Mick, and he had powerful forearms like Mick. He hit like him, too— 18 home runs in 44 games. J.D. took some heckling around the league for holding out, but he always said it was a matter of principle, and it must have been because he signed with us for $750 a month. He didn't hold back, either. Even with all the money that was going to come to him—if he was healthy—he played hard, slid hard, and took chances. He was named Northern League Rookie of the Year for 1997. J.D. was a nice, polite Southern Baptist who didn't smoke, drink, or swear. He moved into an apartment with two or three other guys and slept in a walk-in closet, borrowed an old car from the owner of Gabe's, and ate meals at Gabe's because the players got discounts there. He played with us for a month in '98, too, and would have finished out the season if he hadn't gotten an offer his agent liked. He signed with Saint Louis in early June and by September he was Mark McGwire's teammate, playing for almost $2 million a year.

Ila Borders made the team as a relief pitcher in '97, the first woman to pitch in "men's" professional baseball. She had a nice changeup, but her fastball wasn't fast enough, and she couldn't fool the hitters often enough. Crowds in Saint Paul always cheered for her anyway, and kids lined up to get her to sign their baseball caps. She was very serious and very shy, and all the media and fan attention put a lot of pressure on her. She did better after being traded to Duluth and then Madison, where she was a starting pitcher, and she played a couple more years in other leagues before she retired.

In '97 and '98 we had a talented second baseman named Lamarr Rogers who played the position well, had good hands, and was a smart base runner. Lamarr was a very positive guy and he quickly became a team leader on the Saints. He had played in several organizations, and he was in spring training with the Diamondbacks in 1999 when he collided with another player and injured his head and shoulder, ending his major league hopes. Lamarr was running his own baseball camp and seemed to have a talent for working with players, so in '99 Marty invited him to join the coaching staff. I enjoyed working with him, and when I left, I was glad that he took over my job as first-base coach.

Matt Nokes, the former Tigers and Yankees slugger, spent a couple of years with us as catcher and DH. Matt was a good influence on the team both because of his baseball experience and because he was a nice guy and a family man—he had five kids, some of whom would join us in the dugout. I liked the way he called a game. He'd make the pitchers throw the breaking ball when they were behind in the count. He'd keep sticking down those two fingers, and damned if he didn't convince some of them that they could do it! But his knees were giving him a lot of trouble, so he didn't catch too often. I'll always remember the huge home run he hit to win the division championship in '98. We were tied two games apiece with Thunder Bay, and the fifth game was tied 1-1 in the ninth. The count was full and the next pitch was a fast ball away, but he reached out and sent it high over the right field fence.

One of the team's owners is the actor Bill Murray. Every so often when Bill was in town he would decide to coach either at third base or at first. One night in '97, in the eighth inning against Sioux Falls,

When Saints right fielder Chris Evans married Carey Doar at home plate before the game on July 4, 1998, Twig was on hand—as "bridesmaid" or "witness," depending on one's point of view. Saints manager Marty Scott gave away the bride, and second baseman coach Lamarr Rogers served as best man. *Photo courtesy of the Saint Paul Saints*

Bill decided to wave Lamarr Rogers home instead of stopping him at third. It was a risky call, but Lamarr was able to beat the throw. The Saints had been down 9-2 early in the game, and we rallied to win it 10-9. So from then on, we thought of Bill as being able to inspire a rally. I was surprised to find out that he really was athletic. He was a pretty good hitter, and he had a good strong arm, too—one night when he was about to throw out the first pitch, he decided instead to toss it right over the top of the press box and out into the parking lot. Bill is a funny guy, and he'll do just about anything for a laugh. But most of the time he was there, he was just a regular guy who liked to hang around a ballpark and work out with his two boys and the players.

Other teams around the league—those with which we developed rivalries—often referred to the Saints as "the Yankees of the Northern League." They liked to imply that we violated the salary cap, or that we had unlimited funds to use against them. If we did, I cer-

tainly didn't see it. Midway Stadium had a lot of charm, but by the
time I left Minnesota it was the oldest and one of the smallest in the
league. (Still, it had a lot of charm and if it starts to fall apart, I hope
they put up another one in the same spot.) We rationed batting practice balls and guarded our equipment like anybody else. One day, we
even ran short of uniforms. Early in the 2002 season, I walked into
the locker room and found one of our relief pitchers, Matt Gawer, in
street clothes when everyone else was suited up. Matt—a big guy,
listed at 6-foot-4 and 235—had been roughed up a little in the previous night's game. It wasn't likely that he would be released already,
but I didn't want to risk embarrassing him by asking why he
wasn't dressed. Instead, I went to Barry Moss and asked, "What happened to Gawer? Why isn't he in uniform?" Barry started to laugh.
"We re-signed Richard Bell this afternoon. We want to use him
tonight, but we don't have a uniform that fits. Gawer's in street
clothes because we needed the pants." Even today, when I think
about that story, I have to laugh. It's just the kind of thing that happens in the minor leagues—even to "the Yankees of the Northern
League."

At some point Mike Veeck started to express the Saints' approach
with the slogan "Fun is good." A big part of that philosophy was the
promotions, which sometimes involved the team dressing in special
shirts or caps. For "Saint Patrick's Day" we'd wear bright green caps
or green shirts that said "O'Nokes" or "O'Ruiz" or "O'Terwilliger."
There was a Charlie Brown shirt with zigzag stripes around it. For
some kind of '60s promotion we wore tie-dyed shirts, and some of
the players wore big Afro wigs until just before the anthem. Most of
the players didn't mind the silliness—they appreciated the humor
and realized they would never play in another place with the same
kind of fan support. Sometimes I would take part in a stunt, like
being the guy in the "outhouse" where kids were racing to "deliver
the newspaper." One year a singing cowboy made up a song about
me and sang it at least once every home stand. People wanted me to
smile and wave, but we weren't playing well, so I called a halt to
that.

What really made the Saints special was the involvement of the
fans. On game days, the parking lot would start to fill up two or
three hours before the game. People would bring all kinds of food

and beverages and set up tables and chairs behind their cars for what they call "tailgating." It's an art form, and I've never seen it done with so much enthusiasm anywhere else. I got in the habit of walking around the lot to talk with people and see what they were cooking. There were hot dogs and hamburgers, of course, but also lots of fancier meals—steak, fish, wild game, pasta, chili, you name it. I started to get to know some of the regulars, and before long I had a set of stops to make. One was my friends Peter and Nancy's table, where a few regulars, a couple of coaches, the PA announcer and a changing cast of other guests gathered every night. This group became good friends—they celebrated my birthday every year, brought me gifts of various kinds, listened to my stories, and encouraged me to write this book. But I wasn't out there just to talk to the regulars. I never had to go far; people would recognize me and come over to talk, to get something signed, or to have a picture taken. Sometimes the adults stood back but sent their kids or grandkids to get an autograph. After I would talk to the child a while, the adult would come forward to say hello.

Every year the Saints would sell single-game tickets on a Saturday in April before the season started. I always made a point to be there. Hundreds of people would come out for it. Some of them camped overnight to get a good place in line. Some brought food and made an all-day party of it. The Saints would provide music, and usually doughnuts in the morning and hot dogs around lunchtime. I always got a kick out of driving down Energy Park Drive toward the stadium and seeing all the cars and all the people. I would spend most of the day there talking to folks and looking forward to another season.

> *"The jog [to the first base coach's box] is slower," Terwilliger said, but he takes pride in never walking to and from the box. "I groan like everybody else in the morning when I wake up. By the time I get to the ballpark, I feel pretty good. Coming out to the park . . . does a lot for me."*
> —*Ray Richardson,* Saint Paul Pioneer Press, *June 25, 2001*

In 2001 Marty Scott stopped managing and became an executive vice president of the team. Doug Sisson took the job for a year, and

Northern League umpire Ryan Monteleone gets an earful from Twig in 2002. Because Twig is judicious in deciding which calls to question, fans tend to say, "If Twig is arguing, it must have been a bad call."

Photo courtesy of the Saint Paul Saints

then took a job in the Angels organization. I tried to help the Saints talk Gary Gaetti into being our manager for 2002. He thought about it, especially when I mentioned that he could be a playing manager like Matt Nokes was doing for the Joliet Jackhammers. But instead, Gary decided to be a hitting instructor in another organization. At that point I realized that I would like to try my hand again, but by the time I spoke up, they had already hired someone. Meanwhile, Marty Scott moved to Texas and became president of several teams in a new independent league. Marty came to back Saint Paul for a few days in the winter of 2002, and Lin and I had lunch with him. He talked about his move and half-jokingly mentioned me joining him. Lin told him she would like to move back, mainly to be near her dad, who was struggling with his health. "If we moved, would you really have a job for Wayne?" she asked. Marty said, "Sure, if he's interested." I told him I'd have to think about it. By that same evening I was thinking, "Why not?" Before I knew it, the house had sold, Lin was living in our new house in Texas, and I was telling the Saints I would leave after the 2002 season.

The Saints wanted to hold a special event to say good-bye. I didn't know what my job was going to be, so I couldn't really explain why I was moving, except to be near my wife's family. So once again, it was announced throughout Minnesota that I was "retiring." On Labor Day 2002, a beautiful sunny afternoon in Saint Paul, the Saints gave me a ten-gallon hat and some other Texas-style gifts, read a proclamation, and announced that the number 5, which I had worn as a Saint, would be retired.

Midway Stadium, with its trains going by every other inning or so, is something I'll always remember. The players, the fans, the tailgaters, the guys and gals in the front office for those eight years, I love them all. Mike Veeck was right, "Fun is good."

18
Too Young to Retire

Almost here in fifty-two
Instead went to Saint Paul
Fort Worth Cats and Dodger Blue
Managing again ya'll

"Are you sure you want to do this?" That's what Marty Scott asked when I told him I'd like to be considered as manager of the Fort Worth Cats. I knew what he meant. I was seventy-seven years old and hadn't managed in twenty-two years. Managing would require more time and responsibility than coaching. Long bus rides had gotten a little tougher every year. But I was healthy and energetic, I had been a good manager, and I was pretty sure I could be again. Most important, I still had enthusiasm.

Marty was enjoying life *after* managing. He was back in Texas, taking care of business as president of three teams in the independent Central League—including the Cats—and meticulously tending the grass at Fort Worth's LaGrave Field to relax. I could have relaxed, too, and taken the easy way out by coaching first base. But when the opportunity came along, I couldn't resist throwing my hat in the ring.

In the twenty-two years that I coached with the Rangers, Twins, and Saints—on just about every pitch and every play of every game—I thought about what I would do if I were calling the shots. I always thought I had a pretty good idea what a batter was looking for. In key situations when I thought we had a hitter all set up for a particular pitch, I'd say it out loud. "Got to throw him a fastball now." I didn't say it loud enough for *everyone* to hear, and if they heard, they didn't pay attention anyway. If the pitcher threw a curve and the batter got a base hit, it was all I could do not to say, "I told you so." I had been good at it when I managed before, so why not now? Was I as clever as I thought I was? I was itching to find out, and I was pretty sure I wouldn't embarrass Marty or team owner Carl Bell. They must have agreed, because after a lunch meeting with them, I was named manager of the Fort Worth Cats.

When I took the job at age seventy-seven, I became the oldest minor league manager in history and the second oldest in all of baseball except for Connie Mack, who retired at eighty-seven. People wrote some funny things about my age, including the line about the Cats introducing a seventh-inning nap to replace the stretch—I had to laugh at that one. I wasn't taking the job as a gimmick or a publicity stunt. I took it because it was a challenge, I wanted to be the guy in charge, and I wanted to *win*.

The Cats have a strong sense of their own history, having been a Dodgers' farm club for years. Duke Snider, Carl Erskine, Chris Van Cuyk, Dick Williams, and Cal Abrams, all my teammates on the 1951 Dodgers, were former Cats. So was Danny Ozark, a teammate on the 1952 Saint Paul Saints, the Dodgers' Triple A club. Maury Wills and Sparky Anderson played for the Cats, and Bobby Bragan, a legend in Fort Worth, managed them to their last league championship in 1948—the year the Cubs signed me. The Cats later merged with a Dallas team, and by the time the Rangers arrived in Arlington, the minor league club had disappeared.

The Cats started up again in 2001 and were building their ballpark in stages. They called it LaGrave Field, as in the old days, but the new LaGrave has a wonderful view of the downtown skyline.

Two things were going to be very different from my early managing days. First, I would have a great group of coaches, and second, with no organization to furnish players, we would build our own team. Toby Harrah, a former Texas Rangers infielder who had played with Cleveland and the Yankees, became my third base and hitting coach. Toby lived in the area and would have been a popular choice as manager, but he was more interested in coaching and I was glad to have him. We were on the same wavelength on almost everything, including base running. I had worked with Dan Smith, my pitching coach, while with the Saints; he was a first-round draft pick in 1990 and pitched for the Rangers until running into arm trouble. By coincidence, I was Toby's infield coach when he first played in the major leagues (with the Senators, starting in 1969), and Toby was Dan's manager when he started with the Rangers in 1992. Barry Moss, also a fellow Saints coach, was our director of player personnel, and he came up with some key finds—especially when we needed replacements in the second half of the season. To top it off, I had an ex-big-league trainer, Danny Wheat, who could do a lot more than hand out Band-Aids.

Like the Saints, the Cats had a mix of players—some never drafted, some drafted but hoping for a better offer, some released from other minor league teams—all looking to improve their skills and get another chance to move up. We signed some players from the previous year and picked up a few who had been with the Saints or other Northern League teams. Just before the season, Barry and I attended the 2003 Central League tryout in San Angelo. About 250 players showed up the first day, mostly guys with some experience in college or in minor, semi-pro, or city leagues. Thirty or forty were invited back the second day, and then they held a draft. Picking up one player is considered good. To get two who can start and contribute is almost unheard of, but that's what we did. Bryon Smith became our regular third baseman and carried the team early in the season, both defensively and with his bat. Outfielder Tim Hartshorn caught my eye with speed and aggressive base running. Tim started out on the bench but after a couple of big pinch hits he became our regular left fielder *and* number three hitter in the lineup; he also stole some bases and got some big RBIs down the stretch. We were pleased to have several players who could run. Catcher Brian Moon picked 'em off and threw 'em out. And we had a twenty-nine-year-old minor league veteran and a promising young right-hander to anchor our pitching staff. I had seen the veteran, Angel Aragon, in the Northern League. The youngster, Jermaine Van Buren, looked like a prospect. He was signed by the Cubs right after our season and made their major league team at the end of 2005.

Twig hits fungoes during infield practice in May 2005. He estimates that he has hit 869,850 fungoes in his career and thrown 1,159,800 batting-practice pitches. *Courtesy of Fort Worth Cats Baseball Club (Photo by Bob Haynes)*

As opening day approached, I felt the same old excitement—tinged with nerves—that I always had when I managed. To tell the truth, I felt a little shaky the first couple of games, and losing them both didn't help. But we won the third game with a tenth-inning walk-off home run by first baseman Shawn Greene and things fell into place after that. The game hadn't changed, and things that had worked twenty and forty years ago still worked. We executed the squeeze play eight or ten times during the season, and twice short-stop Ricky Gomez brought the runner home on two-strike bunts. The response of other teams was like old times, too—they complained, threw at Ricky and even hit him in the helmet. The adrenaline still kicked in during the late innings of tight ball games. I confirmed what I already knew: Winning is sweeter and losing is more bitter when you are the skipper. A seven-game losing streak in early June had me losing sleep, but we broke out of it with a seventeen-run game against Shreveport. We finished the first half at an even .500 and then came on strong in the second half.

We practiced and played in hotter weather than I had experienced in a long time. Our temporary clubhouse was a big trailer parked way out behind the center-field fence, and it was a long hike with a bucket of balls in each hand, especially after a tough loss. But the fans were great—on getaway days the booster club served up post-game meals for both our players and our opponents. Dodger the mascot did such a great job entertaining and revving up the crowd that he won a national award, and a bat boy nicknamed Tank had his own following because he never stopped hustling.

With ten teams in the league, we crisscrossed the state of Texas on road trips to places like Corpus Christi, San Angelo, and Amarillo, as well as towns in Mississippi, Missouri, and Louisiana. The bus rides were long, sometimes with a working air conditioner and sometimes without. When the players weren't sleeping, they were usually watching movies—if the DVD player was working—and complaining that the sound was too loud or not loud enough. "Curly," our driver, was a stocky ex-Marine; when he started pounding his forehead with his right palm we knew we either had missed a turn or were lost. But he would do anything for the players, who of course took advantage by asking to be driven around to pick up meals, snacks, or beer. We got to know all the Subways and McDonalds along the way, and we found out which motels were not so bad and which were not so good.

> *[Bryon] Smith said . . . "On the last road trip, someone asked if there was a good restaurant nearby. Twig answered that he found an all-you-can-eat Chinese buffet. We asked him where it was. He said it was three miles down the road. We asked him how he got there. Told us he walked."*
> —Dan McGraw, Fort Worth Weekly, May 25, 2005

Even run-ins with a couple of players didn't spoil my enjoyment. I had a DH named Jason Hill, who had played with the Saints when I was there. Jason could hit, Barry thought he could help us, and I thought I could get more out of him than the Saints had, so we signed him. Jason could be personable and I liked him, but he didn't think it was important to run out fly balls and grounders, and he always had something to say about it. One night during a road trip we were having trouble at the plate, and I gave Jason the take sign on a 2-0 count. He threw his bat and yelled something in my direction. When he got back to the dugout we got into a shouting match. He was louder than me and he wouldn't stop. I'd had enough. He said if I didn't like the way he played I should get rid of him. I did. It was the right move.

I handled an outburst from Angel Aragon very differently. At twenty-nine, he knew his time was getting short if he had any chance to make the majors. He had worked hard to get in shape, losing a lot of excess weight to begin the year. We started him in the bullpen, and then moved him into the starting rotation. He did well, but he was getting a little carried away with himself. One night at Jackson, he was pitching in a late inning of a close game. They had a runner on second, first base was open, and a tough left-handed hitter was at the plate. I saw that he was pitching around the guy, and I saw that a couple of balls in the dirt almost got away from the catcher. Since he wasn't pitching to the hitter anyway, I motioned to our catcher to put the hitter on. When Angel got the sign he huffed and puffed, shook his head, threw the rosin bag down—and finally finished the deliberate walk. He got the next batter out, and the inning was over. As he came into the dugout he fired his glove into the bench not far

If you have participated in more than 7,200 baseball games, you have stood at attention for the national anthem even more times than that. It's still a stirring moment for a Marine who was on the beach at Iwo Jima when he saw the American flag hoisted on Mount Suribachi. *Associated Press*

from where I was sitting and yelled, "Goddammit, let me pitch!" I didn't say a word. He pitched another inning or two, we finished the game. With the road trip over, we got on the bus back to Fort Worth. I held my tongue all the way, and the next day I waited outside the clubhouse. When he showed up, I called him over and asked, "What was that?" He said, "Just let me pitch, that's all. I wasn't going to give him anything to hit." He said he couldn't understand some of the moves I made. I told him if he wanted to manage, he should go to the front office and let the boss know. He didn't say anything useful, but he wasn't challenging me the way that Hill had, and I decided I could live with that. "You don't speak to me and I won't speak to you," I told him. "Just pitch and keep your mouth shut." He did, and he dominated the hitters in July and August. In the next-to-last game of the regular season he pitched a complete ten-inning masterpiece to clinch the second-half championship.

On August 22 we were playing Coastal Bend and the game was all tied up at the end of nine innings. Both teams needed to win to make the play-offs. In the tenth, Tim Hartshorn doubled to put us ahead 3-1. I could have pulled Aragon for our closer, but he was pitching well, he had kept our agreement, and I was determined to stick with him. He retired the side. With the final out, we were the second-half divisional champs and were going to the play-offs.

I took my time getting back to the clubhouse; I stopped to talk with well-wishers along the way and to thank Barry Moss for helping put together a winner. When I finally walked through the clubhouse door, a surprise was waiting. A double line of players stretched from the door through the locker room, each player ready to douse me with champagne or beer. I threw my head back, opened my mouth wide, and shut my eyes as I moved slowly down the line. The bubbly and the beer could not have tasted better. I was proud of my guys and proud of winning. I let the feeling wash over me—literally! What other job brings that kind of feeling? During the celebration, there were hugs all around—I even gave a quick hug to Angel Aragon.

We lost in the first round of play-offs to Jackson, the eventual league champion, but we played a good series and we'd had a good year, finishing 51-43 for the season. I told the players they should be proud, and I meant it. We led the league in attendance; general manager Monty Clegg and all the front office people were great to work with. The whole year had been fun for me. I was already looking forward to 2004.

> *At 78, Twig managed the Fort Worth Cats of the independent Central League to a division title. It was his 55th season in baseball—his career is now eligible for an AARP card—which explains how, as a Washington Senator, he once singled in a game-winning run off . . . Satchel Paige."*
> —Steve Rushin, Sports Illustrated, *October 20, 2003*

Toby Harrah took a job as minor-league hitting instructor in the Tigers system, and we replaced him with Stan Hough, a former catcher in the Mets and Astros organizations who had several years' experience as both a coach and a manager. Dan Smith was back as pitching coach and Barry Moss helped us assemble a team featuring several of the previous year's players.

A couple of things should have told me that 2004 might not be as much fun as 2003. We started spring training with another makeshift clubhouse and showers with no hot water, or sometimes no water at all. But the players handled it with class, and better than I did. Pensacola joined the league in place of Amarillo, which meant we would have one *very* long road trip. Road trips in general were getting more difficult. I kept having to pee much too often. One beer after a game and I could make it to our regular bus stop; two beers meant climbing on armrests over sprawled-out players the whole length of the bus at least once. On the trip to Pensacola—a twelve-hour trip on a shock-less Greyhound—I finally just made the driver pull over to the side of the road a couple of times so I could pee without the climb.

Then one day I took our club trainer aside and asked, "I peed blood a couple of times. Do you think that means anything?" I could tell from his expression that he thought it did. I went to see my doctor, who sent me to a specialist, and a CAT-scan showed I had a tumor in my bladder. I couldn't believe it. I was always so careful about my health—eating right, getting plenty of exercise, washing my hands often—and in spite of it all, I suddenly learn that I have cancer in my body. I was back in uniform five days after surgery—a little weak, but determined not to sit around. The team had gone 1-and-4 in my absence, and we went 7-and-3 when I first got back. That helped my recuperation more than anything else could. My doctor suggested checkups every three months and said as long as they were okay I didn't need chemotherapy. He said the cancer could come back at any time, but I'd probably die of something else.

Meanwhile, we were having some trouble holding our pitching together. Two of our best got picked up by the Phillies during the season, and Angel Aragon was having a fine year until his elbow blew out. Midway through the season, we brought in former major-leaguer Mike Smith. He was tough for me to watch because he would show up umpires and antagonize the other team. But Barry Moss said, "Just put up with him; he'll win for you." It was true; he did a good job for us all through August. We found a lefty out of TCU with a good changeup and sneaky 82-mile-an-hour "hummer." We ran other candidates in and out of the ballpark almost every week but didn't find much other help. On the hitting side Barry got us a rookie from Texas Tech who contributed as a DH, and late in the season he engineered a great trade to bring in veteran outfielder Carlos Adolfo, a class act who played a big role on the team. We ended up with the same record as in 2003—51 wins and 43 losses—but we missed the playoffs. I was disappointed.

Troubles followed me into the off-season. On our last road-trip, I started having back problems. I'd get up in the morning and find that I couldn't straighten up for a couple of hours. With some stretching, it got better and I'd hit fungoes, but it would tighten up again while I sat on the bench. I figured it was the damn soft beds at the motel, but it didn't get any better when I slept on my own good mattress at home. Over the next couple of months, I saw a physical therapist, then a chiropractor, then doctors in Fort Worth and Dallas. I had a couple of MRIs and finally cortisone shots. Just when I was ready to give up and admit that old age was finally getting the best of me, I started feeling some relief. I felt a little better in time for the classy dinner where Marty Scott and I were both inducted into the Texas Baseball Hall of Fame. By the first of the year, I knew I was going to manage the Cats again in 2005.

> When the new season starts this spring, Wayne "Twig" Ter-williger . . . will be out there again throwing batting practice and hitting fungoes. He'll be on the field, as always, before his players, and won't grouse about the 13-hour bus rides to places such as Pensacola."
> —Steve Willstein, The Associated Press, printed in the Tallahassee Democrat, February 4, 2005

We got off to a quick start, winning ten of our first thirteen games, but we only had a two-game lead, so we knew we had to keep playing well. The team really pulled together, and we managed to stay in the lead. A pair of games late in the first half exemplified the character of the 2005 Cats.

First, we had one of those strange, unbelievable games where everything goes wrong. We were at Coastal Bend, playing the second game of a three-game series, battling back and forth and finally taking an 8-7 lead into the bottom of the ninth. Our closer retired the first two batters and had two strikes on the third. His third pitch was

During the Central League championship game in September 2005, Twig has a quick word with infielder David Keesee. "As a player, you love to play for a manager like Twig," Keesee says. "You want to give it your all every day for him. I'm really glad we could win him a championship."
Courtesy of Fort Worth Cats Baseball Club (Photo by Bob Haynes)

a slider in the dirt that the batter swung at for strike three. But the ball got away from catcher Ken Lup. The batter headed to first, Lup retrieved the ball and threw it over the head of first baseman Jordan Foster. The ball rolled down the right field line. The batter kept running and headed for third as right fielder Terrell Merriman chased down the ball. Merriman threw a rainbow over the relay man's head. Foster caught it, and as the runner headed home, Foster had plenty of time to throw him out. But he hurried his throw, it went wild, and the runner scored to tie the game. It wasn't like us. In fact I have never seen anything quite like it!

In the top of the tenth, Foster hit a home run to put us ahead 9-8. In the bottom of the tenth, we again got two outs. Coastal Bend got a runner on and their next hitter blasted one out of the park to beat us 10-9. I stayed in the dugout until all the players left, trying to compose myself and wanting to come up with something to say that didn't sound as if I'd just seen my dog get run over by a car. Our locker room was quiet when I walked in. "Shit happens," I said. "Get 'em tomorrow." It was the best I could do. Needless to say, my beer tasted lousy.

The next night, we pulled out a nail-biting squeaker, 6-5. Everybody contributed in one way or another. We had bounced back from a gut-wrenching loss, struggled through another tough game, and won it. The bus was happy as we headed for Edinburg. We won six of the next seven games, clinching the first-half title.

Actually, it wasn't *quite* that easy. First, we had to overcome a couple of setbacks in the pitching department, where everything had been going well. Kevin Lynn was 5-0, leading the league in every category and making it look easy. Then Kevin was picked up by Tampa Bay—great for him, a problem for us. And rookie Mike Snapp, our closer, had eight saves and looked like a vet, but overnight he lost his control, his coordination, and his confidence. I had seen the same thing happen to major leaguers, and there's no quick fix. We crossed our fingers and moved reliever Juan Figueroa into the closer role, and we won the four straight games that clinched the first half. When we overcame all those problems, I thought to myself, "This team is pretty damn good." My biggest job in the second half would be to keep them motivated.

We started the second half 19 and 6, and I thought we would pile up the wins and clinch the second-half title early. Terence Green had a hot bat and was stealing bases, Adolfo was hitting home runs, and Jordan Foster busted out of an early slump to hit like Barry Moss had said he would. John Allen, the 2004 rookie outfielder, was hitting doubles and driving in runs. Bryon Smith was looking comfortable at second base, a new position for him. Tony Mota was starting to hit like Manny, his dad. Terrell Merriman was catching everything in right field. David Keesee and Arnoldo Ponce were doing the job at shortstop. Ryan Weems, the rookie left-hander who joined us in midseason 2004, was almost unbeatable at home. Big soft-spoken left-hander T.J. Hendricks had been struggling out of the bullpen, and we were about ready to release him when we decided to give him a start. He pitched a complete game winner, followed that with another win and was named pitcher of the week. He ended up with

The 2005 Central League champion Fort Worth Cats. Front row: batboy Matt Treadway, Carlos Adolfo, Arnoldo Ponce, Kevin Lynn, David Keesee, Bryon Smith, Ken Lup, Justin Garcia, Shawn Yarbrough, batboy Tank Ramsey. Second row: hitting instructor Stan Hough, Terrell Merriman, Juan Figueroa, Ryan Weems, Logan Stout, Terence Green, Jordan Foster, Josh Neitz, bullpen catcher Mike Serata, manager Wayne Terwilliger. Third row: trainer Alan Reid, Tony Mota, Jason Radwan, Mike Snapp, pitching coach Dan Smith, Mike Smith, T.J. Hendricks, John Allen, clubhouse manager Cody Strange. Not present: Mike Scanzano, Angel Aragon, Ray Beasley, Dan Grybash, Matt Harrington, Joel Kirsten, Billy Stokley.

Courtesy of Fort Worth Cats Baseball Club (Photo by Bob Haynes)

Twig and the Cats celebrate their championship as Kevin Winn, supervisor of the Central League umpires, presents the trophy.
Courtesy of Fort Worth Cats Baseball Club (Photo by Bob Haynes)

seven wins and all I ever heard him say about it was, "How about them potatoes?" Barry Moss delivered again, with pitchers Dan Grybash, who won six games in the second half, and Joel Kirsten, who struggled some but picked up as the season went on.

Every problem seemed to have a way of working itself out, and life was good. The team never slumped. But I was getting impatient about winning the second half. Finally, on the next-to-last day of the regular season, Mike Smith gutted out a complete game and we threw out the tying run at home plate to win the game and the second-half title. Our record was exactly the same as the first half, and the combined tally of 60 wins and 34 losses was the best in the Cats' history.

A team that wins both halves has a lot to lose in the post-season. You can't be declared League Champions until you win—and if someone else wins, they take the title. We added pressure on ourselves by getting behind in both series. The divisional series, against Pensacola, started at home. We won the first game, lost the second, and got on the bus for another twelve-hour trip, hoping there would be shock absorbers and a working VCR. To keep things interesting, we lost the first game there, then fought back to win the last two for the divisional title. We spent a day at home and then headed to San Angelo, four hours away, for the championship series. Again we won the opener and lost the next two. With Weems and then Kirsten as our starting pitchers, we won the final two and the championship, at home in front of our own fans.

When Juan Figueroa struck out the final hitter, the fireworks began, the players rushed to the middle of the infield to celebrate, the fans cheered, and the music blared. I hugged and congratulated the coaches, and then I stood in front of the dugout watching the celebration. Lin appeared from the crowd and said, "Just like Minnesota." I thought, yes, it was a lot like the Twins' World Series wins, but this was *my team,* and for me that made it something special. It wasn't the big leagues, or the World Series, but it was a bunch of happy independent league ballplayers celebrating a championship, some for the first time and some for the last. They were going to get rings, and tonight they were going to celebrate and revel in the feeling of being a winner. I know that feeling, and it's hard to beat.

He didn't tell his players that he was retiring. No "Win one for the Twigger" speech on his way out, though he was as nervous about clinching the Central title as he was a World Series. But his players know what it meant to him. He wrote each of them a letter last week. Baseball could use a little more of that etiquette.
—*Kevin Sherrington,* Dallas Morning News, *October 16, 2005*

Editors' note: In the summer 2005, the Fort Worth Cats celebrated Wayne Terwilliger's 80th birthday by issuing a second Twig bobble-head, Twig was selected to manage the league's All-Star team against the Can-Am All-Stars, his Cats won both halves and the league championship series, and he was named Central League Manager of the Year. In October he announced his retirement. Then in December he decided he was still too young to retire, and he rejoined the team as first-base coach. The Cats have joined the new American Association, another independent league, named for the Triple A league in which Twig played during the 1950s.

19

'Nuf said

Sometimes too much is written,
too many words are said,
when less is really better;
on patience lest we tread.
—'Nuf said!

What's in a name?

One Sunday afternoon Mother wandered through our kitchen, where Father was making a sandwich and listening to the ball game. The Pirates were playing the New York Giants at Forbes Field. In those days, the Giants had a utility infielder named Wayne Terwilliger. Just as Mother passed through, the radio announcer cried—with undue drama—"Terwilliger bunts one!"

"Terwilliger bunts one?" Mother cried back, stopped short. She turned. "Is that English?"

"The player's name is Terwilliger," Father said. "He bunted."

"That's marvelous," Mother said. "'Terwilliger bunts one.' No wonder you listen to baseball. 'Terwilliger bunts one.'"

For the next seven or eight years, Mother made this surprising string of syllables her own. Testing a microphone, she repeated, "Terwilliger bunts one"; testing a pen or a typewriter, she wrote it. If, as happened surprisingly often in the course of various improvised gags, she pretended to whisper something else in my ear, she actually whispered, "Terwilliger bunts one." Whenever

someone used a French phrase, or a Latin one, she answered
solemnly, "Terwilliger bunts one." If Mother had had, like
Andrew Carnegie, the opportunity to cook up a motto for a coat
of arms, hers would have read simply and tellingly, "Terwilliger
bunts one." (Carnegie's was "Death to privilege.")
—Annie Dillard, An American Childhood, *Harper & Row, 1987*

My name became a household word—in one household, anyway.
In her memoir *An American Childhood*, Annie Dillard tells how her
mother, who was not a baseball fan, came to use the phrase, "Terwilliger bunts one" on a regular basis. The chapter that includes this
story is included in the *Norton Reader: An Anthology of Expository
Prose*, which is used as a text for a lot of college English courses.

In a 2001 mystery called *Soldier's Gap*, a high school principal is
bludgeoned to death by a Louisville Slugger with a Wayne Terwilliger endorsement. And a Wayne Terwilliger at-bat with the Minneapolis Millers is being heard on the radio in the background
during a scene in Garrison Keillor's *Lake Wobegon Summer 1956*. In
Switching Channels, a 1988 remake of *The Front Page*, the character
of the prison warden, listed in the credits as "Warden Terwilliger," is
called "Twig" by another character.

"Terwilliger" is Dutch; it means "near the willow trees." There
was a Richard Terwilliger—also from Michigan and also born on
June 27 but older and no relation—who pitched three innings for
Saint Louis in 1932.

Newspaper guys who made up box scores had to be creative to get
my name to fit. My friend Brian Motiaytis collected some of their
solutions: Terwl'ger, Terwil'ger, Terw'ger, Terwil'r, Terwil'er, Ter-
will'r, Terwlgr, Terwil'g'r, T'wil'g'r, T'w'ger, T'wil'ger, T'wil'gr,
T'w'lg'r, T'williger, T'w'l'ger, Ter'iger, Ter'liger, Ter'ger, Ter'wigr,
Ter'iger, T'rw'g'r, T'r'lig'r, T'lliger, T'rwilgr, T'r'llger.

My parents named me Willard, but when I was seven or eight, a
bully named Willard Britton used to chase me home from school, so
I came to hate the name. I told my mom I wanted to be called by my
middle name, and from then on, I was Wayne. When I found out
that my cousin Loretta, who lived in California, was called Twig, I
latched on to that as a nickname. 'Nuf said.

And suddenly, on the radio, Bob Motley is in a white froth, yelling, "Goodbye, Mama, that train is leaving the station! Whooooooooooooooo-eeee!"—his trademark home-run cry—and Daddy perks up his ears, but it isn't a homer, it's a long fly out for Miller slugger Clint Hardin. ("That ball was on its way out of here, folks! And the wind got hold of it and it's a heartbreaking out to right field for a great ballplayer and just a wonderful guy! What a shame! And now Wayne Terwilliger comes to the plate.") The crowd goes back to sleep. . . .

. . . Wayne fouls off a Toledo fastball . . .

Wayne Terwilliger fouls off another pitch. "It's a waiting game," says Bob Motley. "Wayne's looking for the inside fastball." . . .

. . . Wayne fouls off another pitch. Still looking for the inside fastball . . .

And steady Wayne Terwilliger takes a called third strike ("Unbelievable! Un-believable, folks! That pitch to Twig was in the dirt, ladies and gentlemen! How can a man be expected to hit a pitch like that? In the dirt! And the fans here are letting home-plate umpire Larry Cahoon know they're upset about that call")
—Garrison Keillor, Lake Wobegon Summer 1956, *Viking Penguin, 2001*

The fame game

Everybody remembers Wayne Terwilliger. But nobody can remember exactly why. . . . He couldn't hit his hat size, but he could field every position. . . . He had a good disposition, was always sober, and liked to pitch batting practice—in other words, a manager's dream."
—Brendan C. Boyd and Fred C. Harris, The Great American Baseball Card Flipping, Trading and Bubble Gum Book, *Little, Brown and Company, 1973*

Two guys wrote a funny book about baseball cards—two cards per page, with a little humorous commentary about each. Mostly, they poke fun at lesser-known guys. The very first profile shows my Senators card (1955, Topps, #34), with twenty-four lines of text. Below

In 1939 and 1940, young Wayne Terwilliger collected the signatures of dozens of sports stars and other celebrities. This is a small sampling of those autographs. Pinky Higgins, Hank Greenberg, and Charles Gehringer all played for Twig's favorite team, the Detroit Tigers, at the time.
Wayne Terwilliger personal collection

me is Ted Williams with just six lines, the gist of which was that every male in 1955 America would have given an arm and a leg to be Teddy Ballgame. They say I was a utility man in every way: my face, my build, my outlook on life—even my name. Then they say, "He always looked . . . like the sort of guy you might send for to unplug a drain in a large apartment house." My wife thinks it's insulting, but I see the humor—and there I am paired with Ted, once again.

I had about a dozen major-league cards, most made by Topps. Every year they signed me to a contract and paid a fee and royalties. As I write this, a 1954 check for $50, which I endorsed on the back, is being offered on E-bay for $340! At any given moment, about a dozen of the cards themselves are offered on E-bay, for a lot less than $340.

The only bad part of signing autographs is that sometimes people hand you something grimy to write on, or a pen that feels like it's been through a thousand pairs of hands. I carry my own pen so I know it will work and I know it's clean. Once I finally "grew up" and started signing autographs no matter what mood I might be in, I began to make a point of looking the person in the eye and talking with them a little. If a kid just takes what I've signed and starts to turn away, I ask, "What do you say? How about thank you?" They always say it, and then the parents thank me, too.

I get six or seven letters a week requesting my autograph, and with those I ask for a little money for charity. I ask people to make checks out to Manna, a charity in Weatherford, Texas.

When I turned fourteen, I "graduated" from collecting baseball cards to autographs of athletes and celebrities. I spent a lot of time in 1939 and 1940 writing to football players, sports announcers, actors and actresses, people in government, anybody I got interested in. I'd butter them up a little, or I'd draw a little picture of them hitting a ball—anything to get their attention. I filled several books with the pictures and notes people sent me. One of the first autographs I got came from a utility infielder named Mark Christman. I had written him at the end of the season, and just before Christmas I got a postcard. I read the back: "Best wishes, Merry Christmas." I wondered who sent it, and my mother couldn't figure it out, either. Later I got a postcard from a player and realized that the first one might be from a player, too. That's when I figured out that it said, "Best wishes, Mark Christman." After a while I started sending stamped, self-addressed envelopes. Nobody told me to do that; I may have invented the idea.

I wrote to President Roosevelt and got a nice official letter from the private secretary to the President of the United States, telling me the president is too busy to write. I got a signature from Byron "Whizzer" White, who at the time was a football player and not yet a Supreme Court justice. Bernie Bierman signed his name twice. I heard from Ted Williams, playing his second season in the majors, and from Joe Louis, Tom Harmon, Connie Mack, and Joe Cronin. I drew a picture of Charlie Keller, a Yankee, and he sent it back with his name written underneath. Lou Boudreau tore off the end of a piece of hotel stationary and signed it. Hank Greenberg wrote with a back slant, although he wasn't a leftie. Joe DiMaggio's signature had a lot of loops and looked almost feminine. Charley Gehringer wrote with a beautiful English-style script, "Chas. Gehringer." He was already my idol, and maybe his example is why I have signed my own name so carefully all these years.

Collecting all these autographs gave me a way to approach some of the celebrities who had sent them—I could thank them for responding to a kid's request. In 1953, for example, I was at the Baltimore train station with my teammates when I recognized

As a youngster, Twig drew a picture of Yankee hitter Charlie Keller, who autographed and returned it. Ten years later, a young fan created a remarkably similar drawing for Twig. Note that Twig drew Keller—correctly—as a lefty, and that Joe has Twig swinging from the right. Charlie Keller's brother Hal later hired Twig—twice—to manage in the Senators-Rangers system; Twig stayed eleven seasons each time.
Wayne Terwilliger personal collection

Helen Hayes among the passengers arriving at our gate. She didn't seem to be in a hurry, so I approached and introduced myself as a member of the Washington team and thanked her for the autograph she had sent me in 1940. The First Lady of the Theatre turned out to be a big Senators fan, and she seemed genuinely excited to be meeting *me*. Betty Grable had sent me a snapshot of her and her dog looking out a car window. In spring 1956 when I was with the Giants, she and her husband, Harry James, came to a spring training exhibition game in Phoenix. I introduced myself and thanked her for sending the picture years before. She was very friendly, and Harry James said, "Hey, can you get me a Giants cap?" He barely had the words out before I whipped my own cap off my head and gave it to him. 'Nuf said.

Keep the record straight

If somebody is talking about me, I want the record to be accurate. I don't want more credit than I deserve, and I don't want less. In high school, I was sports editor for the school newspaper. I played three sports and was quarterback of our football team. Every week I wrote about my own plays, and I didn't leave things out if I thought they belonged in the story. But I also made sure I gave credit to the rest of the team—especially the offensive line, since I was going to depend on them in the *next* game.

About a month into the season at Los Angeles in 1949, when I was hitting extremely well, a guy from the *Los Angeles Times* asked me, "How do you account for this sudden success with the bat?" I thought, wait a minute, it's not like I never hit well before. So I said, "The surprising thing was that I only hit .196 at Des Moines last year. Other than that, I've never hit below .300 in my life—not in high school or college, not in the Marines, not in semi-pro ball at Benton Harbor. I can't figure out what happened in 1948." He stared at me for a minute, and then he said, "Okay, that makes sense." He reported what I'd said, and then he added something to the effect that I wasn't bragging, just explaining, because "that's the kind of guy he is."

I thought that was an odd thing for him to write. Of course I wasn't bragging. He asked me a question and I answered it. If somebody is going to write about what I've done, they should give me the credit I deserve, no more and no less. I've kept that attitude all my life. That's why I'm still mad at myself for not correcting Mike Max when he said I'd had "a cuppa coffee" in the majors. On the other hand, a writer in Fort Worth wrote in 2003 that I once got a home run off Satchel Paige. The fact is, I got a game-winning bloop single off Satchel Paige, and I'm very proud of it. I got the writer to print a correction; I don't want credit for something I *didn't* do. 'Nuf said.

Play, don't think

People in Charlotte, Michigan, know me as a high school athlete who went on to play and coach major-league baseball. But I may be best remembered there for a basketball shot I made in the late 1950s. I was invited to participate in an alumni game against a traveling women's team. They had us all lined up and as they introduced each guy he would trot out to center court and stand there. It was taking forever and I was getting bored and embarrassed about the whole thing, so I decided to liven things up. When they called my name, I picked up a basketball that was sitting under my chair, dribbled out to center court, and took a swooping hook shot. It went in, and everybody roared. I stood there as if nothing had happened, trying not to smile. There must have been fifteen hundred or two thousand people at the game, but since that day, five thousand people have told me they saw that shot.

I was grandstanding, and I don't usually do that. Afterwards I thought, what if it had been an air ball? I tried the shot later and couldn't even come close. They say you shouldn't think too much when you play, and that shot might have proved the point. 'Nuf said.

Keep 'em guessing

Six or eight years ago, I started thinking I wanted to swing a bat again. I stood in and took a couple of swings, but then I decided I'd rather have them wonder, "Can Terwilliger really hit it now?" As long as I don't show them otherwise, they have to wonder. But when I want to show off a little, I can still get rid of the ball quicker than a lot of the young guys on the ball club.

I can't watch all the players during practice, but I can make them think I do. When I'm hitting fungoes to the infielders and one of them misses a bad hop, I might say, "Anybody can catch the good hops," and a few smiles will break out. When somebody makes a juggling grab of an easy bouncer, I might say, "Right in the pocket, Ricky." Out of the corner of my eye I might see an outfielder misjudge a fly ball and say, "Nice play, Terrell." It gets their attention and gives them a few laughs, always good for the team. 'Nuf said.

Keep 'em motivated

I once asked Ralph Houk what makes a good manager. He said, "Good players." Period. He's right. All a manager can do is try to help players do their best, keep them motivated, and make the best use of them during a game.

Strategy gets serious late in a close game. With a small roster in the minors, you can't do a lot of pinch-hitting, but you do have to make some decisions about pitchers, and you hope you pick the right one at the right time. If the pitchers do well, they make you look good.

If a game doesn't go well, I might walk into the locker room and say, "Forget that one, we played well, we'll get them tomorrow." But if you lose three or four in a row, you wonder what you can do, and

A Wayne Terwilliger bobblehead, the first of his career, was distributed by random drawing during a Saint Paul Saints game July 8, 2002. Fans entering the game received wristbands in a variety of colors; colors were drawn during the game until 2,500 dolls were distributed. This one has been autographed.

Photo by Nancy Peterson

Mark Johnson of Fort Worth-Dallas CBS affiliate KTVT interviews Twig on June 24, 2005, the day before his eightieth birthday, with the second Twig bobblehead in hand. In this version, given to 1,500 hundred Fort Worth fans, Twigs holds a cake that says "Twig 80."

Courtesy of Fort Worth Cats Baseball Club (Photo by Bob Haynes) sometimes the answer is nothing. They have to do it themselves. It's nice to have a leader or two on the club who can do that.

If you took a vote, I'm sure players would say they want their managers to show a little emotion during a game. You don't have to jump up and run around like some of them, but you need to show you're in the game. When an infielder boots a tough play, I'm going to say, "You should have made that play!" It lets him know I think he's better than the mistake he just made. He already feels bad, so I don't have to beat him up, but I don't have to pat him on the butt, either. If a guy pops up with the bases loaded, I might say, "Okay, stay with 'em, you'll be up there again." When a guy gets a base hit, he knows I'm in the dugout saying, "Atta babe," or something like that. And when he throws a guy out from center field, I'm going to say, "That was a hell of a throw." He already knows it, but he's going to appreciate hearing it.

I see Joe Torre sit in the Yankees dugout with no expression the whole game and I think, "It ain't that easy, Joe." He's one of the most respected managers around and he's probably thinking the whole time, but he doesn't show it. Obviously the Yankees respond to that, but even in the majors most teams need something more. 'Nuf said.

Run, don't walk . . .

Baseball was not intended for walkers. When you're in uniform and on the field you should run, not walk. Players should run to their positions and back to the dugout, and so should coaches. Managers should run to home plate with the lineups and to the mound and back when they deal with the pitcher. When a batter hits a ball down the line that goes foul, he should run back to the batter's box. When a base runner attempts to steal and the batter fouls the pitch, the runner should jog, not saunter, back to the base.

There is one exception, and that's after a strikeout. If a hitter runs off the field after strike three, it looks like he's embarrassed and heading for cover. Walking back, head up, is better body language. You might even give the pitcher a quick look that says, "You got me this time, but I'll be up there again." 'Nuf said.

. . . even if you're not Maury

It's a mistake to think you have to have the speed of Maury Wills to be a good base runner. It's more important to be thinking every minute about how you're going to get to the next base. From the instant you hit the ball until you see it in the fielder's hands, you've got to tell yourself, "There's a chance he'll mishandle it," and run hard all the way. Once you're on first, you should be saying, "How am I going to get to second if there's no base hit? Is the pitcher going to balk? Am I going to get a good jump? The first ball in the dirt, I'm gonna go." You get to second, and maybe a ball is hit to the third baseman. You watch his arm come up, and the instant it starts forward for his throw to first, you take off. By the time the ball gets to the first baseman and he throws back to third, you're sliding in, in a cloud of dirt. You've got to plan for these things so you're not left flat-footed. 'Nuf said.

Life and death

Dying was never something I worried about. I was always much more concerned about being disabled or paralyzed, even though there are a lot of people who are disabled and get along just fine. I'm a little claustrophobic, and that bothers me. Playing high school football, when I'd get tackled and find myself at the bottom of a pile of guys, I'd feel panicky until they got up and I could move again. It lasted maybe 20 seconds, but it seemed like a long time. When I was with the Twins, some players and coaches got together to play touch football, and as I was going after the ball, somebody's knee grazed my head and hit my shoulder hard enough to nearly dislocate it. It scared me at the time, and I still find myself thinking sometimes about how easily something can happen, and how a couple of seconds or a couple of inches can make a life-or-death difference.

In the war, people were getting killed all around me and all I got was a scratch on the knee. On a highway in Wisconsin forty or fifty years ago, I had a guy coming at me head-on. I managed to head for the ditch, and I was fine. When the doctor told me I had bladder cancer in 2004, I was shocked, and it took a long time to accept it. But he told me something else will probably get me before bladder cancer does. (If I had my druthers, I'd like to "die young at an advanced age," as someone said—maybe drop dead from a heart attack while coaching first base just as the winning run cross home plate. But not just yet.)

I was hit in the head three times during my playing career, but they only had to carry me off the field once. I went to the hospital for that and once more when I spiked my own leg turning a double play. In '82 I was throwing batting practice to Rangers outfielder George Wright and didn't get out of the way of a line drive; it splintered two ribs and I spent quite a few weeks in a body brace. And in 2001, I was in the first-base coach's box when a ball ricocheted off the first baseman's glove and hit me just below the temple. I couldn't chew for a couple of days, but an inch or two higher and it could have been much worse. So I think about how lucky I am. You've got to get up in the morning saying, "Let me at 'em. Another day." 'Nuf said.

Anything for the game

The last two years with the Twins, I had excruciating pain in my toes that just killed me when I pitched batting practice. The club doctor couldn't figure out how to help, so I said, "Just cut these two toes off." He refused at first but eventually I talked him into doing one of them, up to the first joint. I thought I could just go to his office and it wouldn't be a big deal. Of course it was. They took me into this room with a whole lot of people around and they deadened my foot, but I could hear everything; I even heard my toe drop into the pan. And the other toe still hurt just as bad, so I had to go through the whole thing a second time. It was all so I could pitch batting practice. 'Nuf said.

Staying healthy

He has wrinkles in his long face and gray in his short hair, and has overcome back problems and bladder cancer, yet he appears, in black T-shirt and jeans, quite fit. "I don't feel 80, not at all," he said. "I can do things that any, any, any 70-year-old can do."
—*Ira Berkow*, New York Times, *December 7, 2005*

I don't eat a lot, but I eat right—broiled fish and chicken, lots of salads, fruit, cereals, and a banana every day, which might be the best food there is. The doctor limits me to two beers in the evening, and Lin and I started having a glass of wine with dinner because it's supposed to be good for the circulation.

All my life I've had a thing about germs. I wash my hands often and I make sure they're clean before I eat. My friends used to laugh about the fact that I carry my own pen for signing autographs, and that if I'm eating I won't sign until I'm finished. What they didn't know was that when I travel, I hate touching things in my motel room, and I put out the "Do Not Disturb" sign to keep maids out because I don't like finding somebody else's hair in the sink. 'Nuf said.

Speaking of travel . . .

In the major leagues, you travel by plane, stay in nice hotels, and eat well. The worst I had to put up with in the majors was a roommate who snored and spit in his sleep. Johnnie Schmitz and I roomed together right after we were traded from the Cubs to the Dodgers, but I couldn't sleep through the noise so I got a different roommate who wasn't a spitter.

In the minors, you spend a lot of time on buses, the lodging isn't nearly so fancy, and especially at the lower levels, meal allowances don't exactly allow for gracious dining.

The worst bus I ever had to deal with was the Black Bus of the 1962 Pensacola Senators, with its broken windshield wipers, its frequent breakdowns, and the water spraying up through a hole in the floor whenever the road was wet. Strangely enough, bus problems also developed when Pensacola became a destination for the Fort Worth Cats in 2004 and 2005; we sometimes found ourselves enduring twelve hours of non-functioning air conditioning and movie equipment—which is a necessity for today's players—or bouncing along with virtually no shock absorbers. When the Saint Paul Saints went into Canada to play Winnipeg or Thunder Bay, we sometimes sat for hours at the border on our return, waiting for authorities to approve the papers of players who were not U.S. citizens.

Hitting the road? Twig tries out Saints fan Randy Haas's Harley in the parking lot at Midway Stadium. To Twig's left are co-authors Peter Boehm and Nancy Peterson, at whose table he and Haas were among the regular pre-game tailgaters. At far left is Abby Boehm. *Wayne Terwilliger personal collection*

In 1963 with Wisconsin Rapids, the team bus hit a Volkswagen almost head-on in the middle of the night. I was in the front with my typewriter doing game reports but I had dozed off, so I didn't see it happen. I had glass and small cuts all over my hands and arms from our shattered windshield. We ran back and found the Volkswagen upside-down in the ditch. An outfielder named Willie Adams, who was one of my favorites, crawled into the car and worked to free the fellow, and a couple of others helped pull him away from the car. The guy was pretty badly injured, and we were relieved to find out later that he survived.

Hotels and motels can vary all over the map. These days, the bad ones are more or less alike—dingy rooms that smell like stale cigarettes and maybe aren't the cleanest you've ever seen. It's worse if the air conditioning doesn't work or there's a lot of noise—which there often is. And it's tough on the players when they're stuck miles from anything interesting to see or do, which also happens a lot because those motels are cheaper.

One place from the old days that stands out was a hotel in Dubuque, Iowa, where the Wisconsin Rapids team stayed in 1963. It was clean but very old, and the floors sagged so much that I felt like I was walking up hill. There was an old steam radiator in each room, and tied to the bottom of the radiator was a long coil of very thick rope. I wondered, what the heck is this for? I soon figured out: it was my fire escape! In case of fire, you were supposed to throw the loose end out the window and slide down. 'Nuf said.

Aluminum socks and other inventions

I've never really liked to go out to eat after a game; I'd rather go to my room and enjoy a beer and a little food where it's quiet. Years ago I figured out a way to have a nice hot meal waiting for me. We were on the road in Charleston, South Carolina, and there was a fried chicken place near our motel. It was a popular place and always busy after the game, so I'd go in the afternoon, just before it was time to leave for the ballpark. I'd buy two or three pieces of chicken, bring them to my room, and wrap them in tinfoil. I'd put the chicken on top of a lamp, put a towel over it, and turn the light on. The light kept the food nice and hot until I came back after the game. I did that pretty often and with different kinds of food. I worried about it catching fire, but it never did.

In all my years on the field, I have never figured out an easy way to keep flies from biting my legs. At Wrigley Field when the wind came from the stockyards it brought swarms of flies, they turned your socks black and they bit. It drove me nuts; I couldn't stand it. Somebody on the Cubs told me to wrap my legs in newspaper, so that's what I did. You wrap a couple of layers of newspaper around each leg and pull up the sanitary socks and then the stirrup socks and try to keep the newspapers smooth. I tried letting my pants hang down over my lower legs, too, but I just couldn't get used to it. A few years ago I tried substituting a layer of aluminum foil instead of newspaper. It was easier to put on, and the flies didn't bite through it, but my legs were really hot after the game so I worried about whether that was bad for me.

In Burlington in 1966, the front office guys were Brody Hood, the general manager who talked fast and ran his words together, and

"The Colonel," who never used any other name, talked LOUD and did a little of everything. Brody, a notorious penny-pincher, introduced me to his "ball-saver"—a wire cage about two feet square, half-filled with little rubber erasers. He would take five or six scuffed and dirty baseballs and put them into the cage with the erasers, then crank a handle to stir them all around together. After a couple of minutes you had smooth, almost white baseballs. They were actually too smooth, so we had to rub them up just to use them in practice.

Sometimes you have to re-use uniforms, too. I mentioned one Saints pitcher having to borrow another pitcher's pants so he could get into a game. At Pensacola in '62 we wore the big-league Senators' old wool uniforms. When I first got to Geneva in '64, the new sanitary socks hadn't arrived. I looked around and found a box of old ones. They were clean, but almost all of them had holes. I spent two hours with a roll of white tape, patching the small holes. I took the ones with larger holes back to the house, and Mary Jane sewed them up. The players weren't thrilled, but we used them until new socks arrived. 'Nuf said.

Lend an ear

I was pretty far into my career when I finally realized that I wasn't going to make the Hall of Fame, I wasn't going to get a base hit every time at bat, or even every day, and I might as well not expect to. I feel bad now just thinking about how I acted before I came to that realization.

But even back then, I was a good listener. My parents told me, "Listen and you might learn something," and they were right. One of the reasons people have liked me is that I look them in the eye and hear them out. I believe it has contributed to what success I've had, and I believe it's true in any line of work. 'Nuf said.

Booze and broads

The musical "Damn Yankees" opened on Broadway in 1955. It was all about the Senators and I had just been one for two years, so I felt like it was about me. It was a great production, and one song I

especially enjoyed was something about booze and broads and putting them aside when it's time to play baseball.

"Booze" and "broads" never played a big role in my life. While I
was growing up, my dad gave me beer at the bar. He probably got a
kick out of it—here's little Wayne drinking beer when his mother
doesn't know. The first time I tasted it I thought, how could anyone
like this? But he kept setting up those little nickel glasses and pretty
soon it got to tasting better.

As a Marine, I once drank a lot and got a tattoo, but I planned
that. Later I got in trouble for stealing beer from the officers' tent
and confessed so other guys wouldn't get punished. Once on liberty I
passed out in town and landed in the brig. It was so unlike me that
when the MPs dropped me off and I walked down the road to my
tent, guys popped out of their tents all along the way and applauded.

I once went for a drink with Hank Bauer, who insisted I try some
awful-tasting stuff called Chartreuse, and Ted Williams introduced
me to a rum concoction called Navy Grog. I had a mai-tai or two in
Hawaii, and the night I was sold to the Yankees and optioned to
Richmond, I had about ten martinis and a jar of olives. But most of
my life, it's been a few beers or a glass of wine, and that's it.

As for girls, I was too shy to talk to them in high school, but I did
look, especially at the legs of the girl sitting behind me in history
class. In my twenties I married the only girl I ever dated, and we
were virgins on our wedding night. I didn't visit any Mexican hook-
ers like some young Marines did, and my visit to a massage parlor in
Hawaii turned out to be just that: a *massage* parlor.

On the road with the Cubs in the early 1950s, I used to room with
Roy Smalley. After the game we would go out to eat, usually with a
couple of other guys, and maybe drink a little beer. We once stayed
at the Fenway Hotel in Boston, with a honeymoon couple right
across the hall. One night they had their transom open, and we could
hear noises from their room. We tiptoed out into the hall and Roy
boosted me up to peek in, but before I could see anything we both
started to giggle and I almost fell. We called off our prank and went
back to our room, where we laughed for a long time. That was a
pretty exciting night for us.

Ball players love to check the stands for pretty women. I always
enjoyed playing in Pittsburgh, partly because Ralph Kiner's wife, a

prominent tennis player, always sat in the front row next to the Pirates' dugout. She often wore her white tennis outfit and sat with her feet up on the railing enjoying the afternoon sun. When I was with the Minneapolis Millers, I liked playing in Indianapolis because one of their pitchers, Don Rudolph, was married to an exotic dancer, Patti Wagon, who would lie in the outfield sunbathing before practice. She was fairly well known so we all got a big kick out of bragging to our friends that we had seen her. With the Senators, we had a favorite fan who put on a show for us. The stands jutted out on one side of the dugout, so we could sit in there and watch the people, and we often recognized people from high up in the government. But our favorite was a woman who always brought a banana. She'd slowly peel it back and put that banana into her mouth. Bucky Harris, our manager, would go, "Ooh, ooh," and the players would all laugh. She knew she was being watched and she was having as good a time as we were.

I usually didn't notice much that went on between players and various women, or I never made it my business. When I married Lin and she started coming to the ballpark, I warned her that she would see a lot of "stuff" going on and she should just try to ignore it. It wasn't easy, but she managed. She's pretty sure there have been women at the ballparks who were flirting with me, but if there were I haven't noticed since I met her. 'Nuf said.

A working guy

Wayne Terwilliger . . . was always the versatile sort. Therefore it comes as no surprise to find him teaching history to high school juniors at Otsego's new school by day, officiating at basketball games by night and running a grade school recreation program at Charlotte on weekends."
—Alex Laggis, The Grand Rapids (Michigan) Press, *January 27, 1963*

For most of my first thirty years in baseball, I worked other jobs to pay the bills. We spent off-seasons in Kalamazoo until we built a house in Charlotte in the early 1950s, and I found jobs in the area. One year I worked in the office of a dairy—and drank enough milk

As Twig was concluding his career with the Saint Paul Saints in 2002, editorial cartoonist Bob Jorgensen contrasted Twig's long-time service to the sport with the greed of some of today's owners and players.
Courtesy of Bob Jorgensen

to go into spring training nearly twenty pounds over my playing weight. Another year I sold sporting goods, and another I did odd jobs in a paper mill. I did some substitute teaching and refereed high school basketball games. One fall I got a job teaching at Otsego, 60 miles away. Jobs were hard to come by, and I figured that teaching experience would be useful if I ever left baseball, so I commuted 120 miles a day and taught U.S. history to high-school juniors. I spent as much time in the library as in the classroom, trying to keep ahead of the kids, who were very sharp. It became a game for them to get me talking about baseball; my part of the game was to keep them talking about history. I enjoyed teaching and I loved making up tests; I worked especially hard to make the final exam interesting and original. The questions were multiple choice and true-false because those are much easier to grade than essay questions, but I made some of the questions rhyme, and I even managed to work in a couple of questions with a baseball slant. On my last day, my students presented me with a school jacket, and I wore it until it fell apart. 'Nuf said.

Jesse . . .

A few days into the 1962 season at Pensacola, we optioned seven players to the Senators' Class D team in Statesville, North Carolina. One was Jesse Snead, a left-handed hitter with a good swing who was golfing every chance he got. Before he left, I told him, "Jesse, you should try concentrating on golf." The next time I heard of him was when I heard about a J.C. Snead winning tournaments on the PGA tour. 'Nuf said.

. . . and Nellie

Nellie Fox and I were both in our early forties when we worked together for Ted Williams, and he became one of my few close friends in baseball. We spent many an hour together after the game; we'd sit at the hotel bar, shoot the breeze, and play liar's poker. The loser bought drinks. Nellie always drank Crown Royal whiskey; I could tell it was the fancy stuff because the bottle came in a purple bag. I was a plain old beer drinker. Somehow, Nellie always seemed to come out ahead! A couple of years after we left the team, Nellie was diagnosed with cancer. He died in 1975, about three weeks before his forty-eighth birthday. He went fast, and much too soon. He was finally elected to the Hall of Fame in 1997; I wish he could have lived long enough to experience that. 'Nuf said.

Gloves on the infield

Baseball is the same game now as when I started to play, but a few things have changed.

We used to leave our gloves on the field, just beyond the edge of the grass, from one inning to the next. Sometime in the '50s we quit doing that—mostly because some outfielder would come by, take out his wad of tobacco, and shove it into the glove.

With Saints owner Bill Murray are Twig's daughter Marcie, granddaughter Terra, son Steve, and wife Lin. Photographed before a 1997 game at Midway Stadium, they seem to be saying "Stop! In the Name of Love," so we will. 'Nuf said! *Photo by Wayne Terwilliger*

Batting helmets came along in about 1952. They were hard to get used to, and the time I was hit in the head *with* a helmet I was hurt more than the two times I got hit without one. But it took away some of the hitter's fear, and I can't imagine facing today's pitchers without one.

It wasn't until 1954 that an outfield fly that scored a run was ruled a sacrifice. Before then, you got an RBI, but you also got an out. I once figured out how many sacrifice flies I would have had to hit from 1949 through 1953 to bring my average up to .300. It was a lot more than I had.

The strike zone has gotten smaller, and the ball—or the bat—has gotten livelier.

I liked the designated hitter at first, because I could get another big hitter into my lineup. But I've changed my mind. There is much more interesting strategy involved when you have to decide whether or not your pitcher will bat in the late innings.

Domed stadiums have exactly one thing going for them: no rain-outs or rain delays.

Free agency was a great change for players, even if it hadn't led to the huge salaries you see now.

Today's high salaries exist because the owners asked for it—they didn't negotiate with the players when they had the chance. When I played, most of us had second jobs because we needed the money. I don't resent today's salaries. On the other hand, we should not treat players like gods, no matter what they earn. And a signed contract should be just that.

Players seem to be getting better all the time. They make some amazing plays. But steroids are making fans wonder who deserves to be admired and who doesn't. 'Nuf said.

Advice

Wayne Terwilliger, c'mon down and accept your award. . . . [One e-mail] summed him up best. . . . "I do admire the man for his honesty, his compassion, his love of country and the fact that, at 80 years of age, he can 'dart' out of the dugout to argue a call probably faster than any [manager]."
—*Jim Reeves,* Fort Worth Star-Telegram, *December 25, 2005, announcing Twig as runaway write-in winner of the first Unofficial Sportsman of the Year award sponsored by Reeves' column, "Postcards from the Ledge"*

I don't go around giving advice on how to live. When I see someone slouch, I want to say, "Stand up straight." That's my dad's influence, along with, "Say please and thank you, look a person in the eye, and give a firm handshake." When I hear folks talk about growing older, I want to say, "Keep your motor running; numbers mean *nothing* when it comes to age."

In terms of real advice, I have just one: *don't give up on your dream too quickly*. My boyhood dream was to become a big-league baseball player and to play second base for the Detroit Tigers, just like my hero, Charlie Gehringer. It seemed far-fetched at the time, and I thought maybe I would be a high school coach or a sports writer. But the more I worked at improving my skills, the more my dream became a possibility, and then a reality. I never played for the Tigers, but I played against them in that great old ballpark, and while I was in the field, I "owned" second base and the space around it, just like Charlie had. So I would say to young people, if you have a dream—whether it's sports or something else—believe in it, work at it, stay with it. 'Nuf said.

Statistics

Major league player: Wayne Terwilliger is often referred to as a "utility infielder." In fact, of his 666 major league games, Twig spent 605 games at second base, had 39 games where he pinch-hit only, and played just 22 games fielding positions other than second. Ten of those occurred in 1954, when the Senators used him at third. His total walks and walks in 1955 each include one intentional pass.

Minor league player: Twig's whole minor-league playing career was spent in Triple A except for 18 games in Des Moines in 1948—right after signing with the Cubs—and one pinch-hitting appearance and one appearance as a relief pitcher during his early managing career.

Managing: The 2005 Fort Worth Cats won the Central Baseball League championship. Twig's other first-place teams lost in playoffs.

Coaching: The Minnesota Twins won the World Series in 1987 and 1991. The Saint Paul Saints were Northern League champions in 1995 and 1996.

Ball Clubs: The list of ball clubs Twig played for, coached for, or managed, and the opponents they faced, is extensive. However, it does not include spring training, exhibition, or post-season teams (or venues), nor does it include opponents of high school, military, college, semi-pro, or winter-ball teams.

Major League Playing Performance

Batting

Year	Team	League	G	AB	R	H	2B	3B	HR	RBI	SB	CS	BB	SO	BA
1949	Chicago	Nat'l.	36	112	11	25	2	1	2	10	0		16	22	.223
1950	Chicago	Nat'l.	133	480	63	116	22	3	10	32	13		43	63	.242
1951	Chicago	Nat'l.	50	192	26	41	6	0	0	10	3	1	29	21	.214
1951	Brooklyn	Nat'l.	37	50	11	14	1	0	0	4	1	0	8	7	.280
1953	Washington	Amer.	134	464	62	117	24	4	4	46	7	4	64	65	.252
1954	Washington	Amer.	106	337	42	70	10	1	3	24	3	3	32	40	.208
1955	New York	Nat'l.	80	257	29	66	16	1	1	18	2	4	37	42	.257
1956	New York	Nat'l.	14	18	0	4	1	0	0	0	0	0	0	5	.222
1959	Kansas City	Amer.	74	180	27	48	11	0	2	18	2	2	19	31	.267
1960	Kansas City	Amer.	2	1	0	0	0	0	0	0	0	0	0	0	.000
9 Season Total			666	2091	271	501	93	10	22	162	31	14	248	296	.240

Fielding

Year	Team	League	Pos.	G	PO	A	E	DP	FP
1949	Chicago	Nat'l.	2B	34	77	103	4	11	.978
1950	Chicago	Nat'l.	2B	126	314	380	24	80	.967
			1B	1	0	0	0	0	
			3B	1	0	0	0	0	
			OF	1	0	0	0	0	
1951	Chicago	Nat'l.	2B	49	136	142	9	37	.969
1951	Brooklyn	Nat'l.	2B	24	31	44	4	9	.949
			3B	1	0	1	0	1	1.000
1953	Washington	Amer.	2B	133	333	395	13	108	.982
1954	Washington	Amer.	2B	90	213	243	13	72	.972
			3B	10	11	24	1	4	.972
			SS	3	3	7	2	1	.833
1955	New York	Nat'l.	2B	78	212	240	7	70	.985
			3B	1	0	0	0	0	
			SS	1	0	0	0	0	
1956	New York	Nat'l.	2B	6	14	9	1	3	.958
1959	Kansas City	Amer.	2B	63	144	166	9	42	.972
			SS	2	0	1	0	0	1.000
			3B	1	0	0	0	0	
1960	Kansas City	Amer.	2B	2	1	1	0	1	1.000
Position Totals			2B	605	1475	1723	84	433	.974
			3B	14	11	25	1	5	.973
			SS	6	3	8	2	1	.846
			1B	1	0	0	0	0	
			OF	1	0	0	0	0	
Total for all positions				627	1489	1756	87	439	

Games with pinch-hit appearances only   39 includes 12 for the 1951 Dodgers and
8 each for 1956 Giants and 1959 Athletics

Minor League Playing Performance

Batting

Year	Team	League	G	AB	R	H	2B	3B	HR	RBI	SB	BB	SO	BA
1948	Des Moines	Western	18	46	10	9	2	0	0	4	2	18	6	.196
1949	Los Angeles	PCL	115	432	80	119	28	2	8	46	13	72	64	.275
1952	Saint Paul	Amer. Assoc.	77	125	32	39	6	0	4	17	1	32	19	.312
1955	Minneapolis	Amer. Assoc.	72	276	51	82	22	0	4	28	6	48	32	.297
1956	Minneapolis	Amer. Assoc.	90	290	39	71	14	3	2	27	10	48	44	.245
1957	Minneapolis	Amer. Assoc.	144	508	84	137	35	4	7	50	18	88	58	.270
1958	Charleston	Amer. Assoc.	146	535	103	144	23	2	2	38	24	101	58	.269
1960	Richmond	International	93	277	41	57	9	0	4	20	5	47	42	.206
1961	Greensboro	Carolina	1	1	0	0	0	0	0	0	0	0	0	.000
1964	Geneva	NY-Penn	1	0	0	0	0	0	0	0	0	1	0	
1967	Hawaii	PCL	7	5	2	0	0	0	0	0	0	2	2	.000
1968	Buffalo	International	2	6	1	1	1	0	0	0	0	0	2	.167
Total			766	2501	443	659	140	11	31	230	79	457	327	.263

Fielding

Year	Team	League	Pos.	G	PO	A	E	FP
1948	Des Moines	Western	2B	18	30	47	2	.975
1949	Los Angeles	PCL	2B	115	297	329	18	.972
1952	Saint Paul	Amer. Assoc.	Inf-OF	77	61	82	9	.941
1955	Minneapolis	Amer. Assoc.	2B	72	153	172	7	.979
1956	Minneapolis	Amer. Assoc.	2B	90	203	231	16	.964
1957	Minneapolis	Amer. Assoc.	2B	144	359	365	9	.988
1958	Charleston	Amer. Assoc.	2B	146	361	397	9	.988
1960	Richmond	International	2B	93	179	259	7	.984
1967	Hawaii	PCL	2B	7	3	5	0	1.000
1968	Buffalo	International	3B	2	3	4	2	.778
Total				764	1649	1891	79	.978

Pitching

Year	Team	League	W	L	G	IP	H	R	K	BB	ERA
1964	Geneva	NY-Penn	0	0	1	2²/₃	1	0	2	1	.000

Managing Record

Year	Team	League	Level	W	L	Pct.	Finish
1961	Greensboro Yankees	Carolina	B	70	68	.507	3rd, 3rd
1962	Pensacola Senators	Alabama-Florida	D	79	38	.675	1st
1963	Wisconsin Rapids Senators	Midwest	A	58	62	.483	10th, 4th
1964	Geneva Senators	NY-Pennsylvania	A	79	51	.608	2nd
1965	Geneva Senators	NY-Pennsylvania	A	65	61	.516	4th, 3rd
1966	Burlington Senators	Carolina	A	76	62	.551	2nd
1967	Hawaii Islanders	Pacific Coast	AAA	60	87	.408	6th
1968	Buffalo Bisons	International	AAA	66	81	.449	7th
1973	Columbus Astros	Southern	AA	69	70	.496	3rd
1975	Lynchburg Rangers	Carolina	A	60	78	.435	4th, 4th
1976	Asheville Tourists	Western Carolinas	A	76	62	.551	1st, 2nd
1977	Asheville Tourists	Western Carolinas	A	81	58	.583	2nd, 2nd
1978	Asheville Tourists	Western Carolinas	A	73	67	.521	3rd, 4th
1979	Asheville Tourists	Western Carolinas	A	75	63	.543	3rd, 3rd
1980	Tulsa Drillers	Texas	AA	75	61	.551	2nd, 3rd
2003	Fort Worth	Central	Ind.	51	43	.542	3rd, 1st
2004	Fort Worth	Central	Ind.	51	43	.542	2nd, 2nd
2005	Fort Worth	Central	Ind.	60	34	.638	1st, 1st
Totals 18 Years				**1,224**	**1,089**	**.529**	

Coaching Record

Year	Team	League	Level	W	L	Pct.	Finish
1969	Washington Senators	American	ML	86	76	.531	4th
1970	Washington Senators	American	ML	70	92	.432	6th
1971	Washington Senators	American	ML	63	96	.396	5th
1972	Texas Rangers	American	ML	54	100	.351	6th
1981	Texas Rangers	American	ML	57	48	.543	2nd
1982	Texas Rangers	American	ML	64	98	.395	6th
1983	Texas Rangers	American	ML	77	85	.475	3rd
1984	Texas Rangers	American	ML	69	92	.429	7th
1985	Texas Rangers	American	ML	62	99	.385	7th
1986	Minnesota Twins	American	ML	71	91	.438	6th
1987	Minnesota Twins	American	ML	85	77	.525	1st
1988	Minnesota Twins	American	ML	91	71	.562	2nd
1989	Minnesota Twins	American	ML	80	82	.494	5th
1990	Minnesota Twins	American	ML	74	88	.457	7th
1991	Minnesota Twins	American	ML	95	67	.586	1st
1992	Minnesota Twins	American	ML	90	72	.556	2nd
1993	Minnesota Twins	American	ML	71	91	.438	tied 5th
1994	Minnesota Twins	American	ML	53	60	.469	4th
1995	Saint Paul Saints	Northern	Ind.	53	31	.631	1st, 1st
1996	Saint Paul Saints	Northern	Ind.	45	40	.529	1st, 1st
1997	Saint Paul Saints	Northern	Ind.	45	39	.536	1st, 2nd
1998	Saint Paul Saints	Northern	Ind.	40	46	.465	2nd, 1st
1999	Saint Paul Saints	Northern	Ind.	38	47	.447	3rd, 2nd
2000	Saint Paul Saints	Northern	Ind.	43	43	.500	1st, 3rd
2001	Saint Paul Saints	Northern	Ind.	37	53	.411	4th, 2nd
2002	Saint Paul Saints	Northern	Ind.	39	50	.438	5th, 4th
Total 22 Years				**1652**	**1834**	**.474**	

Year by Year

1939	Charlotte (Michigan) High School Orioles	third baseman
1940	Charlotte High School Orioles	third baseman
1941	Charlotte High School Orioles	shortstop
1942	Charlotte High School Orioles	shortstop
1943	Out of baseball	
1944	US Marine Corps, 2nd Armored Amphibian Battalion, Saipan	shortstop
1945	US Marine Corps, 2nd Armored Amphibian Battalion, Saipan and Maui	shortstop
1946	Western Michigan College Broncos	second baseman
1946	Benton Harbor (Michigan) House of David	second baseman
1947	Western Michigan College Broncos	second baseman
1947	Benton Harbor Buds	second baseman
1948	Western Michigan College Broncos	second baseman
1948	Benton Harbor Buds	second baseman
1948	Des Moines Cubs	second baseman
1949	Los Angeles Angels	second baseman
1949	Chicago Cubs	second baseman
1950	Chicago Cubs	second baseman
1951	Chicago Cubs	second baseman
1951	Brooklyn Dodgers	second baseman
1952	Saint Paul Saints	second baseman
1953	Washington Senators	second baseman
1954	Washington Senators	second baseman
1955	Minneapolis Millers	second baseman
1955	New York Giants	second baseman
1956	New York Giants	second baseman
1956	Minneapolis Millers	second baseman
1956	Maracaibo Centauros	second baseman
1957	Minneapolis Millers	second baseman
1957	Santo Domingo Leones del Escogido	second baseman
1958	Charleston (West Virginia) Senators	second baseman
1958	Santo Domingo Leones del Escogido	second baseman
1959	Kansas City Athletics	second baseman
1960	Kansas City Athletics	second baseman
1960	Richmond Virginians	second baseman
1961	Greensboro (North Carolina) Yankees	manager
1962	Pensacola Senators	manager
1963	Wisconsin Rapids Senators	manager
1964	Geneva (New York) Senators	manager
1965	Geneva Senators	manager
1966	Burlington (North Carolina) Senators	manager
1967	Hawaii Islanders	manager
1968	Buffalo Bisons	manager
1969	Washington Senators	third base coach
1970	Washington Senators	third base coach
1971	Washington Senators	third base coach
1972	Texas Rangers	third base coach
1973	Columbus (Georgia) Astros	manager
1974	Out of baseball	
1975	Lynchburg (Virginia) Rangers	manager
1976	Asheville (North Carolina) Tourists	manager
1977	Asheville Tourists	manager

1978	Asheville Tourists	manager
1979	Asheville Tourists	manager
1980	Tulsa Drillers	manager
1981	Texas Rangers	third base coach
1982	Texas Rangers	third base coach
1983	Texas Rangers	third base coach
1984	Texas Rangers	third base coach
1985	Texas Rangers	third base coach
1986	Minnesota Twins	first base coach
1987	Minnesota Twins	first base coach
1988	Minnesota Twins	first base coach
1989	Minnesota Twins	first base coach
1990	Minnesota Twins	first base coach
1991	Minnesota Twins	first base coach
1992	Minnesota Twins	first base coach
1993	Minnesota Twins	first base coach
1994	Minnesota Twins	first base coach
1995	Saint Paul Saints	first base coach
1996	Saint Paul Saints	first base coach
1997	Saint Paul Saints	first base coach
1998	Saint Paul Saints	first base coach
1999	Saint Paul Saints	first base coach
2000	Saint Paul Saints	first base coach
2001	Saint Paul Saints	first base coach
2002	Saint Paul Saints	first base coach
2003	Fort Worth Cats	manager
2004	Fort Worth Cats	manager
2005	Fort Worth Cats	manager

Ball Clubs Played For* or Against

Teams on which Twig played, coached, or managed are designated with an asterisk (*). Opposing teams have none. Often teams are listed twice—as Twig's team in certain years and as his opponent in other years. If a team changed leagues, or level, or name, there is an additional listing.

Team	Level	League	Years
Alexandria Aces	Ind.	Central Baseball	2003
Amarillo Dillas	Ind.	Central Baseball	2003-04
Amarillo Gold Sox	AA	Texas	1980
Anderson Rangers	A	Western Carolinas	1975
Arkansas Travelers	AA	Texas	1980
Asheville Orioles	AA	Southern	1973
Asheville Tourists*	A	Western Carolinas	1976-79
Auburn Mets	A	New York-Penn	1964-65
Baltimore Orioles	ML	American	1954,59-60,69-72,81-94
Batavia Pirates	A	New York-Penn	1964-65
Benton Harbor Buds*	S/Pro	Michigan-Indiana	1947-48
Benton Harbor House of David*	S/Pro	Michigan-Indiana	1946
Binghamton Triplets	A	New York-Penn	1964 65
Birmingham As	AA	Southern	1973
Boston Braves	ML	National	1949-51,55-56
Boston Red Sox	ML	American	1953-54,59-60,69-72,81-94
Brooklyn Dodgers	ML	National	1949-51,55-56
Brooklyn Dodgers*	ML	National	1951
Buffalo Bisons	AAA	International	1960
Buffalo Bisons*	AAA	International	1968
Burlington Bees	A	Midwest	1963
Burlington Indians	B	Carolina	1961
Burlington Senators*	A	Carolina	1966
California Angels	ML	American	1969-72,81-94
Charleston Patriots	A	Western Carolinas	1976-77
Charleston Pirates	A	Western Carolinas	1975,78
Charleston Senators	AAA	American Assoc.	1952,55-57
Charleston Senators*	AAA	American Assoc.	1958
Charlotte Orioles*	HS		1939-42
Chicago Cubs	ML	National	1951,55-56
Chicago Cubs*	ML	National	1949-51
Chicago White Sox	ML	American	1953-54,59-60,69-72,81-94
Cincinnati Reds	ML	National	1949-51,55-56
Cleveland Indians	ML	American	1953-54,59-60,69-72,81-94
Clinton C-Sox	A	Midwest	1963
Coastal Bend Aviators	Ind.	Central Baseball	2003-05
Columbus Astros*	AA	Southern	1973
Columbus Jets	AAA	International	1960,68
Columbus Red Birds	AAA	American Assoc.	1952
Decatur Commodores	A	Midwest	1963
Denver Bears	A	Western	1948
Denver Bears	AAA	American Assoc.	1955-58,67

Team	Level	League	Years
Des Moines Bruins*	A	Western	1948
Detroit Tigers	ML	American	1953-54,59-60,69-72,81-94
Dothan Phillies	D	Alabama-Florida	1962
Dubuque Packers	A	Midwest	1963
Duluth-Superior Dukes	Ind.	Northern	1995-2002
Durham Bulls	A	Carolina	1966
Durham Bulls	B	Carolina	1961
Edinburgh Roadrunners	Ind.	Central Baseball	2003-05
El Paso Diablos	AA	Texas	1980
El Paso Diablos	Ind.	Central Baseball	2005
Fargo-Moorhead RedHawks	Ind.	Northern	1996-2002
Fort Worth Cats*	Ind.	Central Baseball	2003-05
Fox Cities Foxes	A	Midwest	1963
Fort Walton Beach Jets	D	Alabama-Florida	1962
Gary SouthShore RailCats	Ind.	Northern	2002
Gastonia Cardinals	A	Carolina	1977-79
Geneva Senators*	A	New York-Penn	1964-65
Greensboro Hornets	A	Western Carolinas	1979
Greensboro Yankees	A	Carolina	1966
Greensboro Yankees*	B	Carolina	1961
Greenwood Braves	A	Western Carolinas	1975-79
Havana Sugar Kings	AAA	International	1960
Hawaii Islanders*	AAA	Pacific Coast	1967
Hollywood Stars	AAA	Pacific Coast	1949
Indianapolis Indians	AAA	American Assoc.	1952,55-58
Indianapolis Indians	AAA	Pacific Coast	1967
Jackson Mets	AA	Texas	1980
Jackson Senators	Ind.	Central Baseball	2003-05
Jacksonville Suns	AA	Southern	1973
Jacksonville Suns	AAA	International	1968
Jamestown Tigers	A	New York-Penn	1964-65
Jersey City Jerseys	AAA	International	1960
Joliet Jackhammers	Ind.	Northern	2002
Kansas City Athletics*	ML	American	1959-60
Kansas City Blues	AAA	American Assoc.	1952
Kansas City Royals	ML	American	1969-72,81-94
Kinston Eagles	A	Carolina	1966
Knoxville White Sox	AA	Southern	1973
Lincoln Athletics	A	Western	1948
Lincoln Saltdogs	Ind.	Northern	2001-02
Los Angeles Angels*	AAA	Pacific Coast	1949
Louisville Colonels	AAA	American Assoc.	1952,55-58
Louisville Colonels	AAA	International	1968
Lynchburg Mets	A	Carolina	1976
Lynchburg Rangers*	A	Carolina	1975
Lynchburg White Sox	A	Carolina	1966
Madison Black Wolf	Ind.	Northern	1996-2000
Maracaibo Centauros	Winter	Venezuelan	1956
Miami Marlins	AAA	International	1960
Midland Cubs	AA	Texas	1980
Milwaukee Brewers	AAA	American Assoc.	1952
Milwaukee Brewers	ML	American	1970-72,81-94
Minneapolis Millers	AAA	American Assoc.	1952,58

Team	Level	League	Years
Minneapolis Millers*	AAA	American Assoc.	1955-57
Minnesota Twins	ML	American	1969-72,81-85
Minnesota Twins*	ML	American	1986-94
Montgomery Rebels	AA	Southern	1973
Montgomery Rebels	D	Alabama-Florida	1962
Montreal Royals	AAA	International	1960
New York Giants	ML	National	1949-51
New York Giants*	ML	National	1955-56
New York Yankees	ML	American	1953-54,59-60,69-72,81-94
Oakland Athletics	ML	American	1969-72,81-94
Oakland Oaks	AAA	Pacific Coast	1949
Oklahoma City 89ers	AAA	Pacific Coast	1967
Omaha Cardinals	A	Western	1948
Omaha Cardinals	AAA	American Assoc.	1955-58
Orlando Twins	AA	Southern	1973
Ozark Mountain Ducks	Ind.	Central Baseball	2003
Ozark/Andalusia Dodgers	D	Alabama-Florida	1962
Peninsula Grays	A	Carolina	1966
Peninsula Pilots	A	Carolina	1976
Pensacola Pelicans	Ind.	Central Baseball	2004-05
Pensacola Senators*	D	Alabama-Florida	1962
Philadelphia Athletics	ML	American	1953-54
Philadelphia Phillies	ML	National	1949-51,55-56
Phoenix Giants	AAA	Pacific Coast	1967
Pittsburgh Pirates	ML	National	1949-51,55-56
Portland Beavers	AAA	Pacific Coast	1949,67
Portsmouth Tides	A	Carolina	1966
Pueblo Dodgers	A	Western	1948
Quad Cities Angels	A	Midwest	1963
Quincy Jets	A	Midwest	1963
Raleigh Capitals	B	Carolina	1961
Raleigh Pirates	A	Carolina	1966
Richmond Braves	AAA	International	1968
Richmond Virginians*	AAA	International	1960
Rio Grande Valley White Wings	Ind.	Central Baseball	2003
Rochester Red Wings	AAA	International	1960,68
Rocky Mount Leafs	A	Carolina	1966
Rocky Mount Phillies	A	Carolina	1975
Sacramento Solons	AAA	Pacific Coast	1949
Saint Louis Browns	ML	American	1953
Saint Louis Cardinals	ML	National	1949-51,55-56
Saint Paul Saints	AAA	American Assoc.	1955-58
Saint Paul Saints*	AAA	American Assoc.	1952
Saint Paul Saints*	Ind.	Northern	1995-2002
Salem Pirates	A	Carolina	1975-76
San Angelo Colts	Ind.	Central Baseball	2003-05
San Antonio Dodgers	AA	Texas	1980
San Diego Padres	AAA	Pacific Coast	1949,67
San Francisco Seals	AAA	Pacific Coast	1949
Santo Domingo Leones	Winter	Dominican	1957
Savannah Braves	AA	Southern	1973
Schaumberg Flyers	Ind.	Northern	1999-2002
Seattle Angels	AAA	Pacific Coast	1967

Team	Level	League	Years
Seattle Mariners	ML	American	1981-94
Seattle Pilots	ML	American	1969
Seattle Raniers	AAA	Pacific Coast	1949
Selma Cloverleafs	D	Alabama-Florida	1962
Shelby Pirates	A	Carolina	1979
Shelby Reds	A	Carolina	1977-78
Shreveport Captains	AA	Texas	1980
Shreveport Sports	Ind.	Central Baseball	2003-05
Sioux City Explorers	Ind.	Northern	1995-2002
Sioux City Soos	A	Western	1948
Sioux Falls Canaries	Ind.	Northern	1995-2002
Spartanburg Phillies	A	Western Carolinas	1975-79
Spokane Indians	AAA	Pacific Coast	1967
Syracuse Chiefs	AAA	International	1968
Tacoma Cubs	AAA	Pacific Coast	1967
Texas Rangers	ML	American	1986-94
Texas Rangers*	ML	American	1972,81-85
Thunder Bay Whiskey Jacks	Ind.	Northern	1995-98
Toledo Mud Hens	AAA	American Assoc.	1952,55,68
Toronto Blue Jays	ML	American	1981-94
Toronto Maple Leafs	AAA	International	1960
Tulsa Drillers*	AA	Texas	1980
Tulsa Oilers	AAA	Pacific Coast	1967
USMC 2nd Armored Amphibian*	Mil.		1944-45
Vancouver Mounties	AAA	Pacific Coast	1967
Washington Senators	ML	American	1959-60
Washington Senators*	ML	American	1953-54,69-71
Waterloo Hawks	A	Midwest	1963
Wellsville Red Sox	A	New York-Penn	1964-65
Western Michigan Broncos*	Coll.		1946-48
Wichita Braves	AAA	American Assoc.	1956-58
Wilson Tobs	A	Carolina	1966
Wilson Tobs	B	Carolina	1961
Winnipeg Goldeyes	Ind.	Northern	1995-2002
Winston-Salem Red Sox	A	Carolina	1966,75-76
Winston-Salem Red Sox	B	Carolina	1961
Wisconsin Rapids Senators*	A	Midwest	1963

Index

About the Authors

Celebrated for his enthusiasm and his love of the game, **Wayne (Twig) Terwilliger** has played, coached, and managed in more than 7,200 baseball games since 1948 when he was first signed by the Chicago Cubs. He still coaches at eighty.

His co-authors and friends, **Nancy Peterson** and **Peter Boehm**, are writers and long-time baseball fans. They can be found tailgating before all Saint Paul Saints home games, and enjoying the action from just behind home plate.

The authors may be contacted through www.wayneterwilliger.com.